Ireland
The Quest for the World Cup
A Complete Record

BOOKS BY CLIVE LEATHERDALE

As Author
SPORT
Ireland: The Quest for the World Cup – A Complete Record
England: The Quest for the World Cup – A Complete Record
Scotland: The Quest for the World Cup – A Complete Record
The Aberdeen Football Companion
Aberdeen – A Desert Island Football History (in preparation)
Wimbledon – A Desert Island Football History (in preparation)

NON-SPORT
The Virgin Whore and Other Chinese Characters – Travels and Traumas
To Dream of Pigs – Travels in South and North Korea
Britain and Saudi Arabia 1925-1939: The Imperial Oasis
So You Want to Teach English to Foreigners
Dracula: The Novel & the Legend – A Study of Bram Stoker's Gothic Masterpiece

As Editor
The Origins of Dracula: The Background to Bram Stoker's Gothic Masterpiece
Treatise on Vampires and Revenants: The Phantom World

About the author
Clive Leatherdale was born in 1949. He is a writer, journalist, lecturer, and publisher, and a person with wide interests. Born with sport in his blood, he has been writing histories and trenchant articles on football for many years. He has backpacked around much of the globe, has lived in Saudi Arabia, China, and Korea, and written histories or travel books on all three countries. He has a Ph.D. in Arabian history and is an international authority on Dracula.

Ireland

The Quest for the World Cup

A Complete Record

Clive Leatherdale

**TWO HEADS
PUBLISHING**

Published in association with
Desert Island Books

This edition first published in 1994 by

Two Heads Publishing
in association with Desert Island Books
12A Franklyn Suite
The Priory
Haywards Heath
West Sussex
RH16 3LB

ISBN   1-897850-80-8

Photograph credits.
Rear cover, pages 107, 119, 137, 141, 155, 159, 175, 195, 205,
217, 221 - Colorsport.
Pages 59, 67, 69, 75, 83, 87, 95 - Jim Connolly.
Front cover -Steve Hale, Tom Jenkins.

Cover design by Doug Cheeseman

Printed & bound by Caldra House Ltd., Hove, Sussex

CONTENTS

Foreword

I first became interested in the Republic of Ireland team through the medium of John Giles who, ironically was one of my predecessors as manager of the Irish team.

We were team-mates at Leeds United at the time and – in a squad dominated by English and Scottish players – John was the only Irishman. Now the thing which intrigued me at the time was the lack of press coverage and the consequent lack of interest in the Irish team among the general public in Britain.

When people like Billy Bremner, Eddie Gray and Joe Jordan went off to play for Scotland, it was easy enough to find out on the television or in the newspapers how they got on. But in the case of the Irish we often had to wait until Giles got back to Elland Road to find out their result.

That I found strange. The Republic of Ireland always had good players, and I think of people like Johnny Carey, Charlie Hurley and Andy McEvoy, who would have fitted into any national team in their time. For all that individual talent, however, they were never able to get it together in a team sense.

As you will read in Clive Leatherdale's book, the Republic came close to qualifying for the 1966 World Cup finals in England, losing out only after a play-off with Spain in Paris. But at that stage, of course, my allegiance lay elsewhere.

I was much more aware of the Republic's misfortune in the preliminaries of the 1982 championship in Spain. On that occasion, they were pipped only on goal-difference for a place in the finals and when you think of the subsequent progress made by the two qualifiers from the group – France and Belgium – it puts the Irish challenge in perspective.

Eoin Hand was in charge of that team, and when you think of it, he had some great players available to him. Liam Brady, Frank Stapleton and David O'Leary were then in their prime. Mark Lawrenson was among the best all-round players in the game at the time, and around them they had people like Mick Martin, Gerry Daly and Don Givens, all of whom were capable of doing a good job.

I liked the look of that side, but the last thing on my mind then was that one day I would inherit many of those players. That came about early in 1986 when, out of the blue, I was asked if I would be interested in taking the Republic of Ireland job.

I accepted, and, as it turned out, it was one of the best decisions I ever made. From day one I liked the response of the football public, and gradually we got things moving in a way which made the Republic of Ireland the envy of many other teams.

Mind you, we got a couple of nice breaks along the way, not least when Scotland beat Bulgaria 1-0 in Sofia and indirectly helped us into the finals of the 1988 European Championship. That was a result which nobody could have anticipated, but I think our subsequent performances in Germany proved beyond a shadow of a doubt that we were the best team in the group.

We beat England in our first game in Stuttgart, had much the better of a 1-1 draw with the old Soviet Union, and were beaten only by a late, late goal by the eventual champions, Holland, in the last of the three group games.

Although we hadn't won anything, we got a great reception when we arrived back in Dublin, and that told me at least one thing. The Irish public sensed that we were in on the start of something big, and I'm delighted to say that we delivered at least in part in the 1990 World Cup championship.

We qualified without too much fuss – the first time the Republic had made it into the World Cup finals – and while we ended up with one of the booby prizes in being grouped with England and Holland in Sardinia and Sicily, we made it into the second phase of the competition.

In all my years in football I had never known anything like the noise generated in Genoa on the day we played Romania for a place in the last eight. It wasn't the prettiest of games, but who will ever forget the drama of those closing minutes when Packie Bonner stopped Timofte's spot-kick, and then David O'Leary sank his effort in the back of the net to give us victory in a penalty shoot-out.

Facing Italy in their own backyard in front of 70,000 of their partisan supporters in Rome's Olympic Stadium was always going to be a huge ordeal. But with the eyes of the world on us, I thought we played well until Schillaci's goal approaching half-time put us out. To many, we had excelled ourselves, but I believe that with a different draw we were capable of going to the semi-finals and possibly the Final itself.

We didn't make the cut for the finals of the 1992 European Championship in Sweden, and that was a pity. In a section which included England, Poland and Norway I felt we deserved to go through. But spurned chances in both legs of the England tie lost us our chance.

If there are many advantages in working with a small country like Ireland, there are also some downsides. Ours is a relatively small pool of players and, when the years caught up with some of our senior citizens, it wasn't easy to replace them. And yet, I knew that somehow we had to repeat our achievement of four years earlier and play in the World Cup finals in the United States in 1994.

In a climate of mountainous expectation in Ireland, the pressures were considerable, and when we slipped to a 1-3 defeat by Spain in Dublin – easily our worst result in the preceding seven years – they even began to get at me.

To make things worse, we had to go to Belfast of all places looking for a 'result' to get us to the States. But after Jimmy Quinn had put Northern Ireland in front, Alan McLoughlin booked our place in the finals with that flamboyant goal which, I suspect, is destined to become a major part of Irish football folklore.

I shall always recall USA '94 as a bitter-sweet experience. Because of the fact that we reached the last eight in Italy four years earlier, anything less than a place in the quarter-finals in America would be a let-down. As it transpired, we failed to reach that target, and yet I think it would be unfair to describe the expedition as a failure.

For one thing, we beat Italy in our opening game in New Jersey, and that had never been achieved in eight meetings between the countries. Personally, that success meant a lot to me as it was fashioned with a brand of football which compared favourably with any in the championship.

Right from the day the draw for the finals took place, I feared the prospect of having to meet Mexico in the cruel heat and humidity of Florida. Those fears proved well-founded in a game we lost 1-2.

That defeat meant we had to take a point from our next fixture with Norway to qualify, and we managed this more easily than the 0-0 scoreline indicated. For me, that fulfilled our primary ambition, to qualify for the knock-out stages, but sadly it merely set us up for a massive anti-climax.

Jack Charlton
August 1994

Author's Note

This book is designed for readers on both sides of the Irish Sea. This presents the author with an obvious headache. The parochialism of British education means that Irish history is little taught in England, Scotland and Wales. As our story takes us back to the 1930s and beyond, to a distant world unrecognisable to today's generation, some basic familiarity is necessary with Ireland's unique constitutional position, her fraught relations with the North, and her cultural antipathy to England and to that 'foreign' game – association football. For decades Belfast called the tune of Irish soccer and Dublin danced to the music. Even the setting up in the South of a breakaway association and league was a matter of tortuous complication, whose ramifications rumble on to this day. Irish readers, of course, were brought up with this knowledge. Many British readers were not. I trust Irish readers will accept with patience and good grace those, to them, superfluous passages relating to the genesis of the game in the twenty-six counties and the maddening handicaps that have hindered it ever since.

But already I fear I have exaggerated the point. No sooner did I commence researching the early history of Ireland's involvement in the World Cup than I unearthed a degree of unawareness even in Ireland. Despite its popularity in Dublin at the time, soccer was relegated to the odd sentence in Dublin's sports pages, and ignored altogether in London's.

Ireland's World Cup bids in the 1930s were, I discovered, almost as little known to the average Irishman as to the average Englishman. Parallels with the United States spring to mind. There, too, soccer was alien, held in low esteem by the mass and ostracised by the sporting press, allowing minds and resources to focus on genuine home-grown sports. To that extent, my brief account of the birth of World Cup soccer in Ireland may enlighten a wider readership than I originally intended.

Ireland's marginal interest in soccer in those early days handicaps the researcher in obvious ways. Match reports are often inaccurate, sketchy, or non-existent. Despite the best endeavours it is difficult to breathe life into matches played half a century ago, with few facts and descriptions available, and those that are seemingly contentious or one-sided. Prior to the Jack Charlton era, books on Irish soccer were few and far between. Without recourse to Donal Cullen's pioneering work – *Ireland: On the Ball* – my own enterprise would have been infinitely more painstaking.

For all these reasons this has been the most challenging of my World Cup histories. This book is the third in a series that already embraces England and Scotland's World Cup quests. The England book married each match with contemporary news and gossip. I have, reluctantly, avoided this framework with the Scotland and Ireland books, partly because the dates for World Cup matches are more or less common to all, and I ran the risk of repetition, partly because the author was denied the benefit of Irish birth, and what knows he of Irish taste in such matters?

Despite this impediment, the author seeks to write with a dispassionate eye, rather than imitate the partisan accounts of Irish colleagues. But he is not wholly an outsider. There runs Irish blood through his veins, enough – were he younger and ever so talented – to represent Ireland on the soccer pitch. If his Irish blood qualifies him to play, it certainly qualifies him to write.

With regard to names and usage, the 'Billy' Whelan of Manchester United is known in Ireland as 'Liam'. I generally bow to this, and other like instances.

What English readers refer to as a 'squad' of twenty-two players is commonly known in Ireland as a 'panel'. Likewise, an English 'free-kick' is an Irish 'free'. In both cases I have stuck with the terms I am accustomed to.

On occasions, I subsume Ireland within the concept of 'British' soccer. In such cases I do not use the term 'British' in a political sense, but as embodying the broad philosophy of football that emanates from these islands, and to which Ireland adheres.

I am deeply grateful to Donal Cullen, for putting his encyclopaedic knowledge of Irish football – not to mention his personal archives – at my disposal, and to Diarmuid Ó Luanaigh, who has delighted so many readers of Ireland match programmes in recent years with his nostalgic pen-portraits of Irish stars of old.

Both of the above read my manuscript and scribbled upon it copiously. Sometimes I heeded their sound advice; sometimes I stuck my neck out and did not. Neither of them is responsible for the views and judgments contained herein.

Clive Leatherdale
September 1994

INTRODUCTION

Strange to say, it was not so very long ago that many of nationalist disposition in southern Ireland professed to detest soccer. Self-respecting Irishmen, they contended, would have nothing to do with it. Nor, despite the best efforts of Jack Charlton and the 'lads', is that attitude entirely laid to rest among older generations beyond the pale, those living beyond the shadow of Dublin.

This is down to history of course, in particular to Ireland's pained relationship with England. Ireland and Scotland might be similar in size and population, and harbour similar suspicions toward governments in London, but with regard to soccer the Scots and Irish reached for drastically opposed solutions. From the start, the Scots sought to beat the English at their own game, claiming authorship of it for themselves, and seeking to rectify historical injustices through victory on the field of play. A Scotland v England international is never 'just a game'. How different in the Emerald Isle, where the game was shunned by many, especially in nationalist GAA (Gaelic Athletic Association) circles, as symbolising the English pestilence.

Soccer had flowed into Ireland in the nineteenth century as part of the psychological baggage of Protestant settlers, seeping ashore in Ulster via the short North Channel from Scotland. As Ulster evolved into a bastion of Protestantism and Unionism, it likewise became the fulcrum of Association Rules football in Ireland.

The (English) Football Association was born in 1872, the Scottish FA one year later. The Irish FA (the IFA) came into existence in Belfast in 1880, implementing as its model the rules and regulations of the SFA, with which it was closely affiliated. An Irish league was formed ten years later, though as all clubs were from the north it was tantamount to an Ulster league. Less restrictive was the Irish Cup, which since 1881 had been encouraging contestants from north and south, east and west, and would even try to entice them from over the sea.

Though Ireland remained until 1922 a single political entity, differences between north and south had been acute for decades, even centuries. The north was industrial, Protestant, seeking to maintain close ties with the UK and its culture. The south was agrarian, Catholic, and desperate to break away. Dublin, with its proximity to the UK and consequent Anglo-Irish heritage, viewed soccer with mongrel eyes. Dubliners both espoused and shunned the Association game. Trinity College had been founded as a Protestant college, and Trinity footballers would be the first from outside Ulster to be selected to play for Ireland.

Inland, nationalist sentiment ran deeper, and so did antipathy to soccer. In the 1900s the oppressive powers of the GAA encouraged the blackballing of what were considered British 'colonial' sports – cricket, hockey, rugby, and, foulest of all, soccer. Association football was disparaged as *the* 'foreign' game, and was anathema to nationalist thinking. Irish youth was indoctrinated into the virtues of Gaelic sport, hurling and Gaelic football, and anyone caught playing the foreign game faced ostracism and banishment. Although the writ of the GAA was resisted in Dublin, the sighting of soccer goalposts in the playing fields of Munster (to the south) and Connacht (to the west) was rare. People thereabouts were exposed to soccer chiefly through British soldiers garrisoned throughout Ireland. Provincial clubs in Athlone, Cork, Limerick, Waterford and elsewhere were heavily dependent on the soldiers' input. This military connotation outraged the GAA still further. When Ireland rose up in rebellion and the British soldier was formally cast as enemy, his pastimes were as loathed as his uniform.

But this is to vault several decades. Ireland's (effectively Ulster's) first international fixture, in what became the familiar yearly cycle of round-robin matches, had been against England in Belfast in 1882. It was won by the visitors – embarrassingly – by 13-0. Internationals were a new phenomenon and selection a casual affair. Players were picked either by virtue of birth or by having lived in Ireland for at least seven years. For British readers accustomed to visualising Ireland's emerald shirts, it may come as a surprise to learn that Ireland traditionally played in blue, not switching to green until 1931.

With Ireland slow to accept the professional ethos that had taken hold in England and Scotland, and not giving way till 1894, results remained poor. When Ireland conceded thirteen goals to England a second time, this time in Sunderland in 1899, Dublin complained that it wasn't a truly Irish team at all, but one drawn from select clubs in Belfast and, in a worrying development, from over in England. Intense lobbying enabled the 1900 match against England to be staged in Dublin, at the home of rugby at Lansdowne Road. A year later, the Dublin club Bohemians opened the city's best-equipped soccer stadium, Dalymount Park, which thenceforth staged several internationals. Meanwhile, the Bohs, followed by another Dublin club, Shelbourne, took the plunge and joined the Irish league.

Yet Irish football was from the start a sickly child. The causes ran deep – sectarianism, professionalism, rivalry between Belfast and Dublin, poor international results, indiscipline on the pitch. For reasons that seem obscure, even trivial, the question of punishment for on-field misdemeanours proved the straw that broke the camel's back, encouraging some clubs to quit the Irish league and try to form a breakaway association.

This was in 1912, by which year tensions between north and south, Protestant and Catholic, Unionist and Nationalist, threatened to rip the nation apart. The last all-Ireland soccer team to play in Dublin, in 1913, had the satisfaction of beating Scotland 2-1. Before the kick-off the Irish band had stoutly refused to play 'God Save the Queen', so a British military band had to step in. The following year Ireland won the British Championship outright, a feat that – as Northern Ireland – they would repeat just twice, in the 1980s.

World War I provided the backdrop to the southern uprising that would partition the island between Northern Ireland and an Irish Free State. When, in 1920, shots were fired into the crowd during a match between Belfast Celtic and the Protestant club, Glentoran, it was clear that Irish soccer as then constituted could not endure.

In this regard, soccer was viewed differently from other sports – rugby, boxing – which happily remained all-Ireland. Soccer was smitten by sectarianism from the start, in Liverpool and Manchester no less than in Scotland and Ireland. Wherever a city boasts two clubs, the one is likely to have Protestant roots, the other Catholic. Burdened by this heritage, unified soccer had an uphill struggle to survive in a divided Ireland. The Belfast clubs, Linfield and Belfast Celtic, for example, mirrored the Rangers-Celtic divide in Glasgow. Partition and sectarianism would later drive Belfast Celtic out of existence.

Yet splitting Ireland's soccer resources between North and South would weaken both, perhaps terminally. If politics suggested division, practicalities and a shared 'Irishness' did not. For that reason it was resisted by many, both in Belfast and Dublin. Not least of the headaches was the fear that any split was unlikely to be watertight. Beleaguered Catholic clubs in the North might wish to seek sanctuary in the South; leading professional outfits in the South might have to look North, where the bigger names played.

Though the decision was not unanimous, southern clubs in 1921 elected to form their own association, the Football Association of Ireland (FAI), and their own league, the Football League of Ireland. There was now an IFA alongside an FAI, to the despair of dyslexics.

At club level, both Ulster and the Free State suffered. However, as most of the big (Protestant) clubs were to be found in and around Belfast, their mutually lucrative fixtures continued as before. Indeed, they were spared the expense and bother of trips to lesser lights in Dublin. In the South, soccer was so marginalised and attendances so small that – without the opposition provided by Linfield and other Ulster giants – professional clubs had difficulty making ends meet. Many Dublin professionals could see no future and went to play in Wales and elsewhere. The exodus hit some clubs particularly hard. Shelbourne, for example, went under for a time. As for provincial outfits, confronted with two-hundred mile round trips to Dublin, on low and diminishing gates, the writing was on the wall.

Nor were the Free State's international prospects any brighter. FIFA had been in existence since 1904. Lancaster Gate initially cold-shouldered this upstart organisation, grudgingly joined in 1906, but withdrew forthwith when told that Scotland, Wales and Ireland could not enjoy separate membership. FIFA reckoned, not unreasonably, that the UK was one country. Today, the idea that Britain could enjoy four members, and four votes on committee, would be laughed out of court. It says much for the muscle wielded by the English FA at that time that by 1910 all four would be ensconced.

The Free State had to tread carefully if she hoped to join FIFA. Independent states were eligible, but partition and dominion status within the British Empire was felt by some to have compromised that independence. By acknowledging the potential allegiance of certain Northern Irish clubs, the Free State muddied the waters still further. Belfast insisted that, as the FAI was a breakaway body, established without the approval or sympathy of the long-established British Associations, FIFA should have nothing to do with the Free State's bid for membership. Gaelic games, not soccer, were the national sports of southern Ireland. Indeed, a visitor to rural parts would be hard pressed to find evidence that soccer was played at all. As for the emotive name 'Ireland', Belfast insisted that this was a legitimate Northern preserve. Dublin retorted that for a tiny rump of the Irish island to claim jurisdiction over the whole was preposterous. In essence, these positions have changed little today.

So powerful was the English Association that – with Belfast kicking at its shins – it was liable to frustrate any FAI move for admission. But other dominions, such as Canada and South Africa, already enjoyed separate membership. The precedent had therefore been set. At the time, moreover, the British Associations had turned their backs on FIFA, objecting to the principle of matches being played against Germany and Austria, the defeated wartime foes.

This further weakened the English FA's hand, and in August 1923 FIFA opened the door to the Irish Free State. After all, in FIFA's eyes she was more eligible than Northern Ireland, which was not even self-governing. The official designation 'Football Association of the Irish Free State' – FAIFS – helped to appease everyone. By this wording, Dublin appeared, at least formally, to renounce any claim to speak for all Ireland.

Having survived a breech birth, the FAIFS was destined for a troubled infancy. There is little point in celebrating international recognition if no one will play you. The Free State yearned to play England and Scotland, football's colossi across the water. These were the matches that mattered, the ones that filled stadiums and coffers, and minimised travelling. Better still would have been an invitation to compete in the Home International Championship, increasing the field to five. The British Associations, predictably, stayed loyal to Northern Ireland. The Free State would have to look elsewhere.

In the 1920s this was not as easy as it sounds. Northern Ireland, for example, would not venture to play east of the English Channel until the 1950s! In football as in other spheres, Ireland's isolation on the fringe of Europe cut her off from the European mainstream. Glasgow Celtic showed solidarity with Catholic brethren by coming to play a Free State XI. The match was a sell-out.

The Free State dipped her toes into international competition at the 1924 Paris Olympics. The soccer tournament was boycotted by Britain, in dispute over what would now be called 'shamateurism'. The Free State's amateurs enjoyed a first-round bye, followed by a second-round victory over Bulgaria, before falling in the quarter-finals to Holland in extra time.

But the Olympics were not the solution, either to the Free State or anyone else. That was why FIFA had been created in the first place. It was top-flight opposition that the Free State craved, not club sides, however prestigious, nor the twilight world of amateur football.

It was Italy who came to the rescue, three years after the Free State was admitted to FIFA. Italy invited the team to Turin for a full international in March 1926, and sent a 'B' team to Dublin a year later. Belgium, Spain and Holland also provided willing opposition in the late 1920s and early '30s.

One consequence of North and South claiming tacit jurisdiction over the whole of Ireland was that both insisted on the right to call upon players from all thirty-two counties, in other words, including those from 'the other side'. Unless this hand was played frugally, however, it could undermine the sensible claims of both Associations. If one or t'other picked a side brimful of imports, what was the point of the split? FIFA was sure to take a dim view of any excessive overlap.

As Northern Ireland played no one outside the UK, and the Free State no one within it, the open door suited both, for it effectively strengthened both. For three decades Northern Ireland happily plundered the cream of the South when contesting the British Championship. These players were clearly the better for the experience, and in that sense furthered the ends of the Free State. Likewise, the Free State could borrow Ulstermen when playing continental opponents, though, in practice, this utilisation of Northerners was less common. Ulster players were generally cagey about turning out for the South, for fear of upsetting their masters.

Within months of the Free State joining FIFA, the British Associations clambered back aboard. But not for long. By 1928 they had yet another fit of pique and stomped out over the vexed question of amateurism. The Free State stayed put. It was around this time that FIFA put forward concrete plans for the first World Cup, to take place in Uruguay in 1930. The British Associations were ineligible, but with their air of pompous superiority probably wouldn't have competed anyway. The Free State took counsel from Lancaster Gate, weighed the matter, and, had the World Cup been staged in Europe, might have signed up. Entry to the tournament was by invitation, there being no need to pre-qualify. Yet, though Uruguay had pledged to pick up the tab of all European entries, the bother of travelling to the southern hemisphere filled the FAIFS with foreboding. The Free State was not alone in declining. At the end of the day just four, mid-ranking, European nations condescended to make the trip.

Given the overall calibre of entrants, the Free State might even have prospered. Belgium were present, but, by the time they set sail, the Free State had beaten them three times out of three. If Yugoslavia and the United States could reach the semi-finals, there was no reason why the Free State couldn't. Who can tell, Ireland might have left their mark on the World Cup map from the start.

1

THE 1934 WORLD CUP

The 1934 World Cup would be contested in Europe, in Italy. Fascism was the flavour of the age. Hitler had taken power a year earlier; Mussolini had been ruling the roost for twelve years already.

For the inaugural World Cup, in 1930, all entrants progressed straight to the finals, without the hassle of an eliminating competition. Four years later the numbers were too great; they had to be pared down to a manageable sixteen. Arrived at arbitrarily, that figure would be the magic number of finalists for World Cups until the 1980s.

A dozen qualifying zones were set up on geographical lines, though several nations scratched in the face of transport difficulties, or real and imagined slights. Holders Uruguay didn't even get that far. They didn't enter at all, angered by the puny European representation at their own World Cup. Nor did they get a chance to defend their 1928 Olympic title; soccer was not on the agenda at the 1932 Games.

The list of starters in 1934 shows the extent to which the world has changed these past sixty years. Lithuania and Estonia, for example, would shortly disappear as national entities, to dramatically reappear in the 1990s. Like Cuba, these east Europeans fancied their chances, though none qualified. Palestine, the sole Asian entry, was not an independent state but a British trusteeship. Egypt, Africa's one entrant, enjoyed scarcely more independence than Palestine. British colonialism weighed heavily in the Middle East. Its spectre, if no actual British team, was sure to infiltrate the World Cup. Egypt needed only to beat Palestine to qualify.

Pools V-XII were reserved for European aspirants. The Free State was placed in Pool XI, alongside Holland and Belgium. Nowadays, nations are asked to play each other home and away. This was not always the case in the early years. Teams in Pool XI would play just once. Ireland would entertain Belgium, then travel to Holland. The Belgians would then host the Dutch in Brussels. For Ireland, the travelling was minimal and the odds favourable. Teams finishing first *and* second would be invited to Italy. Ireland enjoyed 100% records against both opponents. Home and dry, they thought.

Qualifying Pool X1

IRELAND v BELGIUM

Sunday, 25 February 1934   *Dalymount Park – 28,000*

Belgium were true disciples of international football, being one of FIFA's six original signatories in 1904, and providing that organisation with its first secretary-general. Belgium felt honour-bound to take part in the first World Cup, in Uruguay in 1930, but had found themselves one of just four European teams prepared to venture forth. Her high principles did not mean Belgium were any great shakes on the pitch. The Belgians still observed the amateur ethos. Favoured by home soil, and not handicapped by South American participants, their footballers had claimed Olympic gold in 1920. The sprouting of professionalism all around them, however, soon relegated Belgium among the also-rans of European football. They returned from Uruguay without a point or a goal to their name (losing 0-3 to USA, 0-1 to Paraguay).

They might have provided a sterner test had their selectors picked wisely from Belgium's flourishing domestic league. But the Belfast power-brokers who close-shopped the IFA in its early years had able pupils in Brussels. All too often favoured players from favoured Belgian sides were selected irrespective of form or the claims of provincial clubs. By the time they visited Dalymount Park on World Cup business, Belgium's losing run was spiralling out of control. They had plummeted the depths the previous year with a 1-8 hammering by Germany, themselves no world-beaters at that time.

Belgium's accessibility had made them welcome opponents for Ireland and England in the 1920s and '30s. The World Cup-tie constituted Ireland's ninth official international since the creation of the Free State, three of the previous eight having been against Belgium. Ireland had won the lot, and with something to spare. In 1928 the Belgians had been crushed 2-4 in Liege, having led 2-0 at half-time. The following year, in Dublin, Ireland hit another four, this time without reply, and John Joe Flood helped himself to Ireland's first recorded hat-trick. Ireland's third win came in 1930, Jimmy Dunne scoring twice in a 3-1 victory in Brussels.

There were few indications to suppose Belgium would put up a stiffer challenge now, especially in the light of the German debacle. The passage of time meant just two players remained from earlier Ireland-Belgium clashes. Right-winger Versyp had played in Brussels, David Byrne in Dublin.

So few internationals were staged in those days that this was Ireland's first in two years. It was impossible for players to accumulate caps in great numbers, and the five-man Irish selection committee (the 'Big Five') now awarded five first caps. One of these, Peadar Gaskins, was appointed captain.

The most battle-hardened internationalists, David Byrne and Paddy Moore, were each winning their third caps.

February is nowadays an unusual month for a northern European nation to stage a World Cup eliminator. Inclement weather can play havoc with transportation and with the match itself. Ireland's custom – quite alien to England or Scotland's – was to play mid-season internationals on a Sunday. This was from necessity rather than choice. Playing on Saturdays meant that no English or Scottish-based players could be considered; they were needed by their clubs. Sunday matches required players from across the Irish Sea setting off after of their domestic fixtures and embarking on an overnight journey by train and sea. Two matches in twenty-four hours was the price paid for playing for Ireland. Little wonder that few could give of their best.

Although players from the English league were from time to time picked to play for Ireland, none was selected for the 1934 World Cup. But two from the Scottish league were. Joe O'Reilly and Paddy Moore, formerly of Brideville and Shamrock Rovers respectively, were turning it on for Aberdeen in the Scottish first division.

Moore was blessed with a fine football brain and wizardry in his bootlaces. He could also jump like a gazelle. This was just as well, for at 5ft 5½in, centre-forwards usually came bigger than he. Moore didn't set Cardiff City on fire, during a brief stint as a young man, but a torrent of goals for Shamrock Rovers in 1931-32 (forty-eight in all competitions, in a season curtailed by injury) enticed Paddy Travers, manager of Scottish giants Aberdeen, to swoop for Moore and two Rovers team-mates for a combined fee of less that £1,000. Moore was just twenty-three.

Aberdeen was a cosmopolitan home-from-home for many an itinerant footballer in those days. The club was renowned for freely releasing players for international duty, and the goodwill of Merrion Square is evident in a presentation plaque that hangs at Pittodrie to this day.

Playing for Aberdeen, Moore's worth was immediately recognised by the IFA in Belfast, and in 1932 he had been picked at inside-right for Northern Ireland v England at Blackpool. England won 1-0.

Moore was, even then, a Free State international, having scored on his debut in Spain in 1931. One month into his first season at Pittodrie he scored six goals in a 7-0 demolition of Falkirk, ending that 1932-33 season with twenty-seven strikes from twenty-nine games. He started banging them in the next season as well. Aberdeen idolised him.

But Moore's brilliance on the pitch was overshadowed by his growing unhappiness off it. He would be dead by the age of forty-one, and was already drowning his sorrows in drink. Having scored for the Dons on the Saturday, in a 2-2 draw at Celtic, Travers personally chaperoned his prodigy on the all-night journey to Dublin for the big match with Belgium.

Of the Ireland-based players around Moore, none hailed from champions Dundalk, and only one – Peadar Gaskins – from runners-up and perennial Cup winners Shamrock Rovers. Also overlooked were the leading goal-getters of recent seasons – George Ebbs and Alf Rigby of St James's Gate, Pearson Ferguson of Cork, Jack Forster of Waterford.

The selectors seemed to have opted for a regional spread, even calling up two Ulster-based players. Of these, Derry City's Jimmy Kelly was one of those rare creatures to be capped by both North and South. The selectors also chose three players from Dublin sides and four from the city of Cork's two newly admitted clubs.

This Procrustean bed solution left the selectors top-heavy with full-backs, added to which Joe O'Reilly considered himself a right-half, not centre-half. Sages whispered that Ireland might prove to be porous in defence.

A gate of 28,000 paid receipts of £1,700 to see a match that would live in the annals of Irish soccer. Eight goals were scored, a total never subsequently exceeded in an Ireland World Cup-tie. Belgium must have feared the worst, but drew solace from the knowledge that, despite losing, they had scored first against Ireland in Liege and again in Brussels. Spurred by the incentive, they shrugged off Paddy Moore's early disallowed effort to strike twice in the first twenty-six minutes. Outside-right Versyp tussled with Tom Burke, won the ball and swept it across for the unmarked Capelle to score. The winger was also instrumental in Belgium's second goal. His shot was cleared into the sky. Jim Foley punched the dropping ball to the feet of Stanley Vanden Eynde. The Beerschot forward chipped it back over his head.

Belgium had been unable to protect a two-goal advantage in Liege, and their current crew must have sighed deeply when Ireland hit back within seconds. Ulsterman Jimmy Kelly switched the ball to Paddy Moore, who scored just as he was sandwiched between two defenders.

The match was shortly marred by misfortune to Stanley Vanden Eynde, Belgium's left-winger and a real live-wire. Before half-time he broke his leg, whereupon his brother, François, perched on the sideline, stripped off his coat and took his place. Connoisseurs of World Cup history will be aware that substitutes were not permitted by FIFA prior to the 1970 competition. Nor were they hitherto known in Irish or British football. No previous Ireland international had featured a substitute, and England would not experiment with a twelfth man until Jimmy Mullen replaced Jackie Milburn in 1950. England's opponents on that occasion were Belgium!

There is no indication of Irish protest at the sight of a Belgian substitute, who was presumably waved on happily by the English referee, Mr Crew. At a distance of sixty years, the circumstances now appear lost in time.

Whatever its legality, the substitution dramatically affected the outcome of the match. François Vanden Eynde promptly scored two goals. His first came two minutes into the second half, when Van Ingelghem's cross eluded four Irish defenders and reached Saeys, who set up the chance.

Paddy Moore continued his happy knack of whipping the goblet from the lips of a celebrating enemy. He pounced on Billy Kennedy's centre to make it 2-3, then claimed his hat-trick, converting a cross from Kelly on the other flank.

The Dalymount crowd roared lustily and clamoured for the winner, but again Belgium tore up the script. Brichaut passed to François Vanden Eynde, who skipped past Miah Lynch and poked the ball past Foley. Still Ireland weren't done. A corner-kick was cleared only as far as Joe Kendrick, who returned the ball sweetly onto Moore's head. 4-4.

Moore had become the first player anywhere to score four goals in a World Cup-tie. It also remains an Irish World Cup record that might linger awhile yet.

Given the flow of the match, and the fact that they were never in front, Ireland were probably happy to square it, but it was a bad time to surrender their Indian sign over Belgium.

IRELAND (1) 4
Moore 27, 48, 56, 75

BELGIUM (2) 4
Capelle 13, S Vanden Eynde 26,
F Vanden Eynde 47, 63

IRELAND: Foley (CORK), Lynch (CORK BOHEMIANS), Burke (CORK), Gaskins (SHAMROCK R), O'Reilly (ABERDEEN), Kendrick (DOLPHIN), Kennedy (ST JAMES'S GATE), Byrne (COLERAINE), Moore (ABERDEEN), O'Keefe (CORK), Kelly (DERRY CITY).

BELGIUM: Vande Wijer, Pappaert, Smellinckx, Van Ingelghem, Welkenhuyzen, Bourgeois, Versyp, Brichaut, Capelle, Saeys, S Vanden Eynde (F Vanden Eynde).

HOLLAND v IRELAND
Sunday, 8 April 1934   *De Meer Stadium, Amsterdam – 38,000*

Six weeks later Ireland took two boats across two seas to Amsterdam. Some of the players may have pondered the rather longer trip to the finals awaiting them should they succeed. Ireland had already played in Italy, of course, a 0-3 defeat in Turin in 1926 celebrating their footballing independence. It had taken three days to traverse Britain and France, leaving on the Wednesday, arriving on the Saturday, and playing the next day in no fit state to do so. The World Cup finals were now just weeks away – they would commence in late May – and clearly Ireland would need to arrange their travel more sensibly.

Their stay might be brief, for the tournament was organised on knock-out lines. Half the teams would pack their bags after their first match. And if speculation on the finals was counting chickens, so be it. Ireland had no more to fear from the Dutch than they had from Belgium. At least, that was the view of optimists. Pessimists pointed to Holland's recent 9-3 demolition of Belgium in a friendly.

Travelling to Amsterdam was less demanding than travelling to Italy, but it was hardly ideal preparation. Ironically, Ireland had made the same journey to the same stadium in 1932. Their travel itinerary for that match was noted.

'Thursday, depart Dun Laoghaire (Kingstown) 8.00 pm. Arrive Holyhead, 11.45 pm. Mail-train sleeper to London. Arrive Euston Station, 6.00 am. After breakfast at Euston, transfer to Liverpool St for 10.00 am train to Harwich, arriving at 11.30. Board boat for Flushing and on arrival there undertake a four-hour train journey to Amsterdam, arriving 9.30 pm.'

At least, Ireland had the consolation of winning that match 2-0. Joe O'Reilly and Paddy Moore had scored the goals, and both were included this time. They were among six players retained from the draw with Belgium. Of the rest, Harry Chatton and Paddy Byrne were recalled from earlier times. Byrne, too, was making his second trip to Amsterdam. First caps awaited Johnny Squires, Billy Jordan and Paddy Meehan. Squires' club, Shelbourne, was set to fold and be withdrawn (temporarily) from the Free State league, suffering the same fate as Cork Bohemians, who had provided Miah Lynch against Belgium. The Dutch retained five players from that earlier defeat.

Like their Belgian neighbours, Holland were whole-hearted advocates of the World Cup. Well, at least in principle. They had applied to host the first competition, but when that decision went in favour of Uruguay they had little difficulty conjuring up excuses not to travel. The Dutch were stalwarts of Olympic soccer, winning bronze in 1908, 1912, and again in 1920, but once the South Americans took an interest their pedigree faded.

Viewed rationally, Ireland needed only a draw from their travails. Barring a tie between Belgium and Holland, one point would wrap up second place and an invitation to Italy.

For devotees of trivia, the focal point of the first half was the moment Ireland employed a substitute of their own. Billy Jordan shot for goal, fell, and twisted an ankle. The sprain was serious enough to take Jordan from the action. Fred Horlacher of champions Bohemians, another veteran of Ireland's previous outing to Amsterdam, took the field with no evident protest from the Dutch. The correspondent of the *Irish Independent,* who clearly was not at the match, explained: 'Unconfirmed reports have reached me that in the World Cup match on Sunday, W Jordan received an injury to his ankle which necessitated his retirement before the interval. He was replaced by Horlacher. This is the first time that the Free State took advantage of the Continental rule which permits of substitutes replacing injured players.'

Replacing injured players before half-time may have been a Continental 'rule', but it was not a FIFA one. In another qualifying zone, Switzerland vehemently protested that Romania had fielded an 'ineligible' player. Though that player was not a substitute, FIFA cracked the whip. The match, although drawn, was awarded to Switzerland. Clearly then, FIFA had muscle, even in 1934. One presumes it turned a blind eye to the use of substitutions in Ireland's matches, or else was kept in the dark.

(When the author presented this anomaly to refereeing organisations, they could conceive of no explanation. When the author turned to FIFA, they acknowledged that in the dim and distant past private agreements could, and sometimes did, take place between national associations, without FIFA being kept informed.)

The only pity is that Ireland's twelfth man did not match the impact of Belgium's. Horlacher had barely slotted into his inside-left position when Smit fired a cross from Wels into the net. But within two minutes, goal-ace Moore turned goal-maker, setting up a simple chance for Johnny Squires.

Shortly after the turnaround Ireland seemed set for Italy. Goalkeeper Van Male gathered the ball and found himself lifted off his feet by Paddy Moore's shoulder-charge, which took man and ball over the goal-line. Such goals are rightly outlawed today. Indeed, they were never tolerated on the Continent, though the referee in this instance appears to have been satisfied. The goal was credited to Moore, though it is not clear that he even touched the ball.

Had Moore's later lob passed an inch or two lower, Ireland would have led 3-1 and that would have been that. Instead, left-winger Mijnders broke away and squared for Bakhuys, whose shot flew in cruelly off a post.

Even so, Ireland appeared safe, provided they held out. After eighty minutes the score still read 2-2. But, without warning, the Irish defence caved in. Bakhuys headed the Dutch in front, Vente made it four, and, with a flashing drive, Smit put the seal on Ireland's demise.

HOLLAND   (1) 5
Smit 40, 88, Bakhuys 65, 80,
Vente 84

IRELAND   (1) 2
Squires 42, Moore 50

HOLLAND: Van Male, Weber, Van Run, Pellikaan, Anderiesen, Van Heel, Wels, Vente, Bakhuys, Smit, Mijnders.
IRELAND: Foley (CORK), Gaskins (SHAMROCK R), Byrne (DRUMCONDRA), O'Reilly (ABERDEEN), Chatton (CORK), Kendrick (DOLPHIN), Kennedy (ST JAMES'S GATE), Squires (SHELBOURNE), Moore (ABERDEEN), Jordan (BOHEMIANS) (*sub* Horlacher, BOHEMIANS), Meehan (DRUMCONDRA).

The Ireland players trundled disconsolately back home, but still clung to their World Cup hopes. In those days the archaic mechanism of goal-average separated sides level on points. That is, the number of goals scored divided by the number conceded. Should Holland inflict a heavy defeat on Belgium, Ireland might still finish second.

Alas, Holland duly won, but only by 4-2. Ireland's late collapse had cost them dear. Pedants like to insist that Ireland failed to qualify by a mere 0.08 of a goal. But that, of course, is sleight of hand. Ireland failed by one whole goal, Holland's fifth. Without it, Ireland and Belgium would have tied on points and goal-average.

Neither Holland nor Belgium prospered in Italy, falling at the first hurdle. Fielding just four players who drew with Ireland, Belgium squandered a two-goal lead against Germany and collapsed 2-5. The Dutch side was more settled, retaining all but their goalkeeper and outside-left. Two of the Swiss goals that beat them (3-2) were scored by Poldi Kielholz, who played wearing spectacles. Italy duly won the cup, emulating the win-at-all-costs philosophy of the *Duce*. Fascism was the chief beneficiary of Italy's dubious triumph.

For Ireland, they could have competed in Uruguay; they should have competed in Italy. It would be many years before they came so close again.

Qualifying Pool XI

	P	W	D	L	F	A	Pts
HOLLAND	2	2	0	0	9	4	4
BELGIUM	2	0	1	1	6	8	1
Ireland	2	0	1	1	6	9	1

Other group result   Belgium v Holland 2-4

Ireland appearances and goalscorers (substitute appearances in brackets)
World Cup qualifying rounds 1934

	Apps	Goals		Apps	Goals		Apps	Goals
Foley J	2	–	Burke T	1	–	Lynch M	1	–
Gaskins P	2	–	Byrne D	1	–	Meehan P	1	–
Kendrick J	2	–	Byrne P	1	–	O'Keefe T	1	–
Kennedy W	2	–	Chatton H	1	–	Squires J	1	1
Moore P	2	5	Jordan W	1	–	Horlacher F	– (1)	–
O'Reilly J	2	–	Kelly J	1	–			

17 players used   23 apps   6 goals
                                            19 League of Ireland
                                            4 Scottish League

2

THE 1938 WORLD CUP

For most of its history World Cups have alternated between Europe and the Americas. By rights, the 1938 tournament should have returned to the southern hemisphere. Argentina applied to stage it, convinced FIFA would rubber-stamp her application.

But FIFA's bureaucrats had other considerations to weigh. So few European sides had been persuaded to travel to Uruguay in 1930 that the tournament was all but emasculated. Since 1934 FIFA membership had expanded, most of the new intake being European. With Mussolini's shadow skulking over the 1934 World Cup, and Hitler's over the 1936 Olympics, great tact was also required. Spain was stricken by civil war, and Austria was about to be swallowed up by Germany. Neither would compete. Taking the easy option, it was decided to hand the competition to France. This was masked as a tribute to Jules Rimet, the Frenchman instrumental in creating the World Cup. France, too, was happily free from the taint of fascism. No matter how it was dressed up, the choice of venue smacked of expediency.

The South Americans saw it for what it was, and were so outraged that all except Brazil tore up their invitations. Uruguay would again stay behind, having won the only World Cup she had entered. Argentina, so sure that the tournament was hers, sulked for twenty years.

This would be a World Cup enlivened by a dash of exotica. The Dutch East Indies and Cuba would turn up, their qualifying opponents having defaulted. But behind the window dressing, the 1938 World Cup would degenerate into little more than a European Cup.

This may have been bad news to South America and to FIFA, but it was heartening news to Ireland. With England still ostracising FIFA, and therefore unable to host a World Cup, a tournament in France was as near as could be.

Ireland had come so near to qualifying in 1934, failing against sides they were in the habit of thrashing, they must have felt doubly determined to make it this time, especially as like some celestial comet the finals were unlikely to come so close again.

Constitutionally, the Free State was no more, the name Éire ('Ireland' in Irish) being adopted at the end of 1936. FIFA's qualifying procedures looked confusing, but were actually simple. Ireland were placed in Pool II alongside Norway, Poland and Yugoslavia. In practice these were two sub-groups. Ireland would play Norway home and away, the winners going through; ditto Poland and Yugoslavia.

Qualifying Pool II

NORWAY v IRELAND
Sunday, 10 October 1937   *Ullevaal Stadium, Oslo – 19,000*

Norway were competing for the first time. Like the rest of Scandinavia, they were slow converts to the need for a World Cup, and indeed voted against the idea first time around. Norway had never played Ireland before, so this was a new experience for both.

Yet Norway – with no domestic league until 1938, and essentially amateurs until the 1980s – had done themselves proud at the 1936 Berlin Olympics. They put out Hitler's Germany and claimed third place, narrowly beaten in the semi-final by Italy, the World Cup holders and Olympic champions-elect. Norway's reputation was, therefore, higher than at any time in their history. This did not mean Norway were capable of moving mountains. Ireland's task was put into perspective when England travelled to Oslo in May 1937 and won 6-0. They might not win by six, but Ireland surely expected to win.

Had the qualifiers been played a couple of years earlier things might have been different. Since losing in Holland, Ireland had endured a miserable time. They didn't win a game for two years. They failed to exact revenge against the Dutch, who won handsomely, 5-3 at Dalymount Park. But performances from 1936 showed light at the end of the tunnel. Ireland played seven times and lost just once, 2-3 to Hungary, who would shortly reach the World Cup Final. Ireland's victims included Switzerland (twice); Germany (who were flown to Dublin with manager Sepp Herberger aboard a Junkers airliner, only to be hammered 5-2) – and France, in Paris's Colombes Stadium.

With the World Cup Final scheduled for the same stadium one year later, the French match was a useful taster for Ireland. Second-half goals by Davy Jordan and Johnny Brown swung it Ireland's way. Both were Ulstermen. Brown would pick up ten caps for Northern Ireland; Jordan none.

That end-of-season excursion enabled Ireland to field players willingly released from the English and Scottish leagues. Indeed, just two home-based players were represented against France.

One lingering source of friction between Dublin and the British Associations was Ireland's refusal to recognise players' contracts with clubs over the water or in Northern Ireland. Should British-based players find themselves in dispute with their clubs, there was always a team waiting to offer them refuge back home, contract or no contract. This practice undeniably contributed to English lack of cooperation.

Whatever the rights and wrongs, come October, and the trip to Oslo, the top English clubs were once again being obstructive, obliging the selectors to revert to a nine-man domestic contingent. This meant Charlie Turner was the only player to take the field both in Paris and Oslo, a wasteful exercise in terms of continuity and experience.

Indeed, experience seemed to be the last thing on the selectors' minds. Four players were winning first caps, another three their second. Joe O'Reilly, back home after his stint with Aberdeen, and Billy Jordan of Bohemians, would be the only ones to taste a second World Cup. Oddly, Jordan hadn't played between times, and wouldn't play again.

George McKenzie, the goalkeeper, and Charlie Turner, the captain, were the two Anglos, the first English-based players to represent Ireland in the World Cup. Both played for Southend United in Division III (South).

McKenzie was untypical, both as a goalkeeper and in his Irish credentials. He was regarded highly by old-timers at Southend. Yet he stood just 5ft 7in tall and weighed under 10 stone. He is said to have played with a cool head, unlike so many flamboyant goalies. Though born in Dublin he was raised in Scotland, and first drew attention to himself playing in Scottish junior football. He came to Southend via Plymouth Argyle, and quickly came to the notice of the Irish selectors.

This was McKenzie's first cap; Charlie Turner's sixth. Born in Athlone, Turner had come south to Southend from first division Leeds United. His first team appearances at Elland Road had been infrequent, owing to the consistent form of the incumbent centre-half, beefy Ernie Hart. An England international, Hart was in the twilight of his career, having skippered the club and played over 400 games for it. Turner hoped his time would come, but he was overlooked and transferred instead to Southend United. In January 1936 he enjoyed a towering game for Southend in an FA Cup-tie with Spurs at White Hart Lane, which finished 4-4, and was promptly capped in Ireland's next match. By the end of the year he was Ireland's captain. Turner made up for his lack of height with speed of mind and body. He would be an ever-present Ireland captain for two seasons.

With Southend playing on the Saturday, and Ireland on the Sunday, in Oslo, the two players had to be released from club duties. The fact that Southend languished in mid-table may have encouraged their cooperation. Things turned out well, Southend thrashing Torquay 5-1.

Ireland had learned from 1934 to take nothing for granted, even though they were widely expected to roll Norway over. Ireland's chief handicap was the need to shake off the effects of four days' hard travel. To what extent train- and boat-lag affected the outcome is difficult to assess. Suffice to say that Norway, against expectations, steamrollered their presumptuous visitors.

For much of the first half Ireland looked like being overrun. The home side looked to inside-right Radiar Kvammen to ignite their better moves, but it was Kvammen himself who fired Norway in front from a corner.

Ireland rallied, Blohm saved from Jimmy Dunne as a prelude to Matty Geoghegan ramming in the equaliser after Joe O'Reilly's spade-work.

Norway might have restored their lead three times by half-time. The biggest culprit was Holmberg, who frittered away a penalty after Martinsen was tumbled. The spot-kick clipped the outside of a post and flew behind for a goal-kick.

On the balance of play it was almost an affront when, early in the second half, Ireland took the lead. Billy Jordan passed; Jimmy Dunne scored.

Many times in 1934 Ireland had seemed poised to seal a place in the finals. They held the whip hand again, now, but once again found themselves trumped. Intense Norwegian pressure brought its just reward when danger-man Kvammen connected with a left-wing cross from Arne Brustad.

With barely twelve minutes to play Ireland were still level, hanging on for a creditable draw. Geoghegan and Dunne even had chances to put them back in front. But then Isaksen put the ball on Martinsen's toe, permitting the centre-forward to net from close in. By the close Ireland were grateful not to have suffered more. Norway should have had five and might have had ten. George McKenzie's many saves had done his country proud.

NORWAY (1) 3   **IRELAND** (1) 2
  Kvammen 30, 64,   Geoghegan 37, Dunne 49
  Martinsen 78

NORWAY: Blohm, Johannesen, Holmsen, Ulleberg, Eriksen, Holmberg, Frantzen, Kvammen, Martinsen, Isaksen, Brustad.
IRELAND: McKenzie (SOUTHEND), Williams (SHAMROCK R), Hoy (DUNDALK), O'Reilly (ST JAMES'S GATE), Turner (SOUTHEND), Kinsella (SHAMROCK R), T Donnelly (DRUMCONDRA), J Donnelly (DUNDALK), Dunne (SHAMROCK R), Jordan (BOHEMIANS), Geoghegan (ST JAMES'S GATE).

IRELAND v NORWAY
Sunday, 7 November 1937   *Dalymount Park – 27,000*

What Ireland now faced is bread and butter in today's football climate, a two-leg cup-tie, requiring well-versed tactics. Once Ireland had taken the lead in Oslo, they would today have protected the score at all costs. Matters were more slapdash in those happy-go-lucky days. Norway would not come to Dublin to sit back. Both teams would attack, and who knows, scant thought paid to the aggregate scores until the final whistle had blown.

Whatever their reasons, the Irish selectors retained just four players for the second leg – the Southend United pair, the veteran Joe O'Reilly, and Jimmy 'Snowy' Dunne, scorer in Oslo. Dunne's recent return to Shamrock Rovers after many seasons playing in England was a fillip to Irish football. He had enjoyed the bright lights of Sheffield United (during which time he picked up seven caps for Northern Ireland), Arsenal, (with whom he won a champions' medal), and Southampton. He was now home, player-coach at Milltown. Powerful with head and foot, he would inspire Rovers to the league title.

The seven international newcomers contained some young faces, and some not so young. Youngest of all was that of Johnny Carey of Manchester United. 'Jackie', as he was usually known in Ireland, was winning his first cap at the tender age of eighteen. In those days he was considered a forward, and he donned the No. 10 shirt against Norway.

Bohemians' Kevin O'Flanagan was only four months older, an all-rounder who would go on to represent Ireland at rugby and athletics, who would transfer after the war to Arsenal, become a doctor, and later in life become one of Ireland's senior sports administrators.

Harry Duggan was a blast from the past, the first link in a powerful Leeds United connection that continues to this day. Duggan was another of those players capped by both South and the North, proving more popular with the selectors in Belfast than those in Dublin. He had won his first cap for the Free State in 1927, waited three years for his second and another six for his third. Though playing in the same Leeds side as Charlie Turner, both were overlooked for the 1934 World Cup.

With his stocky build and famous coat-hanger ears, Duggan was credited with one of Leeds' most controversial goals, scoring from an 'impossible' angle against Preston, a shot which opposing defenders swore passed through a hole in the net. Pandemonium reigned, and, until their tempers cooled, Preston refused to restart.

Usually an outside-right, Duggan had broken into the Leeds team in 1926 and – unlike Turner – become an integral part of the Elland Road set-up. He had clocked up almost 200 appearances by the time he was snapped by Newport County, whom he would captain to the Division III (South) championship in 1939.

Duggan was one of five Anglos the selectors plumped for. The fifth was Bill Gorman, a full-back with second division Bury.

This was Ireland's first international in which both teams wore numbers on their shirts. The innovation must have seemed as dramatic at the time as the current trend of having players' names emblazoned on their backs. This unprecedented aid to identification duly prompted 27,000 Dalymount Park spectators to whisper: 'Who's that No. 10 for Norway?' The target of their admiration, Kvammen, looked even more menacing than he did in the first leg. Mercifully, Ireland's other tormentor in Oslo, the twinkle-toes winger, Brustad, was missing.

Ireland began brightly, netting after just five minutes. Alas, Kevin O'Flanagan's effort was ruled offside by English referee Gibbs. But when Duggan shortly flicked on Tommy Foy's cross for Dunne to head in, the goal stood, and Ireland had wiped out the deficit.

Unfortunately, that was the signal for Kvammen to turn on the style. He restored Norway's advantage after clever play from Holmberg set up the inside-right to shoot high into the net.

Young Carey had two chances to level before Kvammen appeared to put the game beyond Ireland. Martinsen shot past McKenzie, Billy O'Neill got back to clear, but steered the ball, fatally, straight to Kvammen.

Ireland had to find two goals, just to force a play-off, but four minutes into the second half Martinsen was sent clear by Frantzen to shoot in off a post. Kvammen then had a chance to secure his hat-track, but his shot was wide.

A conundrum for historians of Irish soccer. Why was it that when Ireland turned out in Amsterdam and Oslo they had the air of dead men, but when Belgium and Norway travelled to Dublin the visitors looked fresh as daisies?

With just over half an hour to play Norway still led 6-3 overall. To the credit of the Irish they never flagged. O'Flanagan scored from Dunne's back-header, but the ninety minutes were almost up when Turner sent Carey away, and the latter's cross was converted by Duggan.

There being no away-goals rule, Ireland needed one more to force a play-off, but time ran out. No one disputed the fact that Norway had been the better side twice and fully deserved their place in France.

IRELAND (1) 3	NORWAY (2) 3
Dunne 10, O'Flanagan 62,	Kvammen 16, 33, Martinsen 49
Duggan 88	

IRELAND: McKenzie (SOUTHEND), O'Neill (DUNDALK), Gorman (BURY), O'Reilly (ST JAMES'S GATE), Turner (SOUTHEND), Arrigan (WATERFORD), O'Flanagan (BOHEMIANS), Duggan (NEWPORT), Dunne (SHAMROCK R), Carey (MAN U), Foy (SHAMROCK R).
NORWAY: Nordby, Johannesen, Holmsen, Henriksen, Eriksen, Holmberg, Eeg, Kvammen, Martinsen, Frantzen, Hval.

Norway won on aggregate 6-5.

Although Ireland were out in the cold, England could still have taken part. Following Austria's withdrawal FIFA offered England a wild card. It was, to no one's surprise, politely declined. No other country was invited to fill the breach, so the 1938 World Cup kicked off with just fifteen competitors.

Norway, as it turned out, were well worth their place in France. Their results at the Olympics were shown to be no flash in the pan. It was their misfortune to be paired with Italy, World and Olympic champions, in the first round, in a re-run of the Olympic semi-final.

Norway's stirring encounter in Marseille's spanking new stadium is recorded in the annals of great World Cup matches. Knut Brunyldsen, a towering centre-forward mercifully unemployed against Ireland, tormented the Italians from the first minute till the last. Arne Brustad, that pacy, direct winger, likewise absent in Dublin, scored Norway's only goal (and would shortly receive the accolade of being picked to play for a representative FIFA XI against England), but his equaliser was not enough to save his team. Norway struck the Italian woodwork time and again, and had a goal disallowed, but Italy won through 2-1 in extra time, *en route* to yet another Final, where they beat Hungary 4-2. This marked the first World Cup where the hosts did not win. France had been dumped by Italy in the second round.

For gallant Norway, it would be another fifty-six years before they graced the World Cup finals again. And then they would come face to face with Ireland. Like vintage wine, Irish revenge would be all the sweeter when it finally arrived.

Ireland appearances and goalscorers
World Cup qualifying rounds 1938

	Apps	Goals		Apps	Goals		Apps	Goals
Dunne J	2	2	Donnelly J	1	–	Hoy M	1	1
McKenzie G	2	–	Donnelly T	1	–	Jordan W *	1	–
O'Reilly J *	2	–	Duggan H	1	1	Kinsella O	1	–
Turner C	2	–	Foy T	1	–	O'Flanagan K	1	1
Arrigan T	1	–	Gorman W	1	–	O'Neill W	1	–
Carey J	1	–	Geoghegan M	1	–	Williams J	1	–

* Appeared in 1934 World Cup.

18 players used

22 apps   5 goals
15 League of Ireland
7 English League

3

THE 1950 WORLD CUP

Tension in Europe soon engulfed the whole continent. As if with a premonition of the coming conflagration, Ireland filled the last months of peace with matches against countries soon to be consumed – Czechoslovakia, Poland, Hungary – and which would emerge after the war with the unwanted designation 'East European'. Two draws with World Cup runners-up Hungary helped ease the pain of a 0-6 thrashing by Poland.

Ireland's last match before World War II was against Germany in Bremen in May 1939. The Olympics were scheduled for 1940 and Germany fielded a side, buttressed by Austrian players, with that objective in mind. The match ended 1-1. Germany's goal was scored by Helmut Schoen, team manager of the side which would win the World Cup in 1974.

To the bitter resentment of Britain – and Ulster – Éire stayed neutral during the war. One part of Ireland took up arms, the other did not, fanning the flames of lasting bitterness.

Germany's sporting punishment for her wartime aggression was to be barred from FIFA and hence from competing in the next World Cup. This was designated for Brazil, in 1942, but that tournament and its earmarked successor in 1946 were non-starters. The first post-war World Cup went where it was intended eight years earlier, to Brazil. The trophy was now renamed the Jules Rimet Cup.

The big news from across the Irish Sea was that the British Associations had mended their fences with FIFA, condescended to rejoin, and would take part in the World Cup for the first time. This spelled trouble for the Emerald Isle, if only because two Irelands were now embarked on a quest for the same prize. They would have to call a halt to their habit of picking players willy-nilly from the other side.

In political terms, the split from Britain was finalised in 1949, when Éire declared itself the Republic of Ireland and announced its intention to leave the Commonwealth. The Republic henceforth cut its ties with London. In footballing terms, friction with the North continued awhile, owing to both Dublin and Belfast seeking exclusive rights to the use of the word 'Ireland'.

Not wishing to upset the British Associations, FIFA hedged, deferring a decision for a few more years. In the meantime, the Republic would continue to be officially listed as Éire.

To further kow-tow to the British Associations, FIFA invited them to utilise their own annual championship to determine which *two* of them would qualify for Brazil. This meant that after thirty years Northern Ireland still had played nobody but England, Scotland or Wales. Barred from picking Johnny Carey or any other Republic stars, Northern Ireland had to field players from the six counties. The result – a 2-8 massacre by Scotland, 2-9 by England. With Northern Ireland out of contention, the rules were relaxed for their third qualifier, against Wales. Fortified by their southern brethren, Northern Ireland forced a goalless draw, in which Waterford-born Davy Walsh became the first and last player to play World Cup football for both Irelands.

Ireland were, as usual, thrown to the wider European winds. They were allotted to a pool with Sweden and Finland in the only European section (other than the British one) to comprise more than two nations. Difficulties with timetabling – caused by Scandinavia's long snowbound winters – meant that Ireland's qualifiers would spread from one season to the next.

Qualifying Pool V

SWEDEN v IRELAND
Thursday, 2 June 1949   *Resunda Stadium, Stockholm – 38,000*

Like Ireland, Sweden were World Cup regulars, though they were slow converts to the need for a professionals' championship. Sweden had reached the finals in both 1934 and '38. In 1934 they had overcome Argentina before succumbing narrowly to Germany, who went on to finish third. Four years later, Sweden had been handed a first-round bye (courtesy of England's non-participation), walloped Cuba 8-0 in the second round, and *mirabile dictu* found themselves in the semi-finals. Hungary (1-5), and Brazil (2-4) in the play-off for third place, dispelled notions of grandiosity.

Her wartime neutrality spared Sweden the social and economic dislocation that had ravaged much of the continent. In the 1948 London Olympics, her footballers had swept past the fancied Austrians on their way to taking the title. Olympic champions were customarily strong in the professionals' championship. In the 1930s both Uruguay and Italy went from the one title to the other, and Sweden were keen to emulate them. They enjoyed the perfect preparation, beating England 3-1 in Stockholm in May 1949.

Sweden were big fish in the small Scandinavian pond, but, to aid their development they had turned to an Englishman. George Raynor was a so-so player before the war with Aldershot and Bury, who later found himself posted to Mesopotamia with the Army physical training corps. In 1946 he was recruited from his position as trainer of Aldershot reserves to become Sweden's national coach. His was no here-today, gone-tomorrow appointment. In 1958 he would guide Sweden to the World Cup Final.

The tiny, energetic Yorkshireman was only part of Sweden's international dimension. Although the backbone of the side comprised the usual motley of butchers, bakers, and candlestick makers, half were professionals abroad, mainly in Italy. Naturally, Sweden had won the Olympic title without them.

Ireland might have been celebrating the birth of the Republic, but they had little to celebrate on the soccer pitch. They had played ten matches since the war, seven of them against Spain or Portugal, who had likewise stayed neutral and who were also in a position to quickly resume competition. Nevertheless, Ireland must have been heartily sick of the sight of them.

The breakthrough came in 1946, at Dalymount Park, in England's first fixture against southern Ireland. Only two days earlier England had thrashed Northern Ireland 7-2 in Belfast, and six Irish players who lined at up Windsor Park now did so at Dalymount. Ireland were eight minutes from a draw when Tom Finney pounced. Yet Ireland might have carried a six-game losing streak to Stockholm but for Paddy Coad's penalty against Portugal.

The new era closed the curtain on Ireland sides dominated by Irish-based players, though this was not universally welcomed. The stuffed shirts in Merrion Square were patriotic if nothing else, and still – in all probability – believed their boys in the LOI to be the finest. With the exception of the Johnny Careys and Tommy Eglingtons – of whom there were not too many – the selectors had to scour the English lower divisions and second elevens in search of eligible Irishmen. In the main, the selectors had never seen them play, and had to pick them on the word of those who had, or else on whim.

Scotland, incidentally, would not field an international side comprising a majority of Anglos until the 1970s. One might argue that the Scottish league was stronger than the LOI, but we are talking patriotism, not rationalism.

Though Drumcondra had clung on to the Irish title they first won in 1948, the only intruders into what was, in effect, an English league XI were Tommy Godwin and Paddy Coad of Shamrock Rovers.

This was to be Coad's only outing in the World Cup. To his army of devotees, the war stunted his career. He was twenty-five by the time peace was restored. Coad is revered today as an inside-forward untypical of his kind. Instead of the kick and rush, Coad stroked the ball in the manner of the better continentals. It says much for his calm authority on the pitch that it concealed his comparative slowness of foot. Coad is considered the architect of Rovers' golden era of the 1950s. He would contest eight FAI Cup Finals, score forty-one cup goals, and be talked of with hindsight as the best Irish player never to have been snapped up by a top English or Scottish club.

Of Ireland's English imports, Tom Keane and John O'Driscoll were celebrating Swansea City's promotion to division two. Tommy Eglington's Everton had narrowly missed relegation – and unwelcome fixtures against Swansea the following season. Johnny Carey's Manchester United had finished runners-up for the third time in a row.

Clearly, Sweden would be a tough nut to crack, even though Ireland brought familiar drizzle with them, and even though Gunner Nordahl, feared striker with Milan, was absent. Ireland began brightly, Davy Walsh tucking home from a tight angle after Knut Nordahl failed to clear O'Driscoll's cross. Ireland did not look to sit back, but within half an hour were trailing. Con Martin handled in a goalmouth melee. Sune Andersson converted the penalty, and Hasse Jeppson put the Swedes in front from Johnsson's cross.

Ireland threatened little after that, apart from O'Driscoll's hopeful effort from near the halfway line. Sweden secured the result with an all-Milanese third goal: Gunnar Gren's free-kick was met by Nils Liedholm's head.

SWEDEN (2) 3   **IRELAND (1) 1**
S Andersson 17 pen, Jeppson 37,   Walsh 9
Liedholm 69

SWEDEN: Svensson, K E Andersson, Nilsson, Rosen, Nordahl, S Andersson, Johnsson, Gren, Jeppson, Carlsson, Liedholm.
IRELAND: Godwin (SHAMROCK R), Carey (MAN U), Keane (SWANSEA), Gannon (SHEFF W), Martin (VILLA), Moroney (WEST HAM), O'Driscoll (SWANSEA), Coad (SHAMROCK R), D Walsh (WBA), McGowan (WEST HAM), Eglington (EVERTON).

IRELAND v FINLAND
Thursday, 8 September 1949   *Dalymount Park – 22,479*

While the Swedes were on the up, their eastern neighbours could go no lower. Finland, of course, had suffered mightily in the war, losing much of her north-eastern territory to the Soviet Red Army. The Finns were – and are – the poor relations of Scandinavian football, and to this day have never competed in the finals of the World Cup. They had first entered in 1938, propping up their qualifying section with no points and no goals.

There was every hope that Finland would provide the Irish with their first World Cup win. Ireland had closed the door on the previous season by suffering a thumping home defeat by Spain. That result was unlikely to have any bearing, if only because the Ireland line-up was completely different. Several English-based players happily released in June were kept behind in September. This helped usher in four first caps, including those for Arthur Fitzsimons and Peter Desmond of Middlesbrough.

The newcomers joined in the pre-match ritual that would serve Ireland until modern times. The players would meet up at the Gresham Hotel for lunch, say their hellos, often for the first time, and go off afterwards to play an international football match. Talk about strangers in uniform. There could be no team spirit as such, for there was no team, just an assortment of individuals. As for tactics. What tactics?

It was almost a case of 'what match?' The Finnish FA argued that as their season was so short Ireland should kindly play them in July or August.

Fitzsimons and Desmond nearly celebrated their call-up with a goal apiece, though both were to be denied. Fitzsimons, in fact, had only a team-mate to blame for robbing him of a sensational strike. He had dribbled past two defenders, side-stepped keeper Sarnola, and chipped towards the empty goal. Fellow debutant Johnny Gavin tried to make sure, but headed wide.

The anguish was personal, not collective, for Finland provided only token resistance. They were happy for Ireland to bring on a twelfth man – Pat Daly replacing the injured Brendan Carroll – in the latest episode of Ireland's World Cup substitute saga. Gavin atoned for his earlier blunder by enticing one from Sarnola, who fumbled the winger's corner into the net.

Ireland's second and third goals were claimed by Con Martin, one of the more intriguing characters ever to pull on an Ireland shirt. This was Martin's twelfth international appearance, having already filled six different positions – including goalkeeper in Spain in 1946, where Ireland won 1-0. He was the play anywhere, do anything man of Irish football.

An all-round sportsman, Martin had during the war been 'caught' by the GAA for playing that illegal game, soccer. He was duly suspended, and thereby missed the chance of appearing in an All-Ireland Gaelic football final. It was the army that first introduced him to soccer. He graduated through the ranks from Glentoran to Leeds United for a then record fee of £8,000, before moving on to Aston Villa, where he played the best football of his life. His commanding height made him a natural, if versatile, defender, but when needs be he could score goals with the best of them. He would win thirty caps for Ireland, complemented by six more for Northern Ireland.

Now, in the reshuffle brought about by Carroll's injury, he was switched from centre-half to centre-forward. He was soon entrusted with a penalty-kick, after Asikainen toppled Desmond in the box. He made no mistake, nor with a second-half header that sealed Ireland's win. Martin was denied his hat-trick by Sarnola's fine late save.

IRELAND (2) 3   **FINLAND (0) 0**
Gavin 35, Martin 44 pen, 68

IRELAND: Godwin (SHAMROCK R), Carey (MAN U), Aherne (LUTON), Gannon (SHEFF W), Martin (VILLA), Moroney (WEST HAM), Gavin (NORWICH), Fitzsimons (MIDDLESBROUGH), Carroll (SHELBOURNE) (*sub* Daly, SHAMROCK R), Desmond (MIDDLESBROUGH), O'Connor (SHAMROCK R). FINLAND: Sarnola, Martin, Saarnio, Asikainen, Pylkkönen, Beijar, Svahn, Myntti, Rytkönen, Vaihela, Lehtovirta.

FINLAND v IRELAND

Sunday, 9 October 1949   *Olympiastadion, Helsinki – 13,437*

It was just two weeks later that Ireland beat England 2-0 at Goodison Park. The result entered Irish folklore; the English quickly forgot about it, reasoning that Ireland were not really 'foreigners'. This allowed the myth of English invincibility at home to live awhile longer.

Ireland's victorious side was skippered as always by the incomparable Johnny Carey. It is difficult for outsiders to appreciate what Carey meant to Irish football. He was not just a great player in Irish terms: he was a great player. Full stop. His twenty-nine Ireland caps (and seven Northern Ireland ones) extended over a fifteen-year period while he was on the books of just one club, Manchester United. He was an Ireland international before the war, making his debut against Norway in the World Cup.

After the war he was back, captaining United to the FA Cup in 1948. Twelve months later he was voted English Footballer of the Year. Carey received, perhaps, his greatest tribute in 1947, when he was asked to captain a European Select XI to play Britain's best at Hampden Park.

All this made Carey more than just a mere footballer. To Ireland he was a beacon-light, an icon, a player who could hold his own in any company. A Gaelic footballer in his youth, he was just eighteen when snapped up by the then second division Old Trafford club. Like Con Martin, Carey could and did play anywhere, though as his years went up so his shirt numbers went down. A sprightly inside forward in his younger days, Carey finally settled down as Ireland's right-back.

Like so many superstars of yesteryear, it was the modest and sporting way Carey conducted himself on and off the pitch that took him to people's hearts. No one before or since has enjoyed greater recognition as Ireland's ambassador of football. He was not just captain; he was standard-bearer.

Having enjoyed the plaudits against England, Carey now had to inspire his men against Finland. He had the bonus of an unchanged side, apart from Johnny Gavin, who resumed on the wing, and Timmy Coffey who stepped in for his one international. Ireland had to win to keep the pressure on Sweden.

A sparse crowd endured an eminently forgettable match. A Davy Walsh effort was annulled for a supposed foul on the goalkeeper, while at the other end Asikainen fired against Ireland's crossbar.

Ireland stepped on the gas in the second half, and at last broke through when Coffey fed Peter Farrell. The Everton forward swept past a defender to score. The Irish might even have increased their lead, but were caught out by a heavily-manned raid in the last minute. The ball finished in the Irish net alongside two frustrated Irish defenders. Vaihela was credited with Finland's first World Cup goal, which secured their first World Cup point.

FINLAND (0) 1	IRELAND (0) 1
Vaihela 89	Farrell 65

FINLAND: Laaksonen, Martin, Saarnio, V Asikainen, Pylkkönen, Beijar, Vaihela, Myntti, Y Asikainen, Teräs, Saarinen.
IRELAND: Godwin (LEICESTER), Carey (MAN U), Aherne (LUTON), Coffey (DRUMCONDRA), Martin (VILLA), Moroney (WEST HAM), Gavin (NORWICH), Farrell (EVERTON), D Walsh (WBA), Desmond (MIDDLESBROUGH), O'Connor (SHAMROCK R),

---

IRELAND v SWEDEN
Sunday, 13 November 1949   *Dalymount Park – 41,031*

Vaihela's late strike cast a mortal blow to Ireland's World Cup hopes. Ireland needed to beat Sweden, to give them five points, but Sweden looked likely to overtake that total. They had yet to play Finland, but, with winter upon them, they appeared unlikely to do so.

Once again the Irish selectors were encouraged to make minimal changes. The return of Peter Corr was one; the introduction of Reg Ryan the other. The team that saw off England was given another vote of confidence.

An attendance of over 41,000, by far Ireland's biggest World Cup crowd to date, rolled up to show their appreciation for the Goodison heroics. If they came with expectation in their breast, the dawn of a new age of Irish soccer perhaps, they were to be swiftly disillusioned. Ireland's hopes were bruised after just four minutes, broken by half-time.

Once again George Raynor fielded Hasse Jeppson at No. 9. The English-style game that Raynor imported was alive to players of Jeppson's type, tall, strong, fast, a bagger of goals. So perfectly tailored was he for the bone-crunching British game that, after the World Cup, he played briefly for Charlton Athletic. His priceless goals made the difference between relegation to the second division and survival in the first.

But if Sweden's No. 9 took the eye before kick-off, it was the No. 8 – Karl-Erik 'Kalle' Palmer – who took it thereafter. Could this slight, even frail-looking teenager, an inside forward with Malmö, really be an international footballer? Palmer chose Dalymount Park as the stage for a stunning hat-trick, the first ever to be inflicted upon the Ireland national side.

He served notice almost with his first touch, scoring after Sundqvist's left-wing cross flew straight to his feet.

Twice Peter Corr struck the Swedish crossbar, once, embarrassingly, from just two yards out; later, more commendably, from a sweetly struck free-kick. When Ireland were awarded an indirect kick six yards out, Desmond squared to Carey, whose shot – the crowd bellowed – struck a Swedish hand before it was cleared.

It was to be the crucial turning point. Minutes later Kalle Palmer fired his second goal. It stemmed from one of those phantom 'whistles' from the crowd which were a feature of football matches in times gone by. The Irish defence stopped, Palmer didn't, and English referee Ring pointed to the centre circle. It was not he who had blown.

Ireland were effectively out of the Cup, though when Davy Walsh was impeded by Knut Nordahl, Con Martin's penalty briefly raised their spirits.

They were quickly dampened by Palmer's third goal. A tiring Irish side – several had been in league action the previous day – looked increasingly vulnerable to the counter-attack. Johnny Carey's miscued clearance propelled the ball across his own goal and Palmer pounced.

The Irish rejuggled their formation in an attempt to hit back, but could not stave off their first home defeat in the World Cup.

IRELAND   (0) 1   **SWEDEN   (2) 3**
Martin 61 pen   Palmer 4, 40, 68

IRELAND: Godwin (LEICESTER), Carey (MAN U), Aherne (LUTON), W Walsh (MAN C), Martin (VILLA), Ryan (WBA), Corr (EVERTON), Farrell (EVERTON), D Walsh (WBA), Desmond (MIDDLESBROUGH), O'Connor (SHAMROCK R).
SWEDEN: Lindberg, K E Andersson, Nilsson, Ahlund, Nordahl, Rosen, Johnsson, Palmer, Jeppson, S Andersson, Sundqvist.

Finland needed to beat Sweden twice to leapfrog above them, but the fixtures were never fulfilled, permitting the Swedes to stake their place in Brazil. Had Ireland beaten them, and gone top, one presumes Sweden would have had to meet Finland, somehow. The alternative was to default in favour of Ireland.

This is hypothetical. The problems confronting FIFA were real. Scotland all along had insisted she would travel only as British champions. When England knocked her into second place, she stuck to her pledge. Ireland were invited, it appears, at short notice to take Scotland's place. She declined, as did Portugal. Withdrawals of one kind of another meant that, as in 1930, the World Cup would be blessed with just thirteen starters. One of these was England, about to be beaten by the no-hopers of the United States.

Sweden, meanwhile, were the revelation of the tournament. In their very first match they defeated defending champions Italy (3-2). George Raynor seemed to be unearthing stars by the minute. His latest was Lennart Skoglund, who, while Palmer was banging them in at Dalymount, was toiling away in the Swedish third division. Skoglund bagged two goals against Italy.

Kalle Palmer then took over, scoring against Paraguay, Uruguay, and Spain. Though they suffered a 1-7 mauling by Brazil on the way, Sweden finished up third, one place better than in 1938. When one recalls their Olympic title, Sweden were up there with the best, and this puts Ireland's valiant efforts into perspective.

The twin giants of the 1950 World Cup were Brazil and Uruguay. Each was favoured by good fortune – Brazil, in playing at home (and all but one match in Rio); Uruguay by the draw, which asked them only to see off Bolivia to enter the final phase. Uruguay came from behind to snatch the Cup from Brazil in the final match. Twice Uruguay had entered, twice they had won. This nation of just two million souls was surely something special.

Qualifying Pool V

	P	W	D	L	F	A	Pts
SWEDEN	2	2	0	0	6	2	4
Ireland	4	1	1	2	6	7	3
Finland	2	0	1	1	1	4	1

Other group results
The two Sweden v Finland fixtures were not played.

Ireland appearances and goalscorers (substitute appearances in brackets)
World Cup qualifying rounds 1950

	Apps	Goals		Apps	Goals		Apps	Goals
Carey J	4	–	Farrell P	2	1	Fitzsimons A	1	–
Godwin T	4	–	Gannon E	2	–	Keane T	1	–
Martin C	4	3	Gavin J	2	1	McGowan D	1	–
Aherne T	3	–	Carroll B	1	–	O'Driscoll J	1	–
Desmond P	3	–	Coad P	1	–	Ryan R	1	–
Moroney T	3	–	Coffey T	1	–	Walsh W	1	–
O'Connor T	3	–	Corr P	1	–	Daly P	– (1)	–
Walsh D	3	1	Eglington T	1	–			

	45 apps 6 goals
	9 League of Ireland
23 players used	36 English League

4

THE 1954 WORLD CUP

Four years on, the World Cup returned to Europe, to Switzerland. As the headquarters of FIFA, in the fiftieth year of that organisation's existence, and as a bastion of political neutrality at the height of the Cold War, Switzerland was a prudent choice. It was also an enticing one for Ireland and other would-be European participants.

Ireland's form since the lesson painfully inflicted on them by Sweden showed more low spots than high. Ireland looked particularly fragile on their travels, where they found themselves stuffed 1-5 in Brussels, 0-3 in Cologne, 0-6 in Vienna, and 0-6 once again, this time in Madrid. True, two of those defeats were reversed in Dublin – the Germans (soon to be world champions) 3-2, and Austria, 4-0 – but the overall picture of three wins out of ten told its own story. Among a string of defeats was one inflicted by Argentina (0-1) at Dalymount in 1951, in a match that was Ireland's first against South American opponents. An attendance of 40,000 showed how eagerly the visitors were welcomed, a turn-out that was improbably high only in view of Argentina's persistent shunning of the World Cup. What might the attendance have been for double-champions Uruguay?

Domestically, Irish football was looking healthy. League membership was expanding, and no one club was able to cock a snook at the rest. Three newcomers – Cork Athletic, Sligo Rovers, and St Patrick's Athletic – launched assaults on the championship, facing stiff competition from established clubs, Drumcondra, Shelbourne, and Shamrock Rovers.

When FIFA convened to announce the draw for 1954, Ireland found their path blocked by France and Luxembourg. Matches would not be spread over two seasons, as was the case in 1950, but squeezed within one. Luxembourg were not expected to stand in the way of anybody. France were another matter. She had competed, without distinction, in all three World Cups of the 1930s, but had ostracised Brazil '50 in dramatic fashion. When France lost a play-off eliminator with Yugoslavia, that should have been the end of the matter. But when Turkey rejected the place she had earned, France received a late wild-card entry. France said yes, promptly lost warm-up matches against

Belgium and Scotland, and suddenly got cold feet. When she was then informed that her fixture schedule in Brazil required a two-thousand mile hike from one end of the country to another, with only four days between matches, that provided the pretext for her to pull out.

For Northern Ireland and the other British nations, it was same again. The Home Championship would determine which two would qualify.

Qualifying Pool IV

IRELAND v FRANCE
Sunday, 4 October 1953   *Dalymount Park – 45,000*

Coincidentally, Ireland had entertained France in a friendly as recently as November 1952. For much of that match – marred by trouble in the crowd and on the pitch – Ireland had led by Sean Fallon's goal, only to be pulled back by Roger Piantoni's merited equaliser. The one other meeting between the sides had been back in 1937, Ireland winning 2-0 in Paris.

France were developing into one of Europe's more enterprising sides. They had drawn 2-2 with England at Highbury in 1951 and beaten the coming world champions, West Germany, 3-1. In the World Cup they had got off to a flying start with a 6-1 demolition in Luxembourg, and now kept faith with seven of their earlier Dublin eleven. Glancing through their side, one is struck by names who, four years on, would make such a splash in Sweden. Wing-halves Armand Penverne and Marcel, plus the dashing winger Piantoni, for example. Central pivot Robert Jonquet, Glovacki and Raymond Kopa would line up for Reims in the first, 1956, European Cup Final. The brilliant Kopa, just twenty-two, who could play winger or centre-forward, would soon switch to Reims' conquerors, Real Madrid, and in 1958 be voted European Footballer of the Year. Still, the Irish were not soothsayers. They could have anticipated none of this, and must have hoped, at the least, for a repeat of their earlier draw.

The new World Cup would see a new Ireland, one without the services of its pillar and captain, Johnny Carey. Ireland's most capped player, he seemed to have been around for ever, yet was only thirty-four when he won his last cap. That was in Ireland's last match, at home to Austria in March. It must have felt strange, Ireland taking the field bereft of Carey's reassuring presence. He was now team coach, some might say manager, except that the selectors continued to pull the strings. But at least Carey was looking on, like some benevolent patriarch, able to give a wink here, a nod there, to fashion the side in the right direction.

Everton's Peter Farrell, Ireland's new skipper, wasn't new to the job; he had held it briefly in 1946, and again more recently.

Farrell, Con Martin, Arthur Fitzsimons, Tommy Moroney, Davy Walsh, Reg Ryan and Tommy Eglington made a total of seven players embarking on their second World Cup quest, and three more veterans from 1950 – Tommy 'Bud' Aherne, Eddie Gannon, and Johnny Gavin – would appear before the campaign was out. This suggested a welcome policy of continuity on the part of the selectors. The inclusion of Jimmy O'Neill, in goal, alongside Farrell and Eglington, raised the Goodison contingent to three – though O'Neill was lucky to get a game in Everton's first team. Luton Town players, Seamus Dunne and Tommy Aherne, filled the full-back slots. Aherne's long association with Belfast Celtic had greatly restricted his availability for the Republic. He had also won four caps for Northern Ireland, but that much-maligned open door was now firmly shut. Beginning with Con Martin, one Republic-born player after another had declared for the South, intimating that they were not interested in playing for the North, even if selected, which some of them were.

The one player not mentioned, Frank O'Farrell, would in due course face the unenviable task of succeeding Matt Busby as manager at Old Trafford.

What a feast of football France now turned on before 45,000 awestruck customers. Dalymount Park had never known a larger gate, and never more goals in an international.

There was little early indication of the goal-glut to come. Neither goalie was troubled, other than when Davy Walsh 'punched' the ball goalwards. The referee's whistle stayed silent and Vignal pulled off a flying save. The Racing Club de Paris goalkeeper was back to full fitness. He had been hurt six minutes into the game with Luxembourg and been subbed by Remetter – a further example of unofficial World Cup substitutions.

It was twenty-three minutes before France scored, Glovacki turning the ball in from Kopa's corner. The goal did not dampen Irish resolve and Walsh had a legitimate chance to equalise. It took a second French goal, by Penverne, again set up by Kopa, to puncture Irish spirits.

The second half appears to have been one-way traffic. O'Neill kept out two scorchers, before Hungarian-born Joseph Ujlaki (of Nice) sliced through the Irish rearguard and beat the keeper at his near post.

Ireland reshuffled their formation. Eglington went over to the left, Ryan to inside-right and Moroney to right wing. The switch seemed to have paid dividends when Marcel handled Ryan's shot. Ryan took the penalty himself, Vignal saved, but Ryan lashed in the rebound. He thereby entered the record books as having missed a penalty. But he looked happy enough.

France treated that momentary challenge to their dominance as if it were a fly to be swatted aside. Undaunted, they stormed upfield to score twice more. Ujlaki pounced when O'Neill could do no better than block Piantoni's effort. They scored their fifth while temporarily reduced to ten men. Skipper Roger

Marche was receiving treatment on the touchline when Flamion climaxed the best move of the match. Once again Kopa was at the heart of it.

There were still eighteen minutes to play, and at 1-5 Ireland were heading for humiliation. Perhaps the French team relaxed, for Walsh suddenly headed in from Moroney's cross, and O'Farrell beat Vignal with a flashing shot on the run. The final score suggested a close run thing. It was hardly that.

Belgium, Holland, and now France. This was just the latest instance of Ireland losing to World Cup opponents they were accustomed to beating, but who rose to the big occasion when Ireland could not.

IRELAND (0) 3	**FRANCE (2) 5**
Ryan 58, Walsh 83,	Glovacki 23, Penverne 40,
O'Farrell 88	Ujlaki 50, 69, Flamion 72

IRELAND: O'Neill (EVERTON), Dunne (LUTON), Aherne (LUTON), Farrell (EVERTON), Martin (VILLA), O'Farrell (WEST HAM), Fitzsimons (MIDDLESBROUGH), Moroney (EVERGREEN U), Walsh (VILLA), Ryan (WBA), Eglington (EVERTON).

FRANCE: Vignal, Gianessi, Marche, Penverne, Jonquet, Marcel, Ujlaki, Glovacki, Kopa, Flamion, Piantoni.

IRELAND v LUXEMBOURG
Wednesday, 28 October 1953   *Dalymount Park – 20,000*

Losing at home to one's principal rivals is not a recipe for success. France had run up eleven goals in two games and were almost out of sight. Hitherto, Ireland had always carried their hopes into their final qualifier. Barring an improbable reversal of fortunes in Paris, they were now out after their first.

The shell-shocked Irish selectors panicked, making six changes for the visit of Luxembourg later that month. 'Bud' Aherne and Tommy Moroney were shown the door for good. As their international careers ended, others began. Liam Munroe, George Cummins, and young Noel Cantwell were all given their chance. Munroe would not survive beyond this match; Cummins and Cantwell would play a noble part in Irish soccer for many a year.

In the absence of Peter Farrell, the captaincy passed for the first time to Tommy Eglington. Dubliner Eglington stands as another of those early giants of Irish football. Like others of his vintage, 'Eggo' excelled in his schoolboy days at hurling and Gaelic football, as well as soccer. He was an Irish international at soccer even before Everton snapped him up from Shamrock Rovers in 1946. Eglington was a winger of the old school, head down, swift of foot, haring straight for the corner flag before unleashing those pinpoint crosses. Untypically, however, his job did not end there. Eglington did not wait for the ball to come to him: he hunted it with the tenacity of a latter-day ball-winner. Though he is principally remembered as a 'provider' for Ireland, scoring only twice, it is his goals that are cherished on Merseyside, seventy-six (in the league) in eleven seasons. He once managed five in one match, against hapless Doncaster, surely a record for a winger.

Eglington would earn a total of twenty-four Ireland (plus six Northern Ireland) caps, yet would probably have given half of them up for the one that got away. For reasons that had nothing to do with injury, and everything to do with the politicking of the selection committee, Eglington was omitted from the side that beat England on his beloved Goodison patch in 1949.

The new skipper couldn't have asked for weaker opposition against whom to motivate his troops. Luxembourg were the whipping boys of European football. The tiny Grand Duchy, with a population of just 300,000, had featured in seven World Cup qualifiers since 1934. They had lost the lot and shipped thirty-six goals, an average of over five per match. This, then, was the measure of the motley of amateurs that trotted sheepishly out like lambs to the slaughter. In view of the French result in Dublin, one wonders if they secretly fancied their chances.

The match was hardly a classic, though Ireland won it with few scares. New-boy Munroe might have claimed an undreamed-of success when his corner drifted against a post. The first goal, a gem, was not long delayed. Shay Gibbons, palpably one-footed, engineered a decoy that enabled Arthur Fitzsimons to waltz past three defenders, switch the ball from one foot to the other, and curl it home from an acute angle.

Shortly after half-time Ryan repeated his French trick. He was fouled, won a penalty, and took it himself. This time he did not require a follow-up.

Ireland's third was another wide-angled shot from Fitzsimons, that might have stayed out had it not ballooned off keeper Steffen's body. With precious few defensive duties to perform, Reg Ryan pushed forward to lend weight to the attack. A fourth goal arrived when Eglington's centre was headed against the bar by Gibbons and rebounded for Eglington to finish it off.

So Luxembourg extended their dismal sequence, thankful only that their margin of defeat was slimmer than most.

IRELAND (1) 4   **LUXEMBOURG (0) 0**
Fitzsimons 18, 59, Ryan 48 pen,
Eglington 75

IRELAND: O'Neill (EVERTON), Dunne (LUTON), Lawler (FULHAM), Gannon (SHEFF W), Cantwell (WEST HAM), Ryan (WBA), Munroe (SHAMROCK R), Cummins (LUTON), Gibbons (ST PATRICK'S), Fitzsimons (MIDDLESBROUGH), Eglington (EVERTON).
LUXEMBOURG: Steffen, Speck, Lorang-Trinkes, Fickinger, Spartz, Wagner, May, Meurisse, Kohn, Weydert, Kemp.

FRANCE v IRELAND

Wednesday, 25 November 1953   *Parc des Princes, Paris – 32,265*

Ireland had won on their only previous trip to Paris, but that had been so long ago (1937) as to be a meaningless statistic. Ireland sorely needed a repeat victory. France evidently did not think that was likely, for their side had a distinctly 'reserve' feel to it. They left out six of the side who demolished Ireland in Dublin, including Penverne, Jonquet, and Kopa. Even so, barring an improbable away victory, France were set fair for Switzerland.

For this do-or-die match, the Irish selectors sagely reverted to experience. The three newcomers against Luxembourg were cast aside, though the introduction of Tommy Clinton at right-back and return of Peter Farrell raised the Goodison contingent to four.

Farrell did not reclaim the captaincy from Eglington on this occasion, but his was a special talent, vital to the side. He had been picked for Shamrock Rovers' first team while still a schoolboy. At every stage his career paralleled that of his close friend Tommy Eglington, who was five months younger. They were signed by Everton in 1946 for a combined fee of about £5,000 and illuminated the Merseyside club for eleven years, during which time they played over 800 games between them. Now, in 1953-54, Everton were languishing in the second division. In 1957 the duo would both be transferred to Tranmere.

Like Eglington, Farrell was capped by Ireland while still with Shamrock Rovers. In Farrell's case he achieved the extraordinary honour of captaining his country in his first international. Of medium height, stocky and curly-haired, Farrell was the archetypal wing-half, whether left or right. He was a passer of the ball in an age when passing was considered sacrosanct. To this precious gift he added a willingness to graft, and his general consistency is recognised in his vast number of first-team appearances. Farrell was blessed with such a saintly air, both on and off the pitch, that at one stage he was forced into formally denying rumours that he was set for the priesthood. His greatest moment as an international probably came when scoring Ireland's second goal against England before a stunned Goodison audience in 1949. He had played against England twice before, both times for Northern Ireland, but never before scored or ended on the winning side. His memory on Merseyside is such that he is one of the few footballers to have a street named after him – Farrell Close.

Like other imperial powers – with England, then, a notable exception – France was quick to exploit the native talent of her colonial subjects, Moroccans, Algerians, and anyone else paying allegiance to the French tricolour. Just Fontaine, for example, would become a World Cup superstar in 1958. For the moment, the eye fell on Ben Mohammed Abdelsalem, who twice might have scored when shooting wide of the post, and who saw another effort bravely foiled by O'Neill. Tommy Clinton cleared one shot off the line, Joe 'Robin' Lawler another.

Ireland were not without their moments in this stirring contest. Fitzsimons, Ryan and Walsh might all have pressed French panic buttons. In the second half the unfortunate Farrell was slowed by a knock and limped out time on the touchline. It was while Ireland were thus depleted that France scored the goal they had threatened since the turnaround. Ujlaki clattered into Lawler, who was in possession. The Frenchman appeared to be playing the man rather than the ball, but the referee waved play on. Ujlaki centred, Clinton's defensive header went awry, and Piantoni swooped.

FRANCE   (0) 1   **IRELAND   (0) 0**
Piantoni 73

FRANCE: Remetter, Mihoubi, Gianessi, Marche, Cuissand, Marcel, Ujlaki, Strappe, Abdelsalem, Piantoni, Delarderliere.
IRELAND: O'Neill (EVERTON), Clinton (EVERTON), Lawler (FULHAM), Gannon (SHEFF W), Martin (VILLA), Farrell (EVERTON), Ringstead (SHEFF U), Ryan (WBA), Walsh (VILLA), Fitzsimons (MIDDLESBROUGH), Eglington (EVERTON).

LUXEMBOURG v IRELAND
Sunday, 7 March 1954   Municipal Stadium, Luxembourg – Att: unknown

So France were home and dry – in athletics terms, having lapped all other runners. They followed up their tight win over Ireland by sending out their reserves to inflict an 8-0 mauling on poor Luxembourg. That result left Ireland to engage in their first meaningless World Cup-tie. Many would follow in years to come. The only question now was whether they would grant Luxembourg their first point, or, heaven forbid, points, in twenty years of World Cup endeavour.

It was time for the selectors to look to the future. The team they sent out was so raw that only Con Martin, the captain, possessed more than four caps. Not that the experimentation did any good. Five of the six new boys were promptly discarded. The exception was Pat Saward.

Among the soon to be discarded newcomers were Mick Gallagher and Tom Scannell. Gallagher, of Hibernian, was the first Scottish-based player to be picked for Ireland since Joe O'Reilly and the immortal Paddy Moore twenty years earlier. Gallagher was an unlikely looking footballer, old-fashioned in appearance, with thick-set legs covered by shorts longer than most. But Gallagher formed part of the unsung half-back line that supported Hibs' 'famous five' forwards of the early 1950s. Two successive Scottish championships might have been three but for Rangers pipping them on goal-average in 1953.

Scannell was the second Southend United goalkeeper (after George McKenzie) to represent Ireland. Born in Youghal, Scannell had been at Roots Hall since 1950, but found his place claimed by Harry Threadgold at the start of the present season, during which Scannell had appeared just four times. A year later he drifted out of the Football League, aged thirty.

Scannell was not entirely unknown to the boffins at Merrion Square, having played for an FAI eleven against Glasgow Celtic the previous year. As he was not required by Southend, the club posed no obstacle to his release to play for Ireland. It might be unkind to draw comparisons, but one wonders whether the quality of play offered by Luxembourg rose above that customarily found among English third division reserves.

On this showing, however, one wonders whether the quality of Ireland's play was any brighter. The sight of so many Irish novices gee'd up the home side, who gave the visitors a first-half runaround. Twice Roger Weydert (a civil servant) might have given Luxembourg an early lead. Once he shot wide, on the other occasion Scannell sprinted out to clear. Karier then had the audacity to shoot against an upright.

Ireland tightened up after the break. The match turned just after the hour. At one end, Antoine Kohn (a miner) wriggled free to shoot straight at Scannell. At the other, Cummins fended off Camille Wagner (a railroad clerk) and shot hard and true past Steffen. The goal deflated the home side, who were clearly psyched up to try to break their losing streak. Luxembourg almost lost a second goal when Cummins, in the clear, allowed Steffen to save at his feet.

The final whistle brought the curtain down on what was woefully agreed as Ireland's worst display in twenty years. The only smiling face belonged to Tom Scannell. He had won a cap and kept a clean sheet. Now he was back to Southend's reserves.

LUXEMBOURG (0) 0   **IRELAND (0) 1**

Cummins 62

LUXEMBOURG: Steffen, Mosar, May, Caldarelli, Wagner, Reuter, Meurisse, Peiffer, Kohn, Weydert, Karier.
IRELAND: Scannell (SOUTHEND), Clinton (EVERTON), Traynor (SOUTHAMPTON), Gallagher (HIBS), Martin (VILLA), Saward (MILLWALL), Gavin (NORWICH), Kelly (FOREST), Kearns (WEST HAM), Cummins (LUTON), Hartnett (MIDDLESBROUGH).

France were rewarded by being seeded in Switzerland. That honour was not as rich as its sounds, for half the sixteen competing nations found themselves so labelled. Moreover, for all their promise, the French team failed to set the finals alight. They found themselves up against unseeded Yugoslavia in the opening match, a mismatch of seeds, for Yugoslavia were Olympic Finalists in 1948 and again in 1952, and had recently beaten England in the warm-ups. France never recovered from their 0-1 defeat. A dubious win over Mexico in their next match could not repair the damage, and out they went.

British interest centred on England and Scotland, who had once again finished second in the British Championship, but who knew better than to turn their backs a second time. It might have been better if they had, for Scotland were sunk without trace, 0-7 by Uruguay. The defending champions also accounted for England – 4-2 – in the quarter-finals.

West Germany overturned a 3-8 defeat in their group match to beat the Olympic champions and overwhelming favourites, Hungary, 3-2 in the Final.

Qualifying Pool IV

	P	W	D	L	F	A	Pts
FRANCE	4	4	0	0	20	4	8
Ireland	4	2	0	2	8	6	4
Luxembourg	4	0	0	4	1	19	0

Other group results
Luxembourg v France   1-6   France v Luxembourg   8-0

Ireland appearances and goalscorers
World Cup qualifying rounds 1954

	Apps	Goals		Apps	Goals		Apps	Goals
Eglington T *	3	1	Gannon E *	2	–	Kearns F	1	–
Fitzsimons A *	3	2	Lawler J	2	–	Kelly N	1	–
Martin C *	3	–	Walsh D *	2	1	Moroney T *	1	–
O'Neill J	3	–	Aherne T *	1	–	Munroe L	1	–
Ryan R *	3	2	Cantwell N	1	–	O'Farrell F	1	1
Clinton T	2	–	Gallagher M	1	–	Ringstead A	1	–
Cummins G	2	1	Gavin J *	1	–	Saward P	1	–
Dunne S	2	–	Gibbons S	1	–	Scannell T	1	–
Farrell P *	2	–	Hartnett J	1	–	Traynor T	1	–

* Appeared in 1950 World Cup.   *44 apps   8 goals*
                                                 3 League of Ireland
                                                 40 English League
27 players used   *1 Scottish League*

5

THE 1958 WORLD CUP

It was only in 1954, following the exchange of yet more heated letters on the subject, that FIFA finally bowed to the reality of the Republic's existence. Five years after Dublin's proclamation of a republic, FIFA agreed to refer to its footballers as representing 'The Republic of Ireland'. The new designation was employed for the first time in Ireland's home match with Norway in November 1954.

The mid-1950s were a time of revolution in European soccer. The 1954 World Cup had been the first to be widely televised. Now, Europe's top clubs were able to compete in a Champions' Cup. Irish teams would not participate from the start, but by the time of the next World Cup would be represented.

Football, as it widened its horizons, became more receptive to changes in tactics and fashion. The 4-2-4 formation lay just around the corner. With regard to fashion, the British, typically, one might say, were among the last to respond to the innovations exhibited by Hungary and others at the Switzerland World Cup. Shorts were shorter, boots lighter, shirt collars replaced by trendy V-necks. A move to introduce lighter, water-repellent footballs was initially opposed by the English FA on the grounds that it would mar the essential nature of the game.

Nevertheless, by Sweden '58, modernism had swept all before it. Shirt collars were nowhere to be seen, thigh muscles gleamed under mini-shorts. The footballer as sex-symbol had arrived.

To this extent, Ireland's footballers, stuck on the fringes of the game, were slower to profit than most. They played just seven matches between one World Cup and the next, yet strung together a sequence of results to suggest that they were about to break into the sunlight. Ireland beat Norway twice, Holland twice, and in a brave exhibition in Hamburg lost narrowly, 1-2, to the German World Cup holders. It was Ireland's first exposure to reigning champions, and the scoreline did them credit.

Ireland's one other defeat prior to the 1958 qualifiers came at home to Yugoslavia. The result, 1-4, was less contentious than the fact that the match had been staged at all. It was the first time Ireland had entertained a team from a communist country. Interventions from church and state, citing moral, religious, and practical objections (fearing the cost of mass defections by Yugoslavian players), came close to having the match cancelled.

Aside from this storm in a teacup, Irish soccer had stabilised. The LOI showed a round dozen membership, with Shamrock Rovers and St Patrick's Athletic ruling the roost. Key players from both clubs would play their part in Ireland's new World Cup campaign.

That campaign would be Ireland's most famous yet. The British qualifying zone, in operation in 1950 and '54, had been scrapped. The reasons were clear. The combined performances of England and Scotland in the finals had been so wretched (two wins outs of eight) that they no longer deserved two automatic places. Or even one, some said. European rivals were not slow to complain, as a result of which the British teams found themselves scattered to the wind. All four might qualify, or none at all.

FIFA's lucky dip promptly pitched Ireland against England and Denmark. This was both good news and bad. It was bad, because even the most devout Ireland fan knew in his heart that it would take more than mere footballers to prevent England qualifying. It was good, because Ireland could look forward to two tussles with their mighty neighbours. Without question, these would be the biggest matches in Ireland's history. And who knows, Goliath had fallen once – at Goodison. Ireland drooled at the prospect of a repetition.

Another change of rules meant that all qualifiers had to be completed by the November preceding the World Cup. That pulled the schedules forward, in Ireland's case one whole year. When they kicked off against Denmark, the finals – in Sweden – were still twenty months distant.

Qualifying Pool I

IRELAND v DENMARK
Wednesday, 3 October 1956   *Dalymount Park – 32,600*

This was the first meeting between Ireland and Denmark. Like Norway and Finland, Danish football had yet to come of age. The Scandinavian nations, with the exception of Sweden, inhabited a soccer world of amateur or part-time players and modest aspirations. Indeed, this was the first occasion Denmark had dared enter the World Cup.

This is not to say that soccer was a minority pastime in Denmark. The sport had been introduced in the 1880s, and her amateur players had a proud record in Olympic soccer. They had won gold in Athens in 1896, took silver in 1908 and 1912, bronze in 1948, and would claim silver in 1960, in Rome. But so long as Denmark's domestic league remained wholly amateur, she could not hope for success in the professional arena.

The Irish selectors had gone for a new look. That generation of great post-war players had gone. Only Peter Farrell remained. He had one last bullet to fire, but he would be held back to fire it against England. Of the current crew, four were plucked from the LOI, the most since the war. These were Tommy Dunne of champions St Pat's, Gerry Mackey and Ronnie Nolan of Shamrock Rovers, and Dermot Curtis of Shelbourne.

Jimmy O'Neill, Seamus Dunne and Noel Cantwell were about to see their second World Cup, Johnny Gavin and Arthur Fitzsimons their third.

Fitzsimons first took the eye at Shelbourne. In 1949 Middlesbrough manager David Jack forked out £12,000 to bring Fitzsimons and Peter Desmond to Ayresome Park. Desmond did not last the pace and soon drifted away. Fitzsimons stayed for ten years, through fat times and thin, initially playing alongside the great Wilf Mannion and later, in the second division, with a certain Brian Clough. Fitzsimons was in his first season on Teesside when he had picked up his first cap, against Finland in the World Cup.

He was in modern parlance an attacking midfielder, blessed with great speed over short distances, always seeking to get behind defenders. Still only twenty-seven, he was by some distance the most capped player in the new Ireland side, and much responsibility rested upon his shoulders.

The match proved a nightmare for commentators, Denmark lining up with two Nielsen's, two Jensen's, and two Hansen's. Centre-half Gerry Mackey almost gave Ireland the perfect start. Playing a one-two with Dermot Curtis, he hit the net but found English referee Bond wiping out the goal for pushing. Having an English referee officiate a match in England's group was an anomaly FIFA would never permit today, but football was less fretful, less suspicious, less conspiratorial in those days.

Indeed, Mr Bond was heavily instrumental in Ireland's goals. Ove Andersen had twice come close for Denmark when Ove Hansen deflected a Fitzsimons shot straight to Dermot Curtis who, though looking yards offside, promptly scored. The Danes besieged the referee, though the defender's last touch may have played the scorer onside. The referee later explained that he had allowed the goal because Curtis 'was standing still' and not interfering with play. Bill Shankly might have had something to say about that. So might FIFA, whose 1994 regulations would have backed the referee!

The goal briefly ignited the match. Fitzsimons hit a post at one end while, at the other, Cantwell cleared off the line from Ove Bech Nielsen.

Just before half-time Mr '007' intervened again. Haverty burrowed into the penalty area and had his legs taken by Erling Larsen. On this occasion the Danes did not waste energy protesting. Kaj Joergensen was agile enough to touch Gavin's spot-kick against a post, but it rolled in.

With the result seemingly safe, the second half was much ado about nothing until Denmark tweaked the Irish tail near the end. Andersen beat

O'Neill in a race for a through ball and crossed for Aage Jensen to head goalwards. The covering Seamus Dunne almost, but not quite, headed it out.

IRELAND (2) 2   **DENMARK (0) 1**
Curtis 28, Gavin 44 pen   A Jensen 86

IRELAND: O'Neill (EVERTON), S Dunne (LUTON), Cantwell (WEST HAM), T Dunne (ST PATRICK'S ATH), Mackey (SHAMROCK R), Nolan (SHAMROCK R), Gavin (NORWICH), Whelan (MAN U), Curtis (SHELBOURNE), Fitzsimons (MIDDLESBROUGH), Haverty (ARSENAL).
DENMARK: Joergensen, Linde Larsen, V Nielsen, E Jensen, O Hansen, Olesen, Hansen, Lundberg, Andersen, A Jensen, O Beck Nielson.

ENGLAND v IRELAND
Wednesday, 8 May 1957   *Wembley – 52,000*

One wonders what emotions the Irish players experienced as they contemplated their first trip to Wembley stadium. It was the first occasion its hallowed grass had staged a World Cup encounter. England had already beaten Denmark 5-2 at Molyneux, the home of Wolverhampton Wanderers, and Busby Babes Tommy Taylor and Duncan Edwards had ripped the Danish rearguard apart.

This was England's third attempt to leave her mark on the World Cup. In past qualifiers she had left her mark on Northern Ireland to the tune of 9-2 and 3-1. Qualifying ahead of Scotland both times, England had folded like a damp squib in the finals – beaten by the United States and Spain in Brazil, and drawing with Belgium before losing to Uruguay in Switzerland. These setbacks had produced much soul-searching in the corridors of Lancaster Gate, but like much English soul-searching, nothing came of it.

It was the age of Manchester United, runaway champions twice in succession. In their first attempt at the European Champions' Cup, they had murdered Anderlecht 12-0 on aggregate and withstood the challenge of Borussia Dortmund and Athletic Bilbao before falling to holders Real Madrid in the semi-final.

Notwithstanding the Old Trafford club's dominance, just three 'Babes' were picked to play Ireland, club skipper Roger Byrne, all-action Duncan Edwards, and irrepressible centre-forward Tommy Taylor. But Ireland could call upon one of their own, Liam Whelan. Within a year, all four were dead.

Three of the English side had been around ever since the war, and one of them beyond. Billy Wright, Tom Finney and Stanley Matthews (who was first capped in 1934) were the elder statesmen of English football. Their reputations, at home and abroad, not least in Ireland, were the stuff of legend. Matthews was still turning it on at the age of forty-two.

Another feature of the time was the comparative ease with which players from outside the English first division could be picked for the England international side. Goalkeeper Alan Hodgkinson, half-back Ronnie Clayton, and forwards Johnny Haynes and John Atyeo were all excelling in division two.

Ireland had followed up their win over the Danes with an even better one in November over West Germany, inflicting on the world champions their heaviest defeat (3-0) since their coronation. Four Germans had played in the World Cup Final; seven Irishmen played in the LOI, four of them for Shamrock Rovers.

The side to play England saw Alan Kelly of Drumcondra keep goal. He would still be picking up the odd cap sixteen years hence. Pat Saward had won his first cap against Luxembourg in the previous World Cup. He now won his second. The match would mark the international swan-song for two Everton players, Don Donovan and the restored captain, Peter Farrell. Farrell alone had memories of Goodison '49, and his presence would surely inspire his colleagues.

Elsewhere, there were brothers in arms everywhere to be seen. Alf Ringstead played in the same Sheffield United side as Eddie Hodgkinson, Dermot Curtis alongside John Atyeo for Bristol City, and of course Liam Whelan with England's Old Trafford trio.

For Alan Kelly and Gerry Mackey, the match must have presented particular terrors. They, alone of the Ireland eleven, played in the League of Ireland, and so were strangers to the opposing side as much as they were strangers to their own.

In Mackey's case, he could call upon the experience in playing for an LOI eleven against the Football League at Dalymount the previous September. That match ended 3-3. Then, as now, he was asked to mark mighty Tommy Taylor. Then, as now, Taylor scored against him.

England's national stadium held few fears for Aston Villa's Pat Saward and the quartet from Manchester United. On the Saturday before the international they had competed in one of the FA Cup's best-remembered finals.

Villa had beaten United 2-1 in front of 100,000 spectators. The attendance for the international was barely half that, and was inflated by a healthy Irish contingent. Momentous though the match was for Ireland, it was workaday for England's aristocrats, who doubtless viewed Ireland's footballers as simply eleven more flies to be swatted.

Alas, those who predicted a repeat of Goodison looked fools by the end. Ireland were four down by half-time. Tommy Taylor claimed three of them, to add to his hat-trick against Denmark. He outpaced Saward to reach Haynes' pass for his first, took Finney's through-ball to score past a flat-footed Kelly for his second, and headed in Finney's corner for his third. Just before Taylor's third goal, John Atyeo had ducked to head home after Kelly failed to gather Finney's cross-cum-shot. Atyeo, jealous of Taylor's plunderings, had chances to claim a hat-trick of his own before half-time.

For Ireland, the second half was about damage limitation. With England tottering about as if drunk on success, Ireland saw much of the ball. They salvaged one goal when Haverty out-manoeuvred Jeff Hall and sent the ball across. Irish correspondents insist that Curtis met the centre with a firm header; English ones maintain the ball struck him in the face.

Chances fell at both ends, none closer than when Whelan hit the crossbar. But England went nap in the last minute. Atyeo topped and tailed a move with the assistance of Finney.

The London *Times* adjudged that 'the score looks better on paper than it did in achievement.' It probably did, but try telling that to Ireland's crestfallen footballers.

ENGLAND (4) 5   **IRELAND (0) 1**
   Taylor 10, 18, 40,   Curtis 56
   Atyeo 38, 89

ENGLAND: Hodgkinson (SHEFF U), Hall (BIRMINGHAM), Byrne (MAN U), Clayton (BLACKBURN), Wright (WOLVES), Edwards (MAN U), Matthews (BLACKPOOL), Atyeo (BRISTOL C), Taylor (MAN U), Haynes (FULHAM), Finney (PRESTON).
IRELAND: Kelly (DRUMCONDRA), Donovan (EVERTON), Cantwell (WEST HAM), Farrell (EVERTON), Mackey (SHAMROCK R), Saward (VILLA), Ringstead (SHEFF U), Whelan (MAN U), Curtis (BRISTOL C), Fitzsimons (MIDDLESBROUGH), Haverty (ARSENAL).

IRELAND v ENGLAND
Sunday, 19 May 1957   *Dalymount Park – 47, 600*

One might query whether scheduling the return leg for just eleven days later was in Ireland's best interests. After all, that gave little time to digest the horrors of Wembley or to devise a master-plan for victory. On the other hand, Ireland's players didn't have to pass the summer haunted by that painful scoreline. They had an instant opportunity to redress it.

England, meanwhile, had put their victory to the backs of their minds and travelled to Copenhagen, where they mauled the Danes 4-1. That was on the Wednesday. They turned out at Dublin just four days later.

England had six points from three games; Ireland two from two. Had goal-average been in operation, Ireland would have given up the ghost already. They could hardly hope to overtake England's tally of fourteen goals scored, four conceded. But points were all that mattered. If Ireland could win at

Dalymount, then beat the Danes away, they would force England into a play-off – perhaps in Paris. These hurdles are worth remembering, in view of those of who claim Ireland were just seconds away from the World Cup finals. In fact, Ireland needed not one win but three. England could afford to draw any play-off, after extra time, when goal-average would be invoked.

This was England's first visit to Dalymount Park since winning 1-0 (Finney) in 1946. Finney and Wright were still around, and set to compete in their third World Cup finals. Stanley Matthews had also played in 1946, but he had injured an ankle in Copenhagen and would never recapture his place. Manchester United's David Pegg deputised.

Irish soccer was full of expectancy. Having won the LOI championship, Shamrock Rovers had accepted FIFA's invitation to provide the Republic's first challenge in the European Cup. For Rovers' Ronnie Nolan, now called up to take on England, these must have been among the most exhilarating times of his career.

Nolan was one of the lucky ones. Charlie Hurley of Millwall was another. The selectors backed Hurley to keep his cool during this most daunting of international baptisms. Alan Kelly, however, could hardly hope to keep his place, not after his unnerving afternoon at Wembley. It would take Kelly five years to restore the selectors' confidence, whereupon he would win more caps than any Ireland keeper until the arrival of Pat Bonner.

For the moment, his place went to Tommy Godwin, himself previously banished by the selectors for six seasons. Peter Farrell was done with international football, and West Ham's imposing Noel Cantwell captained the side.

Dalymount Park's previous record attendance had been set against France in the previous World Cup. The venerable stadium was now bursting at the seams with more than 47,000 crammed inside. This enormous gate would suggest that Ireland's soccer public were not too disheartened by the Wembley nightmare. Or if they were, they were confident about exacting revenge.

Those trapped by queues at the turnstiles would have missed Ireland's combustible opening. Ireland were playing towards the tramway end. The match was three minutes old when Fitzsimons, Whelan and Haverty linked exquisitely down the right flank. The cross to the near post was missed by everyone, but fell for the unmarked Alf Ringstead behind them.

The tempo never flagged. Atyeo might have equalised straight away, but Godwin was swiftly out of his goal. The keeper repeated the act later, this time plunging at the feet of Taylor. But the more and better chances were falling to Ireland. Ringstead shot wide, and Hodgkinson saved from Fitzsimons and Haverty. Just before the half-time whistle, Fitzsimons' shot whizzed narrowly wide.

The moment Ireland had waited for. Noel Cantwell and Billy Wright lead out the teams.

It was a different story after the break. Tommy Godwin had already taken his life in his hands, diving where its hurts, amid the flying boots. He was no less heroic at the tramway end, as England steadily tightened the tourniquet around his goalmouth. An Irish breakout might have made the game safe, but when Haverty fired towards a gaping English net, Billy Wright launched himself to head the ball away.

The noise was deafening as the final seconds were consumed. Scottish referee Phillips had checked his watch for the umpteenth time as Jeff Hall cut out Ringstead's pass to Haverty. Hall quickly fed Tom Finney, who went past Saward on the stand-side touchline. Cantwell might have closed him down, but expecting the cut-back onto Finney's left foot he held off. Fatally. Finney dipped the ball to the far post. Taylor and Hurley were drawn to the near, leaving space in their slipstream for John Atyeo to bury the ball in the net. Dalymount went silent as the grave. One Irish newspaper insisted the silence could be heard in O'Connell St.

The goal was officially timed at 92 minutes, ten seconds. Diehards behind the goal claimed Atyeo had ducked and actually 'shouldered' the ball, face-saving, maybe, for English accounts of Curtis 'facing' his goal at Wembley.

Two players from the second division had scored England's goals; Atyeo, in fact, had merely repeated his last-gasp strike at Wembley. England, though, would never call upon him again. Tongue in cheek, perhaps, Atyeo later intimated that had he known his most vital goal would bring down his international curtain, he would have headed it over the bar! Would that he had.

IRELAND   (1) 1   **ENGLAND   (0) 1**
Ringstead 3   Atyeo 90

IRELAND: Godwin (BOURNEMOUTH), S Dunne (LUTON), Cantwell (WEST HAM), Nolan (SHAMROCK R), Hurley (MILLWALL), Saward (VILLA), Ringstead (SHEFF U), Whelan (MAN U), Curtis (BRISTOL C), Fitzsimons (MIDDLESBROUGH), Haverty (ARSENAL).
ENGLAND: Hodgkinson (SHEFF U), Hall (BIRMINGHAM), Byrne (MAN U), Clayton (BLACKBURN), Wright (WOLVES), Edwards (MAN U), Finney (PRESTON), Atyeo (BRISTOL C), Taylor (MAN U), Haynes (FULHAM), Pegg (MAN U).

DENMARK v IRELAND
Wednesday, 2 October 1957   *Idraetspark, Copenhagen – 28,000*

So England were through, leaving Ireland to reflect upon the injustice of it all. As with Scotland's historical grievances against the Sassenach, the soccer pitch had become a theatrical court-house to rectify past ills and rewrite the pages of history. This invests the soccer match with the trappings of war, taken so much to heart by Scottish fans that the annual re-enactment of Culloden at Hampden or Wembley would finally prove beyond the capacities of the police to contain public order. The Scotland v England fixture would come to an end, unmourned except by a few. To that extent, it was perhaps fortuitous that Ireland only played England once in a blue moon.

England, moreover, were not yet done with rubbing salt into Irish wounds. The draw for the European Cup paired Paddy Coad's Shamrock Rovers with Manchester United. Far from ushering in a new age of hope and expectancy, Ireland's European baptism was brutal and harsh. The damage was done in the first leg, which was switched to Dalymount to accommodate another 46,000 crowd. Rovers were overwhelmed 0-6.

Seven days later Ireland took the field for their now-meaningless match in Copenhagen. There were just two new faces from the side which gave England such a fright, Frank O'Farrell and George Cummins coming in for Ronnie Nolan and Liam Whelan.

Denmark were anxious to improve on their earlier home performance, when they had taken the lead before leaking four goals to England. The home side opened sprightly and shaded the first half, thanks to threatening shots by Kjaer, Mosegaard and Flemming Nielsen. Ireland tightened up after the turnaround. Fitzsimons served notice of the new mood by coming close, and it was the same player who loaded the gun for Ireland's first goal. Back to goal, he flipped over a cheeky cross that George Cummins climbed to head in. Some degree of illegality must have preceded or attended the header, for Danish protests obliged the German referee to consult with his linesman before confirming the goal.

A replica 'goal' a few minutes later was chalked off for offside. Irish reports insist the header was good, and blame the referee for an indifferent match. But Irish frustration was soon assuaged. Cummins burrowed his way into the penalty area and set up a strike for Curtis.

Whether Ireland sat on their lead or whether Danish pressure forced them back, the visitors seldom again ventured out of their own half. The Danish crowd became incensed at what they saw as Irish time-wasting, possession tactics, feigning injury. It was the custom in Denmark for injured players to leave the pitch for treatment (interesting, in view of FIFA's 1994 directive), not – as Ireland did – have the trainer running on for minutes at a time. The referee's eccentric decisions infuriated the Danes still further.

In fact, Denmark might have stolen the match with three gilt-edged chances late in the game. Godwin saved from Pedersen; Olesen shot wide; and Hurley cleared off the line.

At the final whistle the spectators refused to disperse. Angry crowds gathered menacingly, and the Irish party had to be spirited away from the stadium via a back door.

DENMARK   (0) 0   **IRELAND   (0) 2**
                                    Cummins 53, Curtis 62

DENMARK: From, Linde Larsen, V Nielsen, F Nielsen, Andersen, Olesen, Pedersen, Jensen, Hansen, Mosegaard, Kjaer.
IRELAND: Godwin (BOURNEMOUTH), Dunne (LUTON), Cantwell (WEST HAM), Saward (VILLA), Hurley (SUNDERLAND), O'Farrell (PRESTON), Ringstead (SHEFF U), Fitzsimons (MIDDLESBROUGH), Curtis (BRISTOL C), Cummins (LUTON), Haverty (ARSENAL).

The Republic were out of the World Cup. Northern Ireland got through, beating Italy, famously, in January 1958 to claim their place in Sweden. Scotland and Wales also made it. After being eliminated by Czechoslovakia, Wales were reprieved when FIFA announced that Israel could not take their place in the finals by default (her scheduled opponents refused to play). Wales' name came out of the hat (it might have been Ireland's), and Wales duly beat Israel in belated play-offs for the one remaining place.

The four-pronged British assault on Sweden silenced those who lobbied for the end of the British qualifying zone. Who knows, success might even have been forthcoming but for the Münich air crash of February 1958, which wiped out a precious Manchester United team. The tragedy also robbed

Northern Ireland of their centre-half (Jackie Blanchflower shattered an elbow), Scotland and Wales of their managers (Matt Busby was convalescing and Jimmy Murphy had to attend to affairs at Old Trafford), and claimed the lives of four of the England side which clinched qualification in Dublin. Though Ireland would not be represented in the finals, the loss of the great Liam Whelan was a bitter pill.

Neither England nor Scotland survived the group phase in Sweden. The unsung Welsh and Northern Ireland marched on to the quarter-finals, leaving the title to be claimed by the magnificent Brazil and the wonder-boy Pele.

Qualifying Pool I

	P	W	D	L	F	A	Pts
ENGLAND	4	3	1	0	15	5	7
Ireland	4	2	1	1	6	7	5
Denmark	4	0	0	4	4	13	0

Other group results
England v Denmark   5-2   Denmark v England   1-4

Ireland appearances and goalscorers
World Cup qualifying rounds 1958

	Apps	Goals		Apps	Goals		Apps	Goals
Cantwell N *	4	–	Whelan L	3	–	Dunne T	1	–
Curtis D	4	3	Godwin T †	2	–	Farrell P *†	1	–
Fitzsimons A *†	4	–	Hurley C	2	–	Gavin J *†	1	1
Haverty J	4	–	Mackey G	2	–	Kelly A *	1	–
Dunne S *	3	–	Nolan R	2	–	O'Farrell F *	1	–
Ringstead A *	3	1	Cummins G *	1	1	O'Neill J *	1	–
Saward P *	3	–	Donovan D	1	–			

* Appeared in 1954 World Cup.   *44 apps   6 goals*
† Appeared in 1950 World Cup.   *7 League of Ireland*
20 players used   *37 English League*

6

THE 1962 WORLD CUP

The League of Ireland's first ventures into the cut and thrust of European competition ended in tears and not a little soul-searching. Shamrock Rovers lost nine goals (over two legs) to Manchester United, Drumcondra thirteen to Atletico Madrid, and Limerick nine to Young Boys of Berne. Now that comparisons could be put to the test, Ireland's clubs were being unkindly compared with the weakest in Europe. These were hardly the sort of results to encourage the Irish selectors to plump for native talent. Ireland's eliminators for the 1962 World Cup – to be held in Chile – were the first to field teams drawn entirely from Anglos.

In this, the selectors were mindful of the opposition. Having tasted the might of England four years earlier, Ireland now came up against the weight of Scotland. In part owing to the bonds between Scotland and Ulster, it was the first time the countries had met on the soccer pitch.

Scotland's World Cup record was abject, in terms of etiquette, common sense, and performance. They had spurned FIFA's invitation to Brazil in 1950, insisting on travelling only as British champions, and refusing to budge once England had knocked them into second place. In 1954 they had taken just thirteen players to Switzerland and capsized under a torrent of seven Uruguayan goals. In Sweden, they had failed to appoint anyone to replace the convalescing Matt Busby, and lined up as the only team without a manager. They had failed to win a game and propped up their group.

By the early '60s, though Ireland were still at the whim of team-selectors, the organisation of Scottish football had advanced a fraction. Ian McColl was their third 'manager', though he too was little more than a coach, able to wield influence but not yet to pick teams of his choice.

The third team in Group 8 was Czechoslovakia. This time there was no whimper of dissent about playing a team of communists. The brouhaha that attended the visit of Yugoslavia in 1955 was forgotten. Besides, Ireland had recently entertained the Czechs in the European Nations Cup.

Ireland had been one of seventeen countries to sign up for this new competition, which was shunned by Italy, West Germany, and the British

Associations. Nowadays, the European Championship is run as a mini-World Cup, with qualifying rounds followed by a final tournament. Its predecessor, the European Nations Cup, staged in 1960 and '64, operated as a straightforward, two-legged knock-out up to the semi-finals. Ireland had been required to play Czechoslovakia in a preliminary tie, winning 2-0 in Dublin but losing 0-4 in Bratislava. The Czechs went on to finish third.

The matches with Czechoslovakia were among eleven that Ireland played between World Cups, of which five were won and four lost. The best of the victories was at Dalymount against World Cup Finalists Sweden (3-2), who arrived fresh from beating England at Wembley, and West Germany (1-0) in Düsseldorf, against a side containing future luminaries Willie Schulz and Helmut Haller. Although Sweden gained handsome revenge (4-1) in Malmö, the signs for the future were brighter than for some time.

Qualifying Group 8

SCOTLAND v IRELAND
Wednesday, 3 May 1961   *Hampden Park – 46,696*

In footballing terms, Scotland were going through one of their xenophobic phases. Just weeks before they entertained Ireland, they had been crushed 3-9 at Wembley. The side was in the melting pot. The Scottish selectors purged the side of Anglos, among them Denis Law and Ian St John, leaving only David Herd of Arsenal. Ibrox boasted five players, among them captain Eric Caldow, the sole survivor from the 1958 World Cup. The fact that the Irish selectors had gone the other way, and packed their side with Anglos, turned the match, in effect, into a Scottish league XI versus an English league XI. Scotland fielded a trio of half-backs which would stand comparison with the best – Pat Crerand, Billy McNeill, and Jim Baxter.

A behind-the-scenes factor affecting Scottish morale was the abolition of the maximum wage in England. England captain Johnny Haynes, of Fulham, had become British football's first £100-a-week player. This unprecedented freedom unsettled senior players in Scotland, where the maximum wage was retained. They listened wistfully to the tales of big money earned by their colleagues in England. Several Scottish players procrastinated over signing new contracts in the hope of receiving lucrative invitations from down south. The combination of a crushing defeat by England and financially frustrated players did not bode well for the coming World Cup campaign.

Given the usual chopping and changing, the Ireland side was reasonably settled. Six players (Cantwell, Hurley, Saward, Curtis, Cummins, Haverty) had seen action in the 1958 World Cup, and Cantwell and Cummins in 1954 as well. Of the rest, young John Giles of Manchester United, blooded at home to Sweden when not yet nineteen, showed rich promise. So did Blackburn's Andy McEvoy, playing for the first time. Noel Cantwell, now at Old Trafford, was still Ireland captain. A towering defender and, when asked, a towering forward, Cantwell was destined for the ranks of greatness. He was one of those who excelled at more than one sport, even playing cricket for Ireland.

The Scottish league proved far too strong for the English league. Cantwell and company found themselves rolled aside. Hurley headed out Caldow's free-kick to Brand (standing in for Denis Law), who killed the ball and drove it back inside Noel Dwyer's right post. The lead was nearly sacrificed when George Cummins' free-kick was misjudged by Lawrie Leslie and slapped against the face of the Scottish crossbar.

Scotland doubled their advantage late in the half. Crerand and Herd created the opening, taken by Brand with a fierce shot. There was time before the intermission for Herd, who enjoyed a memorable duel with Hurley, to connect firmly with Wilson's cross. Dwyer turned the header against a post.

That save gave Ireland hope, for the Scots were not yet over the horizon. The visitors began the second half well, fired up by salvaging a quick goal. Giles escaped from Baxter – who would commit several unseemly fouls on his first Hampden appearance – to cross beyond the far post. Joe Haverty eluded Shearer to shoot past Leslie.

Ireland had snatched the initiative and threatened to square the match. They might have done so but for a magnificent Scotland goal on the counter-attack. The score read 2-1 for just seven minutes when a silky-smooth Scottish build-up was climaxed by Herd's unstoppable drive.

Haverty missed a sitter, when with a cooler head he might have hauled Ireland back into the match. As it was, a scoreline a mite harsh was forced on them in the closing stages. Davie Wilson's header was saved by Dwyer, but the ball spilled from his hands and Herd tapped in.

Scotland's victory was sound enough, but learned discussion dwelt less on the score than on savouring the potential shown by the wing-halves, Crerand and Baxter. The partnership would survive unbroken for eleven matches.

SCOTLAND (2) 4   **IRELAND (0) 1**
Brand 14, 40, Herd 59, 85   Haverty 52

SCOTLAND: Leslie (AIRDRIE), Shearer (RANGERS), Caldow (RANGERS), Crerand (GLASGOW CELTIC), McNeill (GLASGOW CELTIC), Baxter (RANGERS), McLeod (HIBS), Quinn (MOTHERWELL), Herd (ARSENAL), Brand (RANGERS), Wilson (RANGERS).
IRELAND: Dwyer (SWANSEA), McNally (LUTON), Cantwell (MAN U), McEvoy (BLACKBURN), Hurley (SUNDERLAND), Saward (HUDDERSFIELD), Giles (MAN U), Fogarty (SUNDERLAND), Curtis (IPSWICH), Cummins (LUTON), Haverty (ARSENAL).

IRELAND v SCOTLAND

Sunday, 7 May 1961   *Dalymount Park – 36,000*

Four days later the two teams reappeared for Act Two, this time in Dublin. Scotland had not played there since 1913, when, of course, their opponents had been a united Ireland.

Scotland would have fielded an unchanged team, but for the illness that ruled out David Herd. Everton's Alex Young, destined to become a Goodison legend, took his place.

The Irish selectors were more sanguine. Four players were summarily axed. In came the Leeds' centre-forward Peter Fitzgerald. When on the books of Sparta Rotterdam, Fitzgerald had squared up to Rangers in the European Cup. The other three changes saw the return of Phil Kelly at full-back, Fionan Fagan on the wing, and a debut for Mick Meagan.

That the Irish public were not starstruck by the prospect of Scotland's first visit was evident in the disappointing attendance, which had even been exceeded by the recent visits of Czechoslovakia and Sweden.

Ireland had lost just four games out of nineteen at home since 1950. This was a goodish record, and they had to win this match to stay alive in the World Cup. It was not to be. Scotland were quickly two goals up, and Ireland endured the unwelcome, and unprecedented, sound of jeering by supporters.

The ground was hard, the wind was high, and the game was a mess. Scotland played into the gale. In the third minute Brand appeared to be pulled down in the box from behind. The referee, a portly Belgian by the name of Grandain, who put one in mind of Agatha Christie's distinguished detective, Hercule Poirot, saw nothing illegal. Nor did he a minute later when Brand held off Hurley and his flick was nodded home by Alex Young. This time the referee did blow – for a goal. Brand had been arguably offside and Young manifestly so – as the flagging linesman confirmed. Irish shirts buzzed dementedly around the Belgian detective, but he took no notice.

Scotland's second goal, after sixteen minutes, was no less dubious, though this time the Irish shot themselves in the foot. Rather than belt the ball into touch, Phil Kelly found himself dispossessed by Davie Wilson on the touchline. Kelly looked suitably red-faced when Wilson bore down on Dwyer, forced the keeper to come out, and squared for the unmarked Young. Not even the presence of two defenders on the line could keep the ball out.

Scottish-Irish relations were further strained when Cummins took a swipe at Crerand, who exceeded the 'eye for an eye' principle and put the boot in. Monsieur Grandain contented himself with the mildest of admonitions. The more legitimate activity of the half saw Fitzgerald's shot-on-the-run whizz over Leslie's bar, while Fagan's effort struck Leslie amidships and left him winded. At the other end, a Wilson shot was thwarted by an Irish goalpost.

Noel Dwyer saves at the feet of two Scottish forwards.

The second half was yet drearier than the first, though the conditions didn't help. Crerand and Baxter successfully smothered Ireland's attempted resurrection, though Haverty seemed in the clear until caught by McNeill.

It was all too much for the paying customers. Boos and slow handclaps resounded round the stadium. Twice the ball landed in the crowd, and twice it stayed there. That the referee was no Irishman was demonstrated near the end when McNeill up-ended Fitzgerald inside the box and saw Ireland given a free-kick five yards outside.

The game was dead long before Brand's final fling, screwing the ball past Dwyer from a tight angle.

IRELAND   (0) 0   **SCOTLAND   (2) 3**

Young 4, 16, Brand 86

IRELAND: Dwyer (SWANSEA), Kelly (WOLVES), Cantwell (MAN U), McEvoy (BLACKBURN), Hurley (SUNDERLAND), Meagan (EVERTON), Fagan (DERBY), Giles (MAN U), Fitzgerald (LEEDS), Cummins (LUTON), Haverty (ARSENAL).
SCOTLAND: Leslie (AIRDRIE), Shearer (RANGERS), Crerand (GLASGOW CELTIC), Caldow (RANGERS), McNeill (GLASGOW CELTIC), Baxter (RANGERS), McLeod (HIBS), Quinn (MOTHERWELL), Young (EVERTON), Brand (RANGERS), Wilson (RANGERS).

IRELAND v CZECHOSLOVAKIA

Sunday, 8 October 1961   *Dalymount Park – 26,000*

Two heavy defeats. Ireland would clearly not be booking their seats for
Chile. All they could do was help determine which of Scotland or
Czechoslovakia did. Scotland had lost to the Czechs in Bratislava, but beaten
them at Hampden. Now all Scottish eyes were turned on their Gaelic cousins.
If Ireland could steal a point, Scotland would go through. If Ireland couldn't,
it would go to a play-off.

Irish confidence at the start of the new season had not been boosted by the
performances of LOI clubs in Europe. Drumcondra's second venture into the
European Cup saw them torpedoed by nine goals from Nuremberg. St Pat's,
Ireland's first representatives in the Cup-Winners' Cup, fared little better,
savaged by eight goals from the Scottish side Dunfermline.

Scotland's demolition of Ireland's Anglo XI brought the axe down on that
experiment. To curry local interest, Ronnie Nolan and Frank O'Neill of
Shamrock Rovers were installed. Nolan was a veteran of the previous World
Cup; O'Neill was winning his first cap.

Joe Haverty was still an Anglo, though he was no longer with Arsenal.
Having broken into St Patrick's Athletic first team, he soon came to the
notice of David Jack, Arsenal hero of old, then managing Shelbourne. It was
Jack who gave the nod to his old club, and in the summer of 1954 Haverty
was on his way. Haverty proved the perfect inheritor of Tommy Eglington's
No. 11 Ireland shirt, first wearing it in Rotterdam in 1956 – a match which
Ireland won 4-1 and in which Haverty scored. Haverty always reckoned his
finest match came a year later, when Ireland were sunk 1-5 at Wembley. An
English reporter, indeed, credited him with being the best footballer on the
pitch.

The diminutive Haverty, 5ft 3in, according to match programmes, was one
of those players who demanded that the ball be played to feet, and who
would then set off down the wing as though flames were licking his heels. He
relished the dummied back-heel, performed at full-throttle, which fooled full-
backs more often than not, and which would gain him several yards.
Nowadays, of course, with the aid of TV and video, defenders would be wise
to these tricks. Besides, changes in tactics have rendered the old-fashioned
winger obsolete. Haverty was among the last of a breed.

Still only twenty-five, and having spent seven productive seasons at
Highbury, Haverty was, in the summer of 1961, transferred north to
Blackburn Rovers. The move didn't work out and – apart from a brief spell
with Glasgow Celtic – Haverty was soon doing the rounds of lower-division
football. Throughout his comings and goings, the selectors kept faith in him.
Come World Cup '66, he would be playing for Shelbourne.

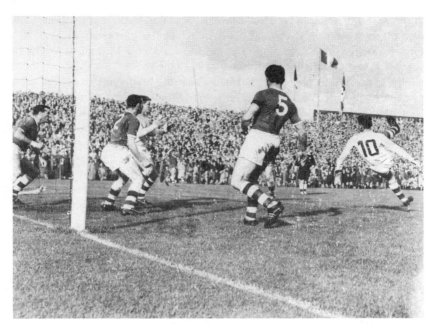

Four Irish defenders are needed to keep out this Czech effort.

His task now was to prise open a stubborn Czech defence. Insofar as the Czechs embodied Iron Curtain soccer, they were dismissed as shamateurs, exploiting loopholes in regulations to enable them to compete in the Olympic Games. Their football was dismissed as a reflection of their culture, drab, stereotyped, defensive.

Czechoslovakia's 1934, pre-communist side had advanced to the World Cup Final, losing to hosts Italy after extra time. They had qualified for the finals in 1954 and 1958 but were eliminated quickly from both tournaments. In 1958 they were put out by Northern Ireland, who beat them twice, 1-0 (Wilbur Cush) in the group, and 2-1 (Peter McParland 2), after extra time in a play-off.

The Czechs, of course, were no strangers to Dublin, having lost 0-2 in the first leg during the 1960 European Nations Cup. Czechoslovakia had overturned the deficit (4-0) in the second leg, and then swept past Denmark and Romania on their way to the semi-finals. There they lost out to the eventual winners, the Soviet Union.

Three Czechs took the field in Dublin a second time, Jiri Tichy at full-back, plus giant stopper Jan Popluhár and midfielder Svatopluk Pluskal. A newcomer to Dublin, though not to the Czech side, Josef Masopust had twice faced Northern Ireland in Sweden. Son of a miner, Masopust was a stocky, thirty-year-old left-half for Dukla Prague, a major in the Czech Army, and part of an awesome Czech midfield in which he partnered Pluskal in a forward-looking 4-2-4 line-up. By the season's end Masopust would be voted European Footballer of the Year (1962).

With Scotland as desperate as Ireland that the home side avoid defeat, it came as a mighty blow when Scherer scored after just three minutes. It was a wretched goal, too, Dwyer covering the shot until it glanced off Hurley. Not wishing to be lumbered with an own-goal, Hurley was happy to accredit it to Scherer.

New boy O'Neill wasted two chances to restore parity before Giles, from out of the blue, did so with a twenty-five yard thunderbolt. Vilem Schrojf got both hands to the ball, high to his left, but couldn't keep it out. The Czechs should still have gone in a goal up, but Andrej Kvasnak miskicked horribly.

The second half was all Czechoslovakia. British football was only slowly throwing off the shackles of the WW formation, and Czechoslovakia's 4-2-4 brooked no challenge. That second period brought two Czech goals. Kvasnak vultured the remains after Dwyer couldn't hold Rudolph Kucera's fierce cross-shot, and shortly afterwards Kvasnak headed another from Vaclav Masek's corner. Three more Czech efforts were denied by the goal-frame.

IRELAND   (1) 1   **CZECHOSLOVAKIA   (1) 3**
Giles 40   Scherer 3, Kvasnak 61, 69

IRELAND: Dwyer (SWANSEA), Kelly (WOLVES), Cantwell (MAN U), Nolan (SHAMROCK R), Hurley (SUNDERLAND), McGrath (BLACKBURN), Fitzgerald (CHESTER), Fogarty (SUNDERLAND), O'Neill (SHAMROCK R), Giles (MAN U), Haverty (BLACKBURN).
CZECHOSLOVAKIA: Schrojf, Tichy, Hledik, Popluhár, Pluskal, Masopust, Pospichal, Scherer, Kucera, Kvasnak, Masek.

CZECHOSLOVAKIA v IRELAND
Sunday, 29 October 1961   *Strahove Stadium, Prague – 30,000*

What Ireland couldn't do at home they were unlikely to accomplish away. Scotland's automatic place in Chile looked to have died in Dublin.

And so it proved. If the Czechs had looked good in Dublin, they looked sublime in Prague. They needed two more points to force a play-off with Scotland, and never looked in the slightest doubt of being denied them. Despite the stiffening qualities that Cantwell and Hurley brought to bear, Ireland simply caved in. A popular photograph shows the Ireland party assembled by their propellered aircraft after touchdown in Prague. In their ties and overcoats they are shown standing and squatting, and in the case of Johnny Giles and Ambrose Fogarty, clearly amused about something.

The Czechs were celebrating sixty years of soccer. Television schedules were interrupted to show highlights of great victories over the decades. Hour in, hour out, an avalanche of goals poured from the screen. There are those who claim that this orgy of goals went to the Czech players' heads. Either way, Czechoslovakia battered Ireland to their heaviest World Cup defeat to that day or since.

The Czechs exploded into life, bringing first half goals for Kvasnak (two), Scherer and Jelinek. Best of the four was the third, from Jelinek, the winger embarking on a mazy run from the halfway line that took him past five Irishmen before finishing off with a mighty shot.

Goal-difference did not apply, and as the points were safe there was no need for the Czechs to go chasing goals in the second half. Even on half-throttle they still managed three more. It was Ambrose Fogarty who stung the Czechs into life, snapping up Fitzgerald's cross. But Pospichal hit back within seconds, Dwyer perhaps at fault. When Masopust and Scherer brought the tally to seven with a quarter of an hour remaining, Ireland must have feared being buried by ten. But the Czech thirst was quenched.

In a spirit of heady intoxication, Czech journalists voted Charlie Hurley man of the match.

CZECHOSLOVAKIA (4) 7   **IRELAND (0) 1**
Kvasnak 8, 36, Scherer 24, 75,   Fogarty 56
Jelinek 30, Pospichal 57,
Masopust 61

CZECHOSLOVAKIA: Schrojf, Hledik, Tichy, Pluskal, Popluhár, Masopust, Pospichal, Scherer, Kvasnak, Adamec, Jelinek.
IRELAND: Dwyer (SWANSEA), Kelly (WOLVES), Cantwell (MAN U), Nolan (SHAMROCK R), Hurley (SUNDERLAND), McGrath (BLACKBURN), O'Neill (SHAMROCK R), Fogarty (SUNDERLAND), Fitzgerald (CHESTER), Giles (MAN U), Haverty (BLACKBURN).

Four matches, four defeats, seventeen goals conceded. These were the worst figures Ireland had ever posted in the World Cup. For ever-presents Dwyer, Cantwell, Hurley, Haverty and Giles, the humiliation must have seemed almost personal.

England were Britain's sole representatives in Chile, the smallest British representation ever. Scotland put up a brave show in their play-off, leading Czechoslovakia with eight minutes to play and falling (2-4) only after extra time. The Czechs had impressed all who had seen them, and their strength, pace, and all-round verve carried them to the World Cup Final itself. There they met Brazil, who had put England out in the quarter-finals. The Czechs took the lead before succumbing 1-3. Measured by such standards, Ireland's defeats became easier to bear.

Qualifying Group 8

	P	W	D	L	F	A	Pts
CZECHOSLOVAKIA *	4	3	0	1	16	5	6
Scotland	4	3	0	1	10	7	6
Ireland	4	0	0	4	3	17	0

* Czechoslovakia qualified after play-off with Scotland.

Other group results
Czechoslovakia v Scotland 4-0   Scotland v Czechoslovakia 1-4

Ireland appearances and goalscorers
World Cup qualifying rounds 1962

	Apps	Goals		Apps	Goals		Apps	Goals
Cantwell N *†	4	–	Fogarty A	3	1	O'Neill F	2	–
Dwyer N	4	–	Kelly P	3	–	Curtis D *	1	–
Giles J	4	1	Cummins G*†	2	–	Fagan F	1	–
Haverty J *	4	1	McGrath M	2	–	McNally B	1	–
Hurley C *	4	–	McEvoy A	2	–	Meagan M	1	–
Fitzgerald P	3	–	Nolan R *	2	–	Saward P *†	1	–

* Appeared in 1958 World Cup.   *44 apps   3 goals*
† Appeared in 1954 World Cup.   *4 League of Ireland*
18 players used   *40 English League*

7

THE 1966 WORLD CUP

The 1966 World Cup was the one for which Ireland – plus Scotland, Wales and Northern Ireland, come to that – were desperate to qualify. The reason was simple. The finals would be held in England. Not only would fans flood across the Irish Sea in their thousands; there was a better chance of performing well in England than anywhere else. Who knows, Ireland might even win it. Stranger things have happened.

Ireland were buoyed by reaching the last eight of the 1964 European Nations Cup. This time the numbers had been swelled by the inclusion of most of Europe's major footballing powers. Ireland had put out Iceland in the first round, Austria in the second (with the aid of a last-minute Cantwell penalty), and lined up against Spain with a place in the semi-finals at stake. Spain, who had already eliminated Northern Ireland 2-1 on aggregate, proved much too strong, winning 5-1 in Seville, 2-0 in Dublin. Spain went on to take the Cup, albeit enjoying home advantage in the semi-final and Final.

Ireland's unexpected success on the European stage convinced few that the national side was marching forward rather than back. 'Twixt one World Cup and the next, Ireland lost more than they won, and entered the 1966 campaign having lost five of their last seven.

The story was no brighter in European club competition. Though the margins of defeat were mercifully narrowed, no Irish club survived the first obstacle in the Champions' or Cup-Winners' Cups. Only the Fairs' Cup offered solace. LOI representatives first competed in 1962-63, whereupon Drumcondra promptly registered Ireland's first triumph. Squeezing past the Danes of Odense, they signalled a famous 1-0 first leg triumph over Bayern München in the second round. Alas, the tables were turned, 0-6, in München. In 1964, in the same competition, Shelbourne beat Belenenses of Portugal after a first-round play-off.

Having faced England in the 1958 World Cup and Scotland in 1962, there were those who wondered whether FIFA would throw up Wales or Northern Ireland this time round. That didn't happen. Instead, Ireland's opponents were listed as Spain, which was bad news, and Syria which was good. The idea of playing Syria was as surprising as it was mouth-watering. Syria, as every schoolboy knows, is in Asia. All but two Asian entries were properly bracketed in the Africa-Asia group. But when it became known that just one nation would qualify from two continents, everyone – apart from North Korea – withdrew in pique. The two Asian exceptions, Israel and Syria, had been allocated to European sections – Israel, because no Asian states would play her, Syria, for 'geographical reasons'. Anyway, Syria didn't fancy being European after all, withdrew from the World Cup, their first, leaving Ireland and Spain to fight out a double-header.

This was a whopping bonus for Ireland. Most European groups comprised four nations, Ireland's just two. The twin towers of Wembley loomed high in the Irish imagination.

Qualifying Group 9

IRELAND v SPAIN
Wednesday, 5 May 1965   *Dalymount Park – 40,772*

In view of Spain's current standing in European and World football, it comes as a surprise to learn that she was among the last European nations to embrace the kicking game with a round ball. Bull-fighting dominated Iberian sporting culture till well into the twentieth century. Not till 1928 did Spain set up her own professional league, boosted – at the end of that first season – by inflicting upon England her first ever defeat by a continental side, 3-4 in Madrid.

Spain were making a habit of being asked to play Arab countries in World Cup qualifiers. In 1962, FIFA had experimented by setting up several mixed Africa-Europe groups. Spain overcame Wales, and then put out Morocco.

Spanish club sides were the talk of Europe. Real Madrid or Barcelona had contested every European Cup Final bar 1963. The 1965 trophy would also be headed elsewhere, for Real Madrid had lost out in the quarter-finals to Benfica. The players at Spain's disposal were prominent in the European Hall of Fame. Feliciano Rivilla, Severino Reija and Adelardo were veterans of Chile '62. Ignacio Zoco had lined up in the last Real Madrid side to contest the European Cup Final, in 1964, when they had been overcome by Internazionale. Captain Fernando Olivella had played, and lost, in Scotland during the 1958 qualifiers. Seven of the eleven who won the European Nations Cup in 1964 – José Iribar, Rivilla, Olivella, Zoco, Marcelino, Pereda, and Carlos Lapetra – were selected to play in Dublin.

But this was clearly a Spanish side in transition. The superstars of the 1950s and early '60s – di Stefano, Kubala, Santamaria, Gento, Suárez – were either finished or past their prime, and the gaps they vacated were huge.

The centre-circle is a centre-cross, and Spain agree to use an English ball.

Even with that crop of great names, Spain had performed feebly in the World Cup. Given the stature of Real Madrid and the players at Spain's disposal, hers was a miserable record in the global championship. Spain had beaten England 1-0 in 1950 but gone on to lose 1-6 to Brazil, had failed to qualify in 1954 and 1958 (when they had been put out by Scotland), and in 1962 had finished bottom of their group in Chile. The soccer-mad Spanish public was becoming restive.

For this match, history pointed firmly to Spain. Not only had they cruised to a six-goal aggregate triumph in the European Nations Cup, they had won five of the last six meetings, the other being drawn. Ireland's only pleasant memories were of two victories immediately after the war.

By scheduling the current match for the close of the league season, the Big Five were able to call upon Anglos who might otherwise have been denied them. They made six changes to the team beaten 0-2 by Spain at Dalymount a year earlier, with Shelbourne's Jackie Hennessy and Shamrock Rovers' Frank O'Neill representing the LOI.

The selectors called up four Manchester United players, two Dunne's, two debutants, two full-backs. Pat Dunne's performances between the posts had done much to bring the English championship to Old Trafford. He was making his Ireland debut, along with eighteen-year old right-back Shay

Brennan. Though born in Manchester, Brennan was eligible for the Republic under FIFA's new 'parentage' ruling. Left-back Tony Dunne had won ten caps over the previous three seasons. The fourth United player was also its skipper. Noel Cantwell was now embarking on his fourth World Cup, his third as captain, and his first as centre-forward.

John Giles was a vital cog in the Leeds United side that, upon promotion to the first division, finished runners-up on goal-average to Manchester United. He was now winning his nineteenth cap. All of Ireland looked to his magic. He did not disappoint.

Dalymount Park received the European champions with yet another mammoth crowd. Goal-average, once again, had no part to play. A win for Ireland would guarantee a money-spinning play-off, at the very least.

Playing towards the school end, Charlie Hurley 'scored' after just eight minutes, but Cantwell had fouled. Andy McEvoy was then sent clear, but Iribar blocked with his feet and Zoco thumped away the loose ball.

Spain pressed at the close of the first half and the start of the second, so it was somewhat against the tide that Ireland scored. Giles was fouled out wide. O'Neill flighted in the free-kick, for which Cantwell, Zoco and Iribar rose as one. Iribar won the race, but the ball spilled from his grasp and dropped into the net. One wonders if O'Neill had half a mind to claim the goal, rather than have it accredited to the twenty-two year old Atletico Madrid goalkeeper.

Predictably Spain pressed till the end. Dalymount held its breath for fear of an Atyeo-style late snatcher. Guillot and Adelardo almost saved the day for Spain, and Jesus Glaria missed a sitter, but Ireland held out for a momentous victory.

IRELAND (0) 1   **SPAIN (0) 0**
Iribar 63 (o.g.)

IRELAND: P Dunne (MAN U), Brennan (MAN U), A Dunne (MAN U), McGrath (BLACKBURN), Hurley (SUNDERLAND), Hennessy (SHELBOURNE), O'Neill (SHAMROCK R), Giles (LEEDS), Cantwell (MAN U), McEvoy (BLACKBURN), Haverty (BRISTOL R).
SPAIN: Iribar, Rivilla, Olivella, Zoco, Reija, Glaria IV, Ufarte, Guillot, Marcelino, Adelardo, Lapetra.

SPAIN v IRELAND
Wednesday, 27 October 1965   *Sánchez Pizjuán Stadium, Seville – 29,452*

All that Ireland needed was a draw. One little draw, however ill-deserved, and Ireland would be on-stage at the World Cup finals for the first time.

Spain does not possess a national stadium, as such, preferring to spread internationals around her major cities. Over the years, Seville's Sánchez

Pizjuán Stadium had become renowned for its patriotic fervour in times of need. The crowd was separated from the pitch by no more than the width of a matador's cape. It was in this very stadium that Ireland had been tortured 1-5 the previous year.

The new domestic season was under way long enough for Drumcondra and Limerick to tumble in the various European competitions, and for Merrion Square's international selection committee to return to the drawing board. Four new players had to be summoned, with players chopping and changing position to the confusion of everyone.

Of the four newcomers, only Eric Barber was a fresh face. Two-footed, pacy, good in the air, Barber was one of the best forwards ever to emerge from the Shelbourne stable. It was his goal in Portugal that had toppled Belenenses from the Fairs' Cup the previous year. A schoolboy boxer, his hot-head reputation on the field had impeded his international prospects. He was lucky to play at all in Seville. Before flying out he had dashed to the dentist with toothache and almost missed the team's plane.

The other changes involved returnees – Mick McGrath of Blackburn, who were headed for the drop; Mick Meagan of second division Huddersfield. Theo Foley's club, Northampton Town, had scaled the heights, all the way to the first division. Come May, they would be spiralling back to the fourth. Foley recalls how he learned of his international call-ups. The FAI never made contact with him. Instead, he would be rung at home by the secretary of the Cobblers' supporters club, who had heard it on the radio.

'Hey Theo,' he would say. 'You've been picked to play for "Eerie" again!'

In the absence of that man-mountain, Hurley, Cantwell dropped back to centre-half. Giles and McEvoy swapped shirts and numbers.

Spain's objective was to beat Ireland twice. Anything less, and Spain's highly paid stars would go into hiding. Imagine, then, local feeling when – having seen Spain press unavailingly for twenty-five minutes, Theo Foley clearing off the line from Pereda, and Pat Dunne turning Marcelino's header onto the bar – Andy McEvoy volleyed Giles' cross past Antonio Betancort. It was the Real Madrid goalkeeper's first cap, and Betancort must have been mortified. Indeed, the damage could, perhaps should, have been worse. Frank O'Neill had not enjoyed his time at Highbury, for whom he played just two league games in two seasons. Shamrock Rovers brought him back home for an LOI record fee. Now it was O'Neill's misfortune to slip a quick free-kick to Mick McGrath, who smashed it into the net. It all happened too fast for Portuguese referee Freitas, however, and he ordered that the kick be retaken. Needless to say, nothing came of it.

Nevertheless, Ireland were in the luxurious position of knowing they could concede one goal with impunity. They had scarcely dreamed of being ahead, so it was vital they reached the dressing room intact, from which vantage point they could plan their second-half strategy.

The best laid plans of mice and men ... Half-time was still four minutes distant when disaster struck. Carlos Lapetra's teasing cross was missed by Marcelino and Cantwell at the near post and ran to Pereda at the far. Pereda made no mistake. Spain were fired up now, and seconds before the half-time whistle scored again. This time it was Spain who took a free-kick quickly, though not so quickly as to concern Mr Freitas. Zoco shot, Dunne parried, Pereda followed up.

The Irish dressing room must have resembled a morgue. Ireland had to unearth an equaliser or live through the furnace of a play-off. Unfortunately, Spain were now spilling forth like a tidal wave. Cantwell cleared off the line from Ufarte before the scourge of Ireland, Pereda, latched onto a long ball to notch his hat-trick from the tightest of angles. Spain's fourth, from Lapetra, mattered to no one but the statisticians.

SPAIN   (2) 4   **IRELAND   (1) 1**
  Pereda 40, 44, 58, Lapetra 63   McEvoy 26

SPAIN: Betancort, Rivilla, Olivella, Zoco, Reija, Glaria IV, Ufarte, Pereda, Marcelino, Suárez, Lapetra.
IRELAND: P Dunne (MAN U), Foley (NORTHAMPTON), A Dunne (MAN U), McGrath (BLACKBURN), Cantwell (MAN U), Meagan (HUDDERSFIELD), O'Neill (SHAMROCK R), McEvoy (BLACKBURN), Barber (SHELBOURNE), Giles (LEEDS), Haverty (SHELBOURNE).

SPAIN v IRELAND

Wednesday, 10 November 1965   *Colombes Stadium, Paris – 35,731*

The play-off was scheduled for a fortnight later. Much behind-the-scenes whispering preceded the choice of venue. The Irish fancied Wembley; the Spanish, not unreasonably, did not. In geographical terms Paris seemed a reasonable compromise, though it helped turn the match into a virtual home tie for Spain, with up to 30,000 Spaniards travelling to lend their vocal support. There was much talk of money changing hands in return for the FAI's 'cooperation'.

Hurley was still out, but Shay Brennan, missing in Seville, returned at right-back. One debutant, made way for another. Eamon Dunphy, later to prove such an articulate thorn in Jack Charlton's backside, won his first cap in place of Eric Barber. Barber had insisted on playing in Seville, despite the effects of penicillin injections, and he had had a stinker. In years to come, Eamon Dunphy would serve Millwall with distinction. For the moment he was fighting a losing battle to keep York City in the third division.

There must have been many who believed Ireland had blown their hopes when failing to protect McEvoy's strike in Seville. It is doubtful whether the players gave it a thought at the time, but their second-half collapse in Seville threatened to cost them dear. Although goal tallies played no part in the two group games, they would be called upon to separate the sides should the play-off end all square after extra time. In short, Ireland had to win in Paris; Spain only to draw.

Ireland began in a rush, hoping to catch Spain cold. Foley's free-kick was headed wide by Giles and McEvoy's header also gave Spain the flutters. Spain soon recovered their equilibrium, seizing territorial command, and José Ufarte blazed frivolously wide. Yet Ireland's break-outs continued to threaten. McEvoy's drive was too good for Betancort, but it ricocheted off Zoco and out for a corner.

Spain ended the first half on top in everything but goals. So it continued in the second half, with Ireland being forced back, and hoping to catch Spain on the counter. Pat Dunne excelled with a double-save from Marcelino and Ufarte. Theo Foley took a knock and had to retire for running repairs. He hadn't long been back on board when Spain broke the deadlock. Only eleven minutes remained when Pereda outpaced Tony Dunne and squared. Suárez miskicked, Cantwell and Meagan were wrong-footed, and Ufarte was unmarked.

A bizarre footnote. This match would be Noel Cantwell's last in the World Cup. At the time, he was Ireland's leading international goalscorer, with fourteen, but not once had he found the net in the World Cup.

SPAIN (0) 1   **IRELAND (0) 0**
Ufarte 79

SPAIN: Betancort, Rivilla, Olivella, Zoco, Reija, Glaria IV, Suárez, Ufarte, Pereda, Marcelino, Lapetra.
IRELAND: P Dunne (MAN U), Brennan (MAN U), A Dunne (MAN U), Foley (NORTHAMPTON), Cantwell (MAN U), Meagan (HUDDERSFIELD), O'Neill (SHAMROCK R), Dunphy (YORK), McEvoy (BLACKBURN), Giles (LEEDS), Haverty (SHELBOURNE).

Spain were not yet through with breaking Irish hearts. Shamrock Rovers had, with the aid of a first-round bye, progressed to the second round of the Fairs' Cup. No Irish club had ever reached the dizzy heights of a third round place in Europe, and Real Zaragoza stood in Rovers' way. Zaragoza had won the Fairs' Cup in 1964 and now, two years on, were destined for the Final again. Full-back Severino Reija, together with forwards Carlos Lapetra and Marcelino, enjoyed a double celebration at Ireland's expense, though Rovers ran their opponents close. It was 2-2 on aggregate and only twelve minutes remained when Zaragoza clinched victory.

So Ireland were out of the World Cup and out of Europe. Although Scotland and Wales seldom threatened in their eliminating groups, Northern Ireland came almost as close as the Republic. Victory in Albania in their final qualifier would have forced a play-off with Switzerland, but Northern Ireland could only draw. England, of course, as hosts, were not subject to the vagaries of qualifying. Reaping the benefit of home advantage and a myopic Russian linesman, they strode on to lift the World Cup for the one and only time. Spain showed that hers was no extraordinary team, losing to West Germany and Argentina, and on their bikes after the first round.

The two Finalists, England and West Germany, both chanced to play Ireland prior to the finals. Ireland lost 1-3 to England in Dublin in 1964, to a team fielding five of the eventual champions. Jack Charlton was not yet an international. In May 1966, during their pre-tournament preparations, West Germany cruised to a 4-0 win at Dalymount, with seven of their Final team included.

Qualifying Group 9

	P	W	D	L	F	A	Pts
SPAIN *	2	1	0	1	4	2	2
Ireland	2	1	0	1	2	4	2
(Syria withdrew)							

* Spain qualified after play-off with Ireland.

Ireland appearances and goalscorers
World Cup qualifying rounds 1966

	Apps	Goals		Apps	Goals		Apps	Goals
Cantwell N*†‡	3	–	McEvoy A *	3	1	Meagan M	2	–
Dunne A	3	–	O'Neill F *	3	–	Barber E	1	–
Dunne P	3	–	Brennan S	2	–	Dunphy E	1	–
Giles J *	3	–	Foley T	2	–	Hennessy J	1	–
Haverty *†	3	–	McGrath M	2	–	Hurley C *†	1	–
						(own-goals)		1

* Appeared in 1962 World Cup.   *33 apps   2 goals*
† Appeared in 1958 World Cup.   *7 League of Ireland*
‡ Appeared in 1954 World Cup.   *26 English League*
15 players used

8

THE 1970 WORLD CUP

Now that European and World championships were alternating every two years, Ireland were given a quick opportunity to return to competitive action. Czechoslovakia, Turkey, and – once again – Spain completed the section, in which Ireland finished third. Turlough O'Connor's late winner in Prague, in Ireland's final match, hauled Ireland off the bottom and knocked the Czechs off the top. To their astonishment, Spain went through instead. The Czechs would never forget, or forgive, Ireland for what they had done.

The victory was proud, yet Pyrrhic for Ireland, for it could not disguise a slump in morale and fortunes so profound that no ray of sunshine peeped through the clouds. Both at club and international level, defeat followed defeat with monotonous regularity. The Prague mirage was Ireland's solitary win in seven matches, as they prepared for the new World Cup.

On the club scene, Ireland's participants in Europe had slipped back to old ways. In successive seasons in the European Cup, Waterford lost twelve goals to Vorwaerts of East Berlin, Dundalk nine to Vasas Budapest, Waterford ten to Manchester United. Ireland's only plusses amounted to Shamrock Rovers' win over Spora Luxembourg in the Cup-Winners' Cup and Dundalk accounting for Utrecht in the Fairs'. Dundalk were made to pay: Glasgow Rangers swept nine past them in the second round.

At long last a whiff of modernisation permeated the corridors of Merrion Square. The English FA had appointed Alf Ramsey as its first full-time manager, enjoying full autonomy over team matters, back in 1962. Though the FAI had, ever since he stopped playing, enjoyed the services of Johnny Carey in an ill-defined coaching capacity, the Big Five made no gesture to surrender their prerogative over team-selection. But the day was not far off. Carey had had enough. Charlie Hurley was asked to take over, combining coaching with captaincy of the national side. An international 'player-manager' we might call him these days. Hurley could be expected to throw in his tuppence-worth over the choice of players to play alongside him, even if he was short-changed. But once the dam was breached, the Big Five would be swept away in a flash.

Qualifying Group 2

The finals of the 1970 World Cup would be staged in the controversial setting of Mexico, which had also been granted the 1968 Olympics. Altitude and heat would affect all participants, even to the extent of threatening their health. Mexico couldn't possibly hold the same attractions as England, and to that extent Ireland did not look forward with feverish expectation. How could they, in the light of recent results? On the other hand, the televising of England '66 had brought soccer to the mass attention of Ireland as never before. Those previously ignorant of the game, or antagonistic to it, were won over in their thousands. The GAA's antipathy to soccer was shown to have outlived its usefulness, and in a few short years its ban would be lifted.

To take part in Mexico, Ireland had to stave off the challenge of Denmark, Hungary and Czechoslovakia. It was the first occasion Ireland had found themselves in a four-team group; the odds against qualification correspondingly lengthened. Few gave the Republic much of a chance.

Ireland had hoped to set things rolling with a home tie against Denmark, the least daunting opposition. But fifty-one minutes into the match the fog thickened and the fixture was abandoned at one goal apiece.

IRELAND v CZECHOSLOVAKIA
Sunday, 4 May 1969   *Dalymount Park – 32,002*

Ireland's *de facto* programme began with the visit of Czechoslovakia, still seething over Ireland's demolition of their European dreams. Having fought their way to the 1962 World Cup Final, the Czechs harboured high hopes for England '66. Alas, they never even got there. Portugal ran away with their qualifying section, leaving Czechoslovakia stalled at the starting blocks. The chance to make amends in Euro '68 had been dashed by Ireland. Small wonder the Czechs were fired up this time. They already had four points in the bag, courtesy of two wins over Denmark.

Whether they picked up two more depended in large measure on how Ireland applied themselves. Looking through the Ireland team-sheet, one is struck by the mixture of new and old – and has-beens. Here was Alan Kelly, the same Alan Kelly who saw five slip past him at Wembley back in 1957. He had played for Ireland, on and off, since his restoration in 1962, but now, at last, came his second World Cup opportunity, twelve years after his first. Shay Brennan, Charlie Hurley, Frank O'Neill and Johnny Giles were other old hands to steady the ship, but the rest were new to World Cup football.

Two of them were new to international football. Paddy Mulligan and Mick Leech played alongside O'Neill for Shamrock Rovers. Leech was a predatory goal-machine, albeit against LOI opponents, but he had only just returned

Help me somebody! Charlie Hurley under pressure against Czechoslovakia.

after seven weeks out with knee-ligament damage. Mulligan had excelled against Real Zaragoza in 1965. Now both grabbed their big chance. A fourth LOI slot went to Limerick's Al Finucane.

International football in the 1960s and '70s was often a brutal business, with referees unwilling or unable to stamp out physical excesses. Insofar as Irish football was shaped and moulded by the English game, which is nothing if not physical, Ireland could hardly plead innocent. But certain East European teams, in particular, specialised in a cynicism that shocked even the muscular Irish. Czechoslovakia, having lost the stars who had carried them so far in 1962, were one of these. The Czechs took the field with their sleeves rolled up, figuratively if not literally, and flayed about them, felling Irishmen one after the other with fist or boot. Astonishingly, no names entered the Portuguese referee's black book, which only encouraged the Czechs all the more.

Perhaps the Czechs were only responding in kind. Mick Leech, in particular, seemed determined to leave his mark, and an early clash with goalkeeper Vencel – unpunished by the referee – may have sowed the seeds for what followed.

On the quarter hour Ireland, who had been pressing strongly, deservedly scored. Giles' slide-rule pass to Ray Treacy sliced through the Czech's offside trap. Treacy squared to O'Neill, who returned the ball onto Eamonn Rogers' head.

Tempers flared. A minute before half-time Leech was sent crashing by a disgraceful, over-the-top tackle by Plass and was stretchered off. The 1970 World Cup was the first in which substitutes, two per side, were officially permitted – in qualifiers as well as finals, at any stage of the game, for any reason. Accordingly, as one debutant left the battle, another, Portsmouth's Eoin Hand, joined the fray.

The future Ireland manager's baptism was not a joyous occasion. The Czechs steamrollered forward in the second half with a momentum Ireland found impossible to contain. Jurkanin's centre was deflected onto the post by Shay Brennan, but bounced back for Kabat to pounce. Treacy had a chance to reclaim the lead, but couldn't keep his shot down, and Jurkanin sent Adamec sprinting clear to seal the points. The Czechs were avenged.

IRELAND (1) 1	**CZECHOSLOVAKIA (0) 2**
Rogers 15	Kabat 51, Adamec 65

IRELAND: Kelly (PRESTON), Brennan (MAN U), Hurley (SUNDERLAND), Dempsey (CHELSEA), Mulligan (SHAMROCK R), Finucane (LIMERICK), Giles (LEEDS), O'Neill (SHAMROCK R), Leech (SHAMROCK R) (*sub* Hand, PORTSMOUTH), Treacy (CHARLTON), Rogers (BLACKBURN).
CZECHOSLOVAKIA: Vencel, Dobias, Plass, Horvath, Hagara, Szikora (Hrdlicka), Kvasnak, Vesely, Jurkanin, Adamec, Kabat.

DENMARK v IRELAND
Tuesday, 27 May 1969   *Idraetspark, Copenhagen – 26,195*

The Czechs were now six points clear of Ireland, who were almost out of the 1970 World Cup before it had begun. Nothing less than a win in Copenhagen could resuscitate those fading dreams.

Ireland had done the double over Denmark in the 1958 qualifiers, and must have fancied themselves this time. The Danes had never come close to qualifying for a World Cup. Their domestic league was weak and, though their best pros were reaping rewards in other leagues in other lands, they showed no sign of gelling their talent for common cause. Few even bothered to press for international release.

The match provided international baptisms for two more fresh-faced hopefuls, Billy Newman, who would not last long in Ireland colours, and Don Givens, who would. Young Givens was sampling World Cup football before he had pulled on a first-team shirt at Old Trafford, upgrading from Manchester United's youth side, which he captained, to international football overnight.

The third change to the side saw the reintroduction of Eamon Dunphy. To the amazement of many, Johnny Giles was dropped. He would not be recalled for the duration of the campaign. With Hurley in the party as coach, or so he thought, not player, John Dempsey was promoted to captain. Only when he arrived at the airport did Hurley learn that he had been named as a substitute. But he hadn't brought his boots with him. Such mishaps perfectly illustrate the slapdash world of Irish football at the time.

Ireland's one previous visit to the Idraetspark, in 1957, had inflamed the crowd, who took exception to the visitors' negativity once they had gone in front. The Irish team, it appears, had the capacity to inflame passions, for on this occasion their robust play provoked a one-woman pitch invasion. Dempsey had to be rescued from her advances, which one presumes were anything but amorous. When Paddy Mulligan wrestled Ole Soerensen to the floor, the Irishman was the target of a bottle tossed from the crowd. Thankfully it missed. Oddly, the tally of bookings after ninety minutes stood at just one apiece, Madsen for Denmark, Dempsey for Ireland.

Unproductive skirmishes at either end preceded Denmark's first goal. Mulligan was initially at fault, losing out in midfield to Bengt Jensen. The Dane homed in on goal, skipped past Newman, and set up Ole Soerensen.

Ireland's best chance of saving the game arrived immediately after the change of ends. Givens raced into the danger zone and took aim for the bottom corner. Engedahl was equal to the shot, pushing it behind.

Hurley sent on Frank O'Neill in place of Billy Newman, whose international career lasted precisely fifty-five minutes. But it was Denmark who scored next. Madsen did the spade work with a fine run, setting up Ole Soerensen for his second goal.

Ireland had lost to Denmark for the first time, and could forget Mexico.

DENMARK   (1) 2   **IRELAND   (0) 0**
O Soerensen 35, 67

DENMARK: Engedahl, Larsen, Nielan, Andersen, H M Jensen, Moeller, B Jensen, O Soerensen, Madsen, L Soerensen, Le Fevre.
IRELAND: Kelly (PRESTON), Brennan (MAN U), Finucane (LIMERICK), Dempsey (CHELSEA), Mulligan (SHAMROCK R), Newman (SHELBOURNE) (*sub* O'Neill, SHAMROCK R), Dunphy (MILLWALL), Treacy (CHARLTON), Leech (SHAMROCK R), Givens (MAN U), Rogers (BLACKBURN).

IRELAND v HUNGARY
Sunday, 8 June 1969   *Dalymount Park – 17,286*

When qualifying groups are first announced, there follows much verbal argy-bargy and secret trade-offs among the competing national associations.

Agreeing a fixture list to the satisfaction of all is fraught with wheeling and dealing. Everyone wants to get off to a flying start. Most nations, England certainly, like to get cracking with a home tie against duff opponents. Get those first two points in the bag, is the axiom.

For weaker nations – such as Ireland, pre-Jack Charlton – a gentle start can make all the difference to whether a campaign is sustained awhile or is stillborn. It is no use winning matches at the end if early defeats have left you without hope. Public interest will already have been eroded.

Wales, for example, in the 1970s and '80s exploited the useful habit of visiting the tough guys last. By so doing, they often kept themselves in contention till the end. Predictable defeats at the climax permitted Wales to bask in the myth of their misfortune.

1970 was the first occasion Ireland had opened with a home fixture, against Denmark, they truly expected to win. Had the fog lifted, and had Ireland won, things might have looked brighter. As it was, their position was now beyond recall, leaving them with a string of meaningless internationals useful only for the blooding of new talent.

For the moment, they were booked to entertain the Hungarians for the first time in thirty years. The sides had met five times in the 1930s, but Ireland had never come out on top. The fabulous Magyar side of the early '50s had fallen apart in the wake of the Hungarian Revolution. Hungary (1938, 1954) and Czechoslovakia (1934, 1962) shared the distinction of never having won the World Cup, but having played in, and lost, *two* Finals. Holland (1974, 1978) have subsequently joined that select club.

It was now the second week in June, when soccer appetites were at their lowest. The attendance, barely 17,000, reflected the disenchantment. It was Dalymount's lowest for a World Cup-tie, yet Hungary provided attractive opposition. They were reigning Olympic champions, having retained in Mexico the title they won in 1964. They had been World Cup quarter-finalists in 1966; Farkás, who would now appear as a substitute, had scored a breathtaking goal against Brazil; and in Florian Albert, Hungary boasted the European Footballer of the Year 1967.

Hungary had commenced their programme with a vital home win over the Czechs, setting up a tumultuous challenge with their neighbours for the one ticket to Mexico.

Charlie Hurley was back in the Ireland side, for what would be his international swan-song. The return of Manchester United's Tony Dunne and Fulham's Jimmy Conway were the other changes.

The sparse crowd could enjoy the bright sun if not the dull football. Hungary opened and concluded the scoring, going ahead with the messiest of goals. Kelly couldn't hold Ferenc Bene's shot, Mulligan's clearance flew back off Bene, and the ball dropped for Dunai.

Substitute Frank O'Neill, second from left, heads towards Hungary's goal.

As in Copenhagen, Hurley brought on Frank O'Neill at half-time, this time taking himself off. Jimmy Conway might, and Mick Leech should, have equalised before Dunphy won the ball on the edge of his own penalty box and sent O'Neill clear down the wing. Givens chested down O'Neill's cross to volley past Szentmihályi, one of five Hungarian veterans of England '66. That number rose to six with the introduction of Farkás, who repaid his manager's faith by laying on the cross from which Bene volleyed past Kelly.

One interested spectator in the stands was Chelsea boss Dave Sexton. He was rumoured to be eyeing up Mick Leech. But Leech missed a great chance when one on one with the keeper. Mulligan took Sexton's fancy instead, and a few months later moved to Stamford Bridge.

IRELAND (0) 1   **HUNGARY (1) 2**
Givens 59   Dunai II 23, Bene 80

IRELAND: Kelly (PRESTON), Brennan (MAN U), Finucane (LIMERICK), Mulligan (SHAMROCK R), Dunne (MAN U), Conway (FULHAM), Dunphy (MILLWALL), Rogers (BLACKBURN), Leech (SHAMROCK R), Hurley (BOLTON) (*sub* O'Neill, SHAMROCK R), Givens (MAN U).
HUNGARY: Szentmihályi, Káposzta, Mészöly, Szucs, Ihasz, Göröcs, Albert, Zambo, Bene, Dunai II, Kozma (Farkás).

CZECHOSLOVAKIA v IRELAND

Tuesday, 7 October 1969   *Sparta Stadium, Prague – 32,879*

Three games, no points, and Ireland's players couldn't wait to be off on their hols. When they reconvened in the autumn it was to greet Mick Meagan, former player-manager of Drogheda, as Ireland's full-time manager. It appears that pressure from senior players helped persuade the selectors that their time was up and that they should hand over to a pro. Meagan had control of tactics and team-selection, bringing Ireland belatedly into line with the rest of Europe. In his first match, against Scotland in September (1-1), Meagan picked himself, but thereafter left the donkey work to others.

LOI champions Waterford had looked forward to registering Ireland's first ever win in the European Cup in thirteen years of trying. Drawn against the Turks of Galatasaray, they had surprised themselves, losing home and away.

The Ireland side to face Czechoslovakia in Prague had a raw look about it. Kevin Fitzpatrick in goal and Terry Conroy out wide were new to international football. Alfie Hale of Waterford and Spurs' Joe Kinnear – later to manage Wimbledon – sampled World Cup action for the first time.

Hale had first been picked for the Republic in 1962, while with Aston Villa. Breaking through at Villa Park was hard work, and, after spells with Doncaster and Newport, Hale returned home. Supporters of Waterford would be glad that he did, for Hale played an integral part in the club's run of championships in the late '60s. A natural scorer, and surprisingly good in the air for one of modest height, Hale had scored dramatic late equalisers in friendlies against Poland and Austria, and Meagan looked to him to puncture the Czech defence.

Ireland's most-capped player was the new skipper, Shay Brennan, with twelve. With four players from the LOI, plus another, Johnny Fullam, coming on as sub, Meagan was clearly turning to home comforts, rather than having to beg, steal and borrow from English clubs who, as ever, released players grudgingly, if at all. English league clubs were obliged to release players for the England national side, but not, at that time, for anyone else.

The top of Group 2 was too close to call. From the start it had been a two-horse race, which initially swung Hungary's way, with their win over Czechoslovakia, then tilted towards the Czechs when Hungary amazingly lost in Copenhagen. In September Hungary made up ground with a 3-3 draw in Prague. This was the Czechs' final match. Victory was imperative.

Meagan's 'I'm backing Ireland' campaign backfired wretchedly. Adamec bagged a first-half hat-trick. He launched the Czechs into a quick lead, seizing on Kabat's flick; almost burst the net with his second, from Kvasnak's short free-kick; and – after Vesely's corner had been chested down to him – drove in his third from fifteen yards.

Damage limitation dominated Meagan's thoughts in the second half. He took off Givens, sent on Johnny Fullam, and packed his midfield. No further goals resulted, but that was scant relief. The horse had already bolted.

CZECHOSLOVAKIA   (3) 3   IRELAND   (0) 0
Adamec 9, 37, 44

CZECHOSLOVAKIA: Viktor, Pivarnik, Migas (Hrivnak), Horvath, Hagara, Kvasnak, Kuna, Vesely, Jurkanin (Jokl), Adamec, Kabat.
IRELAND: Fitzpatrick (LIMERICK), Brennan (MAN U), Finucane (LIMERICK), Mulligan (SHAMROCK R), Carroll (IPSWICH), Kinnear (SPURS), Conway (FULHAM), Conmy (PETERBOROUGH), Givens (MAN U) (*sub* Fullam, SHAMROCK R), Hale (WATERFORD), Conroy (STOKE).

IRELAND v DENMARK
Wednesday, 15 October 1969   *Dalymount Park – 19,603*

This match should have been played ten months earlier. Then it would have carried weight. Now it had lost all purpose. It couldn't even carry the tag 'wooden spoon stakes'. Denmark already had four points, Ireland none.

A sparse crowd watched apathetically as Meagan blooded Southampton's Tony Byrne at centre-back. Ireland scored quickly – Don Givens controlling Eamon Rogers' cross to net – and thereafter they pummelled the Danish goal.

In the second half Munk Jensen cleared off the line from Ray Treacy, and Poulsen thrillingly foiled one of Rogers' better efforts. But, as often happens when one side is in undisputed control, the team on the receiving end raced upfield to score. The game had been yawning to a close when Kelly brought down Madsen. Bengt Jensen made no mistake from the penalty spot.

IRELAND   (1) 1   DENMARK   (0) 1
Givens 8   B Jensen 85 pen

IRELAND: Kelly (PRESTON), Kinnear (SPURS), Byrne (SOUTHAMPTON), Mulligan (SHAMROCK R), Brennan (MAN U), Conway (FULHAM), Dunphy (MILLWALL), Rogers (BLACKBURN), Conroy (STOKE), Givens (MAN U), Treacy (CHARLTON).
DENMARK: Poulsen, Larsen, Nielsen, Thorst, H M Jensen, Moeller, Praest, Michaelsen, B Jensen, Andersen, Roemer (Madsen).

HUNGARY v IRELAND
Wednesday, 5 November 1969   *Nep Stadium, Budapest – 23,620*

And so to Budapest. Hungary needed two points to force a play-off with Czechoslovakia, yet, despite the importance of the match, the imposing Nep

Stadium was no more than a third full. Ireland were not exactly crowd-pullers. The return of Tony Dunne saw him rewarded with the captaincy. Apart from the first five minutes, Ireland rarely showed as an attacking force, and Tamas in the home goal had hardly a shot to save. His opposite number, Kelly, was sorely overworked, as he and his defenders conceded a rash of corners to keep the Magyars at bay. The breakthrough came just after the half hour from yet another corner. The Irish defence failed to clear and Halmosi profited. Ray Treacy substituted for Terry Conroy before half-time.

Three minutes after the break Zambo outstripped Dunne down the flank, and curled in a cross from which Bene scored fiercely. Hungary had the points – and the appointment with Czechoslovakia – sewn up, but still they ploughed forward. Number three arrived when Fazekás headed Kelemen's free-kick goalwards. Kelly got his hands to the ball, but Puskás (namesake of an earlier Hungarian hero) was on hand to poke back the loose ball.

Bearing in mind that, for Hungary, the result was safe, it is strange to read that the game boiled over in its final minutes. No sooner had Kocsis notched Hungary's fourth than John Dempsey was penalised for fouling Bene. The defender reacted angrily, flung the ball at the Yugoslavian referee, and was ordered off, the first Ireland player ever to be dismissed. Dissatisfied with the judicial response, Szucs shortly flattened Treacy. Szucs, too, was shown the way to the tunnel.

HUNGARY (1) 4   **IRELAND   (0) 0**
Halmosi 31, Bene 48, Puskás 72,
Kocsis 81

HUNGARY: Tamas, Kelemen, Pancsics, Szucs, Ihasz, Göröcs (Kocsis), Halmosi, Fazekás, Bene, Dunai II (Puskás), Zamabo.
IRELAND: Kelly (PRESTON), Brennan (MAN U), Dempsey (CHELSEA), Mulligan (CHELSEA), Dunne (MAN U), Conway (FULHAM), Kinnear (SPURS), Dunphy (MILLWALL), Rogers (BLACKBURN), Conroy (STOKE) (*sub* Treacy, CHARLTON), Givens (MAN U).

All things considered, these were among Ireland's most abject results in their World Cup history. To finish four points adrift of Denmark meant that the Irish patient was sickly indeed. Shay Brennan and Paddy Mulligan were the only two ever-presents.

Northern Ireland, George Best and all, put up a much better show and gave the Soviet Union a run for their money. Wales finished pointless in their group, and Scotland were outmanoeuvred by West Germany in theirs. England qualified automatically as defending champions.

Czechoslovakia had been unable to see off Hungary in either of their group clashes, but did so when it mattered in the play-off. In Mexico, the Czechs, notoriously bad travellers, finished bottom of a group that included

Brazil, Romania and England, to whom they lost 0-1 to a doubtful penalty. Brazil, playing rapturous football, won the Cup, beating Italy in the Final.

Qualifying Group 2

		Home					Away				
	P	W	D	L	F	A	W	D	L	F	A	Pts
CZECHOSLOVAKIA*	6	2	1	0	7	3	2	0	1	5	3	9
Hungary	6	3	0	0	9	0	1	1	1	7	7	9
Denmark	6	2	0	1	5	5	0	1	2	1	5	5
Ireland	6	0	1	2	3	5	0	0	3	0	9	1

* Czechoslovakia qualified after play-off with Hungary (4-1, Marseille).

Other group results

Denmark v Czechoslovakia 0-3	Denmark v Hungary 3-2
Czechoslovakia v Denmark 1-0	Czechoslovakia v Hungary 3-3
Hungary v Czechoslovakia 2-0	Hungary v Denmark 3-0

Ireland appearances and goalscorers (substitute appearances in brackets)
World Cup qualifying rounds 1970

	Apps	Goals		Apps	Goals
Brennan S *	6	–	Dunne A *	2	–
Mulligan P	6	–	Hurley C *†‡	2	–
Givens D	5	2	O'Neill F	1 (2)	–
Kelly A	5	–	Byrne A	1	–
Rogers E	5	1	Carroll T	1	–
Conway J	4	–	Conmy O	1	–
Dunphy E *	4	–	Fitzpatrick K	1	–
Finucane A	4	–	Giles J *†	1	–
Treacy R	3 (1)	–	Hale A	1	–
Conroy T	3	–	Newman W	1	–
Dempsey J	3	–	Fullam J	– (1)	–
Kinnear J	3	–	Hand E	– (1)	–
Leech M	3	–			

* Appeared in 1966 World Cup.
† Appeared in 1962 World Cup.
‡ Appeared in 1958 World Cup.
25 players used

71 apps   3 goals
19 League of Ireland
52 English League

9

THE 1974 WORLD CUP

Ireland's bleak results in the 1970 qualifiers were trumped by those in the 1972 Euros'. Though pitched into a tough group – with Italy, Austria and Sweden – Ireland once again finished bottom, once again taking just one point. They concluded their programme with home and away ties against Austria. When Austria rattled in four at Dalymount, it proved the last straw for the mandarins of Merrion Square. Mick Meagan had been in office for two years, overseen a dozen internationals, lost nine and not won any. This truly was Ireland's darkest hour. Meagan had to go.

The torch passed to Liam Tuohy, like Meagan an Ireland international, but unlike Meagan someone who had played most of his football in the LOI. He had in the past taken control of LOI representative sides. 'Rashers' Tuohy knew little about the English or continental game, other than when spending three in-and-out seasons with Newcastle United, and playing the odd match in Europe. As an Ireland international he was best described as a 'bits and pieces' player, winning eight caps, but spreading them over ten years. But for the selectors' keenness for Joe Haverty, Tuohy would surely have won more.

A hero with Shamrock Rovers for his pace and his eye for goal, Tuohy was an outside-left in an age when wingers were becoming obsolescent. In the fullness of time he moved into management with Rovers and then Dundalk, before receiving the call from Merrion Square.

Tuohy knew perfectly well that the FAI was bedevilled by amateurish shilly-shallying, and that the Ireland team's greatest bugbear was the lack of preparation before international matches. To some extent, given players' obligations to their English clubs, that was unavoidable and always had been. But Tuohy could remember a time when team talks consisted of an exhortation to gaze at the tricolour and to 'remember you're Irish'. No wonder the team got hammered. Tuohy wielded a new broom, but that did not necessarily mean it would sweep clean.

He wore the guv'nors cap for the first time when taking the team over for the return match with Austria, in Linz. In the face of English obstruction, he sent out six debutants, a seventh coming on as substitute, in a side that, with the exception of Paddy Mulligan – now with Chelsea – was extracted entirely from the LOI. Instead of looking forward, Tuohy had had his arm twisted into turning the clock back to the 1930s.

Tuohy's baptism was hellish. Ireland were swept away under a torrent of six goals. He swung the axe again during a summer tournament in Brazil, competing for the Brazilian Independence Cup. Ireland had never previously participated in close-season tours of this kind, and it was a welcome innovation, sure to educate both manager and players. When Ireland beat the nondescripts of Iran in their first match, it heralded their first victory in five years, a run of twenty-one matches. They followed up with another win, over Ecuador, before losing to Chile and Portugal. Yet so low was the morale of Irish soccer, that no newspaper bothered to cover the tournament.

The Irish club scene was as depressing as the international one. Waterford continued to dominate the LOI, and to Waterford fell the honour of a first Ireland triumph in the European Cup. The victory was all the sweeter as it came against Glentoran from the North. The LOI champions reverted to type in the second round, being hammered for ten by Glasgow Celtic. The following season Cork Hibs briefly took up the baton, but their interest in the competition was brief. Borussia Moenchengladbach ran in seven. It was not the defeats that hurt so much, but the sheer weight of goals conceded.

Though Ireland had no direct interest in Mexico '70, the magnificence of Brazil, highlighted by the introduction of colour television, brought the genius of Jairzinho and Pele into countless thousands of Irish homes. Kids took to soccer in unprecedented numbers. No longer could it be dismissed as a heretical sport, disparaged as that 'foreign' game. Pressure from within obliged the GAA to rescind the ban that had been in place since the dawn of the century.

Irish soccer was clearly in the throes of revolution, first shaking off the Big Five, then the GAA, and now Dalymount Park. Bohemians' grand old stadium had served the nation well, but it was poorly equipped, in need of restoration, and was little better than many English fourth division grounds. The stadium was an embarrassment to the protocols of international football, and, as such, was detrimental to the advance of the Ireland team.

The trouble was, Ireland had no national soccer stadium, no Wembley, no Hampden Park. Where Gaelic games had Croke Park, and rugby Lansdowne Road, soccer had had no alternative but to use club grounds. If the Ireland team was to play elsewhere it would have to ground-share. The GAA stayed aloof, refusing to countenance the contamination of hallowed Croke Park, but the rugby authorities at Lansdowne Road proved more amenable. Given the improbability of Scottish soccer internationals ever being staged at Murrayfield, or English ones at Twickenham, this marked something of a triumph. With Lansdowne from now on having to serve two masters, friction was never far from the surface, and even today ferments acrimoniously from time to time.

Ireland's first international at Lansdowne Road of modern times was against Italy in the European Championship. Having been the first country ever to play the fledgling Free State, both in Italy and in Dublin, Italy now chalked up a hat-trick of historical 'firsts'.

Italy were World Cup runners-up, yet despite their star billing they attracted an audience of just 25,000. Clearly, the idea of soccer at Lansdowne raised doubts in some quarters and would take some getting used to. At first, the atmosphere seemed dissipated in such an 'open' stadium, and some fans mourned the loss of the famed 'Dalymount roar', which they reckoned was worth a goal start. In view of Ireland's dreadful results, some considered the move suicidal for that reason alone. This debit was cancelled out by the state of the pitch. Being suited to rugby, it was not at all conducive to good soccer. It was too bumpy and the grass too long, handicaps that might take the wind out of the sails of visiting exhibitionists. In any case, Ireland would alternate between Lansdowne and Dalymount for some years yet.

The 1974 World Cup was earmarked for West Germany. Ireland needed to squeeze past France and the Soviet Union, a feat that, in the light of form and history, seemed improbable in the extreme. Even if they succeeded, Ireland were not sure of a place. The winners of European Group 9 were scheduled to play-off against the winners of South American Group 3, which comprised Chile and Peru. Many air miles awaited Ireland if they hoped to take part.

Qualifying Group 9

IRELAND v SOVIET UNION
Wednesday, 18 October 1972   *Lansdowne Road – 25,000*

This was a double-first for Ireland. A footballing clash with the largest state on Earth, and Ireland's first World Cup-tie to be staged at Lansdowne Road.

David versus Goliath. A country of three million inhabitants taking on an empire with a population some one hundred times greater.

For all its size and resources, the Soviet Union has rarely punched its weight in World Cups. The Soviets were politically quarantined for the first forty years of their existence, and first competed for the Jules Rimet Cup as late as 1958, when they were confident they would do themselves justice and not discredit socialist perfection. Since then they had, without exception, qualified for the finals, and only once failed to progress beyond the group phase. Three times – 1958, 1962, 1970 – they had fallen at the quarter-finals, advancing to the last four in 1966. While this might show consistency, it did not suggest that the soccer world was about to beat a path to Moscow's door.

Terry Conroy doesn't connect properly with this header against the Soviets.

The Soviets were typecast as eschewing free-flowing creativity, which was presumed to be a prerogative of the Free World. Defeat brought shame upon the socialist ideology, therefore defeat was prohibited. Though Soviet club sides lagged behind their national team, Dinamo Kiev, pre-eminent for some seasons, would stay afloat in the European Cup till the quarter-finals.

The Soviets had set Group 9 in train by subsiding 0-1 in Paris, and desperately needed a two-point haul from Dublin. Caution extended to team-selection as to everything else. Anchoring the side were five of the team beaten 0-1 by Uruguay in the 1970 quarter-finals. Critically, two stars from Mexico were missing, centre half Shesterniev and striker Anatoli Bishovets.

For Ireland, Liam Tuohy installed the most experienced side he could muster. In the absence of Mulligan and Giles, he passed the captaincy to forty-two-cap goalkeeper Alan Kelly. Aside from Tommy McConville, Mick Martin, and Noel Campbell, he swallowed his pride and reverted to players from the English league. Campbell was playing with Fortuna Cologne, and hence became Ireland's first continental player to appear in the World Cup.

Ginger-haired, bleached-skinned Terry Conroy was exciting spectators the length of England with his lissom performances for Stoke City, while Steve Heighway, the university graduate dubbed 'Big Bamber' by his Liverpool team-mates, had come to prominence with his leggy runs down the flanks.

One of these had brought him an FA Cup Final goal against Arsenal. Three other members of the side would make a name for themselves as managers, Ray Treacy, with a number of Irish clubs, latterly Shamrock Rovers, Joe Kinnear, at Wimbledon, and Eoin Hand, of the Ireland national team.

On the face of it, Tuohy possessed a team capable of upsetting opponents who took them lightly. Ireland put up a fight, but Soviet firepower told in the end. The first half was goalless, though Kelly earned his corn, saving from Muntian, twice, Fedotov and Euryuzhikhin. The visitors had the upper hand after the break, but their first goal arrived unexpectedly. Puzach found himself all alone as he took a pass from Fedotov to beat Kelly.

Tuohy sent on Mick Leech in place of Rogers, switching to 4-2-4, but no sooner had the substitute taken the field than the Soviet Union doubled their lead. Ireland's bare midfield was exposed as cheeky Soviet interplay allowed Muntian to cross for Kolotov – possibly offside – to head into the net.

The deficit might have been three or four before Ireland summoned a late flurry. Kinnear's header went close; then Leech set up Conroy to bullet Ireland back into contention. The visitors held out for the final eight minutes.

IRELAND (0) 1	**SOVIET UNION** (0) 2
Conroy 82	Puzach 55, Kolotov 65

IRELAND: Kelly (PRESTON), Kinnear (SPURS), McConville (WATERFORD), Hand (PORTSMOUTH), Carroll (BIRMINGHAM), Campbell (FORTUNA COLOGNE), Martin (BOHEMIANS), Rogers (CHARLTON) (*sub* Leech, SHAMROCK R), Heighway (LIVERPOOL), Treacy (SWINDON), Conroy (STOKE).
USSR: Pilgui (Rudakov), Dzodzvashvili, Khurtsilava, Kaplichny, Lovchev, Kolotov, Muntian, Semenov, Fedotov, Puzach, Euryuzhikhin.

IRELAND v FRANCE
Wednesday, 15 November 1972   *Dalymount Park – 30,000*

As with the previous World Cup, a home defeat in the opening match was likely to be irretrievable. It would be hard to accumulate the five or six points necessary to qualify. Already, sceptics were looking ahead to 1978.

This was the second time Ireland had been paired with France in World Cups, the foetus of a relationship that would later become almost incestuous in its frequency. In 1953 the French had romped to a 5-3 victory at Dalymount. They had flourished in the 1958 finals, but had lapsed since those heady days of Just Fontaine and Raymond Kopa. France had failed to reach two of the next three World Cups, the exception being 1966, where they failed to win a game. The fortunes of club and national teams are often symbiotically intertwined, as both Ireland and France knew to their cost, and England would shortly know to theirs. France's domestic game was in tatters,

Reims had fallen on hard times, and no other French clubs were making waves in European competition.

By the 1980s France would have built a fine team. The first of these future stars lined up now, Marius Trésor, an ebony sweeper from Mauritius. If France could build on their win over the Soviet Union, they would be in pole position and would take some shifting.

With hindsight, the game marked something of a watershed for Irish football. Spirits were rock-bottom, not least because Ireland hadn't beaten anybody in Dublin for seven and a half years, since defeating Spain with the assistance of an Iribar own-goal in May 1965.

The health of a nation's football is gauged principally through the fortunes of its national side. The antipathy of the GAA might be softening, but if soccer were ever to take off in Ireland it was imperative that the national side start winning occasionally, and, sooner rather than later, qualify for a major tournament. It might be too late to aim realistically for Germany '74, but before this match Tuohy spelled out the consequences to his players, not just in the short term, but in the long.

The manager's words appeared to have entered one of Kinnear's ears and exited from the other, for it was his sloppy back-pass that went wide of Kelly and, mercifully, the post. Revelli's header flew past, Larque's strike soared over, and Revelli struck a post.

Tuohy had axed five of the team bowled over by the Soviets, brought back Givens, Mulligan and Giles, and handed Giles the captain's armband. Coventry's Jimmy Holmes, four days past his nineteenth birthday, became the youngest player ever to play World Cup football for Ireland.

On the evidence of the first twenty-five minutes, Ireland were heading for another fall. But with their first shot on goal they went in front. Giles took a free-kick. Trésor headed it out, Giles headed it back. The ball finally broke to Conroy, who smashed it into the net via the underside of the bar.

France looked less assured now that they had fallen behind. Trésor almost did a 'Kinnear', but his wayward back-pass was salvaged. Conroy brought the first half to a close by striking the crossbar.

Having seen Ireland score against the run of play, France followed their example. Substitute Molitor, having barely shaken the cobwebs from his feet, crossed into the danger zone for Larque to volley past Kelly.

Still Ireland pressed. Mulligan shot wastefully high. Hand beat Rostagni in a race for the ball and centred for Treacy. The ball appeared to come off the back of Treacy's head, but it beat Carnus to put Ireland back in front. Giles and Conroy had chances to tie up the win, before France launched a late riposte, encouraged by a referee who added four minutes injury time. Never mind. Ireland had won a match at last. But never again would Dalymount Park reverberate to the cheers or groans of World Cup football.

IRELAND (1) 2	**FRANCE (0) 1**
Conroy 28, Treacy 75	Larque 66

IRELAND: Kelly (PRESTON), Kinnear (SPURS), Mulligan (PALACE), McConville (WATERFORD), Holmes (COVENTRY), Hand (PORTSMOUTH), Giles (LEEDS), Byrne (SO'TON) (*sub* Campbell, FORTUNA COLOGNE), Conroy (STOKE) (*sub* O'Connor, BOHEMIANS), Treacy (SWINDON), Givens (QPR).
FRANCE: Carnus, Broissart, Quittet, Trésor, Rostagni, Huck, Adams, Loubet (Molitor), Revelli, Larque, Bereta.

SOVIET UNION v IRELAND
Sunday, 13 May 1973   *Lenin Stadium, Moscow – 70,000*

Ireland had enjoyed a famous but probably futile victory. They now needed to reap something from the trip to Moscow six months later.

Whether they did so or not depended in large measure on how the players reacted to the bombshell that Liam Tuohy was quitting at the end of Ireland's World Cup itinerary. Business pressures were cited as the reason. With a more-or-less full squad from which to choose, Tuohy made just two changes, preferring Tommy Carroll to Joe Kinnear and Mick Martin to Tony Byrne.

The Soviets introduced a tall, ungainly youth to the No. 11 shirt. Come 1975, he would be voted European Footballer of the Year. He would still be terrorising international defences – a hundred and more caps to his credit – in the 1986 World Cup. His name was Oleg Blokhin.

Ireland had little choice but to back-pedal early on, though they restricted the hosts to just two chances, both capably repulsed by Kelly. Tony Byrne and Miah Dennehy took the field for the second half, both Giles and Conroy having laboured with hamstring strains. A Soviet goal was not long delayed. Andreasan shot over when he should have scored. A minute later Muntian crossed, Carroll failed to clear, leaving Onischenko in the clear.

After that, the hosts came nearer to extending their lead than the visitors did to erasing it, but Kelly was equal to shots from Blokhin and Onischenko.

Ireland continued their continental tour, losing 0-2 to a Polish side about to boot England from the World Cup. And on to Paris.

SOVIET UNION (0) 1	**IRELAND (0) 0**
Onischenko 58	

USSR: Pilgui, Dzodzvashvili, Kaplichny, Khurtsilava, Lovchev, Kolotov, Muntian (Olchanski), Kuznetzov, Andreasan (Fedotov), Onischenko, Blokhin.
IRELAND: Kelly (PRESTON), Carroll (BIRMINGHAM), Mulligan (PALACE), McConville (WATERFORD), Holmes (COVENTRY), Hand (PORTSMOUTH), Giles (LEEDS) (*sub* Byrne, SO'TON), Martin (MAN U), Conroy (STOKE) (*sub* Dennehy, FOREST), Treacy (SWINDON), Givens (QPR).

FRANCE v IRELAND
Saturday, 19 May 1973   *Parc des Princes, Paris – 40,463*

Ireland were not yet formally out of contention, though they needed to win in Paris and then hope for a French win in Moscow. That would leave all three nations deadlocked on four points.

As Giles and Conroy were still on the mend, Tuohy began with the eleven who had finished the match in Moscow. Mulligan was captain.

The outgoing manager was rewarded with a spirited Irish show, which resulted in Ireland's first away point in the World Cup for sixteen years, since winning in Denmark in 1957.

Ireland saw an early share of the ball. Treacy shot over at one end, Bereta at the other. Both sides made early substitutions. John Herrick took the place of the limping Tommy Carroll, but when Chiesa replaced Larque the Romanian referee flourished a yellow card. Chiesa had not waited to be summoned onto the field. By full-time Don Givens and Ray Treacy had also been cautioned, in their case for physical misdemeanours.

Three times France might have gone in front before half-time, the nearest being when Revelli struck Kelly's post.

Ireland held their own in the second half, though the French substitute, Chiesa, seemed to have stolen a win, flicking in Floch's corner. Defeat would have been hard on Ireland, and they deservedly levelled. Miah Dennehy hoodwinked two defenders and shot against the crossbar. Mick Martin was in the right place to net with a downward header.

FRANCE (0) 1   IRELAND (0) 1
Chiesa 79   Martin 84

FRANCE: Carnus, Domenech, Quittet, Trésor, Rostagni, Michel, Adams, Floch, Revelli, Larque (Chiesa), Bereta.
IRELAND: Kelly (PRESTON), Carroll (BIRMINGHAM) (*sub* Herrick, SHAMROCK R), Mulligan (PALACE), McConville (WATERFORD), Holmes (COVENTRY), Martin (MAN U), Hand (PORTSMOUTH), Byrne (SOUTHAMPTON), Dennehy (FOREST), Treacy (SWINDON), Givens (QPR).

France tumbled to a 0-2 defeat in Moscow, enabling Ireland to escape the wooden spoon for the first time since 1958. The Soviet Union thereby topped Group 9 and duly entertained Chile in the first leg of the aforementioned play-off. The game ended goalless. The second leg was the stuff of farce. Cynics said the Soviets didn't fancy their chances in the feverish atmosphere of Santiago, and were seeking any excuse to pull out. The official Moscow line cited political difficulties. The match was scheduled for Santiago's national stadium, employed by President Pinochet for the torture and execution of former President Allende's communist-sympathisers.

FIFA refused to switch the venue, the Soviets stayed at home, and Chile took the field unopposed. At which point the players of the Brazilian side Santos trotted sheepishly into view, having been secretly invited to fill the void. Santos thrashed Chile 5-0. Chile failed to win a game in Germany.

England, Wales and Northern Ireland never even got there, falling by the wayside. This left the British spotlight on Scotland. The Scots were appearing in their first finals for sixteen years, finished unbeaten, but fell foul of the swings and roundabouts of goal-difference and returned home early.

Brazil's third triumph in 1970 had entitled them to retain the Jules Rimet Cup in perpetuity. A new trophy was on show, simply named the 'World Cup'. West Germany won it, though many sympathised with Holland.

Qualifying Group 9

	P	W	D	L	F	A	Pts
SOVIET UNION	4	3	0	1	8	3	6
Ireland	4	1	1	2	4	5	3
France	4	1	1	2	3	5	3

Other group results
France v Soviet Union   1-0   Soviet Union v France   2-0

Ireland appearances and goalscorers (substitute appearances in brackets)
World Cup qualifying rounds 1974

	Apps	Goals		Apps	Goals
Hand E *	4	–	Byrne A *	2 (1)	–
Kelly A *	4	–	Giles J *†‡	2	–
McConville T	4	–	Kinnear J *	2	–
Treacy R *	4	1	N Campbell	1 (1)	–
Carroll T	3	–	M Dennehy	1 (1)	–
Conroy T *	3	2	Heighway S	1	–
Givens D *	3	–	Rogers E *	1	–
Holmes J	3	–	Herrick J	– (1)	–
Martin M	3	1	Leech M *	– (1)	–
Mulligan P	3	–	O'Connor T	– (1)	–

* Appeared in 1970 World Cup.   *50 apps   4 goals*
† Appeared in 1966 World Cup.   *7 League of Ireland*
‡ Appeared in 1962 World Cup.   *41 English League*
20 players used   *2 German League*

10

THE 1978 WORLD CUP

When Liam Tuohy stepped down he took with him the memory of three wins from the ten matches he had supervised, a mighty improvement on the record of poor Mick Meagan, but hardly the stuff of headlines. The miracles would have to wait. Sean Thomas stepped briefly into the vacuum, in that quaint phrase, in a 'caretaker capacity', and promptly stepped out of it following a 1-1 draw in Norway. By the new season the FAI had the man they wanted.

Ireland's fourth manager in four years was Johnny Giles. Thus began Ireland's most prosperous epoch prior to the arrival of Jack Charlton. For seven years Ireland would hold their own on the international stage, without quite achieving the breakthrough Giles had promised.

Giles was appointed player-manager. The FAI's enthusiasm for this most demanding of double-acts is hard to account for, especially as there were few precedents in British football, and fewer successful ones.

At the time of his appointment Giles could only offer his services on an absentee basis. He was, after all, still under contract with Leeds United, though nearing the end of his time at Elland Road. Though lacking managerial experience, Ireland welcomed him as a mother might welcome a son returning after many years at sea. If Johnny Carey was the inspiration behind Ireland international sides of the 1940s, there is no doubt Giles was Ireland's superstar of the '60s and '70s. It was unfortunate that Giles' summer coincided with Ireland's long winter. Otherwise, goodness knows what havoc he might have wrought on opposing defences.

He was thirty-two now, past his best to be sure, but so far ahead of his peers that he was able to pick himself without demur until his thirty-ninth birthday loomed. By then he had been an international footballer for twenty years. Giles was so good, at a time when Ireland were so bad, that one inevitably felt for a player denied the appropriate arena for his talents. Giles would have been a certainty for England, as would George Best, and there are not too many Irishmen of whom, hand on heart, that might be said.

That Matt Busby could consider Giles – then a right-winger – dispensable at Old Trafford remains a rare blot on that great man's judgment. Manchester

United's loss was Leeds United's gain. Don Revie promptly built a team around the Giles-Bremner axis. Having stormed into the first division in 1964, Leeds – bolstered by an immovable giraffe in the back four – lorded it over English football for the next ten years and more.

Two league championships seems meagre reward for the domination that Leeds exerted in their golden years. Five times they were runners up, often denied the big prize by margins cruelly small. Leeds won the FA Cup, the Fairs' Cup, and in the eyes of many would have won the European Cup had the referee properly awarded a penalty against Bayern Münich for a foul on Allan Clarke.

One might think that the English soccer public would have taken Leeds to their hearts, not only for their consistent excellence, but because they so often seemed genuinely unlucky. Without an offside decision here, a penalty there, a goalkeeping gaffe or two, Leeds might have won half a dozen championships, never mind two.

Yet, truth to tell, Leeds were more despised than revered. No one would quibble with their talent – Giles was just one of numerous aces up Revie's sleeve – but people did question the application. Revie brought a ruthlessness to Leeds' play, one might almost say a meanness of spirit, which in the process turned 'professionalism' into an ugly word. Winning was all, and if enemies were made the length and breadth of the land, so be it. When, in 1974, Don Revie believed he could employ the same methods on England's behalf, he came a mighty cropper. He would not be the only England manager hounded from office, but he would be the only one to leave England in the lurch, and the only one to bury his hands in Arab gold. In comparison with those other builders of football dynasties, Bill Shankly and Matt Busby, Revie's death – outside Leeds – did not unleash a tide of tributes.

All this is important, for it helps to unravel the complex emotions heaped upon Leeds United and its exemplars. Even today, the Elland Road club struggles to shake off the Revie legacy. It wants his success, but not the opprobrium that accompanied it.

So well schooled were Revie's players in the mechanics of winning that many moved smoothly into management. Bremner, Clarke, Trevor Cherry, Terry Cooper, Norman Hunter, Eddie Gray, all took charge of, usually, northern outfits, some of them Leeds itself, with greater or lesser success. Joe Jordan tried his hand in Scotland. Three players reached the heights of international management, Terry Yorath, with Wales, Giles, and of course Jack Charlton, with the Irish Republic.

As a player, Giles was a scheming mastermind, small, dapper, hugely intelligent, switching play this way and that. He would score over one hundred goals for Leeds, a dimension to his play understandably lacking in the ramshackle Ireland teams of his time. Articulate and persuasive, Giles as manager was thought to be a natural ambassador to promote the cause of Irish football.

But not even Giles could escape the Leeds stigma, that even today clings to him like a stain. Sure, he is remembered for that defence-splitting pass, for those priceless goals, but – along with Billy Bremner and Norman Hunter – he too often seemed at the heart of his team's intimidatory tactics. These tactics were executed in the cause of the Leeds 'family', though 'Mafiosi' seemed to some a better description. Either way, Giles committed his share of shameful fouls and crippling, over-the-top tackles. He even confessed, when he would have been better advised not to, his aptitude for the cunningly executed disabling tackle. Giles might be a genius, but to some that genius was tainted.

This reputation, of course, was forged in England. Reputations do not travel well, and even devils can become saints in their homeland. In the same way that Jack Charlton could start afresh in Ireland, unencumbered by the baggage of English critics, so Giles could bask in the glory of Irish boy made good. Few in Ireland knew of his double-edged reputation, and fewer cared.

At the very least, Giles would bring a professional's mind to bear. His aim was to imbue Ireland with a soccer culture, to see progress at club level in Europe, and international progress on the World and European stage. But the one must not interfere with the other. Giles had no time for sentimentality. In his view, LOI players had neither the fitness nor the know-how to cope with international soccer. In effect, Giles told LOI hopefuls to go over to England if they wanted to blossom. The only LOI player he ever picked in the World Cup was himself, when playing out his days with Shamrock Rovers. Irish folk had better get used to the idea: from now on the teams representing them would be exiles.

In all this, of course, one can see the embodiment of Jack Charlton. Big Jack would have done the same. Wee John did it for him.

Giles' players enjoyed a winning start, beating a Polish side on cloud nine after humiliating England. Giles furthered Ireland's education with a second close-season trip to South America, two years after the first. Defeats by Brazil (1-2) and Uruguay (0-2) were partially offset by victory over Chile.

Ireland's breakthrough into the soccer sunlight so nearly arrived with the 1976 European Championship. Stacked into a group with the Soviet Union, Turkey and Switzerland, the Irish completed their programme top of the pile, leaving the Soviets requiring two points from their concluding two matches to overhaul them. Sadly, for Ireland, they got them.

By this time Giles had severed his Leeds links and transferred to West Bromwich Albion. If he hoped to lead Ireland to their first World Cup finals – set for Argentina – he would have to see off France, again, and Bulgaria. His players prepared with the help of a friendly against England at Wembley, meriting their 1-1 draw. Three years into the job, Giles had already made his mark. Ireland had lost just four of fourteen matches under his care, and won five in a row at home. Giles, himself, was embarking on his *fifth* World Cup.

In the European Cup, LOI sides were still in the abyss, tumbling at the first hurdle. Cork Celtic let in seven goals to Ararat Erevan of the USSR, Bohemians five to Glasgow Rangers, Dundalk seven to PSV Eindhoven. In the UEFA Cup, Finn Harps had been left traumatised, losing 1-4 at home to Derby County, 0-12 away.

Qualifying Group 5

FRANCE v IRELAND
Wednesday, 17 November 1976   *Parc des Princes, Paris – 50,000*

In 1974 the French challenge had fizzled out, permitting Ireland to leap-frog over them. Indeed, there was little to suggest that a French revival was in the offing. They had been washed away in the Euro '76 eliminators, and kicked-off the new World Cup campaign with a 2-2 draw in Sofia.

With hindsight, France were on a slow-burner. The key to their upsurge was Saint Etienne. An unfashionable club, compared with the likes of Reims, Marseilles, Nice, they had come to the fore in the mid-1960s and would claim eight championships in little more than a decade. France had never won a European trophy, but in 1975 Saint Etienne progressed to the semi-finals of the European Cup, losing to holders Bayern München. A year later they faced the Germans again, this time at Hampden Park, this time in the Final, but lost, a mite sadly, 0-1.

Saint Etienne had won admirers, if not first prize. Now, five months later, Michel Hidalgo, the new French manager, promised to build the national side around the pillars of that great team. That included Dominique Rocheteau, he of the flowing locks and artistic frills. Marseille's Marius Trésor was also included. So was Michel Platini, France's phenomenal young talent, who had shot from nowhere to be voted fourth in the recent poll for European Footballer of the Year. Platini had stepped out on the path to greatness at the Montreal Olympics, and was now banging them in for Nantes.

Giles picked a side brimming with experience to do battle at the Parc des Princes. Giles himself, Mulligan, Martin, Heighway, Holmes and Givens had all seen World Cup action in their time. Of the newcomers, all eyes focused on Highbury's trio of hopefuls, each of whom was destined for Ireland's Hall of Fame. David O'Leary and Frank Stapleton would still be featuring in Ireland's World Cup plans into the 1990s. Liam Brady, a regular for two years already, and Gerry Daly of Derby ensured that Ireland's midfield was a match for anyone. Skyscraper Mick Kearns – bridging the gap between

English third division and World Cup football – for the time being fended off the mounting challenge of Gerry Peyton for the goalkeeper's jersey.

The confidence with which Ireland began the match endured only till half-time. Ireland contained well enough, but posed little threat. The first half was notable more for bad tempers than good football. Bernard Lacombe scythed O'Leary; O'Leary exacted revenge on a French player; and Kearns indulged in excessive time-wasting. All three miscreants were booked.

Upon the change of ends, Platini treated the crowd to one of his soon-to-be-famous free-kicks. It was turned behind, one of several fine saves by Kearns. The corner was cleared, but shortly afterwards Giles, of all people, was caught playing silly buggers in midfield. Jack Charlton would have given him a flea in his ear about that. Giles was dispossessed by Didier Six, who sent Platini away to score.

France were buzzing, and when Trésor finished off a flowing move it seemed Ireland were done. This time, referee Maksimovic came to Ireland's assistance, ruling that Dominique Bathenay had handled.

The Yugoslav official was shortly to forfeit Irish goodwill. Brady danced past two defenders, Stapleton headed in his cross, but a linesman waved his flag. Stapleton he adjudged to be offside, but it was a hairline decision.

Ireland now carried the game to their opponents. First Daly, then Giles might have levelled, before Ireland were caught on the hop two minutes from time. Platini passed to Bathenay, who bulged the net from twenty yards.

FRANCE   (0) 2   **IRELAND   (0) 0**
Platini 48, Bathenay 88

FRANCE: Baratelli, Janvion, Lopez, Trésor, Bossis, Bathenay, Platini, Keruzore, Rocheteau, Lacombe (Rouyer), Six.
IRELAND: Kearns (WALSALL), Mulligan (WBA), O'Leary (ARSENAL), Martin (WBA), Holmes (COVENTRY), Daly (DERBY), Giles (WBA), Brady (ARSENAL), Heighway (LIVERPOOL), Givens (QPR), Stapleton (ARSENAL) (*sub* Walsh, BLACKPOOL).

IRELAND v FRANCE
Wednesday, 30 March 1977   *Lansdowne Road – 48,000*

Away defeats do not hurt nearly as much as home ones. For that reason Ireland rightly viewed the result in Paris as a bruise to their World Cup hopes, not a fracture. In any case, matters could be rectified when France came to Lansdowne Road in the spring. Ireland's home form under Giles suggested the tables could be turned. To that extent, the brickwork of Irish confidence was chipped in February, when Spain came a-visiting and won 1-0.

Ireland had the memory of the Dalymount victory over France last time round to send them out in good heart. Same opponents; different stadium. France's soccer players would need to take a leaf from her rugby stars and get used to Lansdowne Road, with all its peccadillos – the railway line that runs beneath the main stand, the cute little signposts by the corner flags, the cottage club-houses at either end.

The match was *de jure* all-ticket, 36,000 of which had been printed. Such was the demand to see Giles' crusaders that the *de facto* attendance was put at 48,000, a then record for a soccer match in Ireland. This, in spite of the match being shown live on TV. Lest anyone be in doubt, soccer had arrived in the Republic. And clearly, few of the multitudes who rolled up gave a hoot whether their heroes earned their living in Ireland, England, or Timbuktu.

Meanwhile, the Saint Etienne bubble had burst. Paired with Liverpool in the quarter-final of the European Cup, the French team's first-leg advantage had been overhauled at Anfield. Liverpool would march on to lift the trophy for the first time. Janvion, Lopez, Synaeghel, Bathenay, Rocheteau – five Saint Etienne stars were included to play Ireland at Lansdowne.

Giles was almost able to field an unchanged World Cup team, but when Stapleton stood down, Ray Treacy stood in. Treacy was a team-mate of Giles at the Hawthorns, along with Mick Martin and Mulligan. The West Midlands might be a home-from-home for the Irish, but since when had an English second division club ever provided four internationals in the same team?

The roar that deafened Dublin 4 told of an early goal. Giles had taken a free-kick. French sweeper Christian Lopez headed it out, but only to Brady. The French back line rushed out *en masse* to catch Irish forwards offside, whereupon Brady waltzed past Lopez and Bathenay to slide the ball under Andre Rey. Rey had been preferred to Baratelli in goal, as he was considered better able to withstand the aerial buffeting of Stapleton and Givens. But he was as powerless as his predecessor against such a sublime goal, one to enhance Brady's already burgeoning reputation.

Thereafter it was, as they say, end to end stuff. When the Martinique full-back, Gerard Janvion, toppled Givens the crowd hooted for a penalty. No such luck. A Giles piledriver then cannoned off the woodwork, soared into the air and fell for Givens, who headed over the bar. Giles had the ball in the net, but a linesman flagged against Gerry Daly.

France had their moments, too, and in the second half were decidedly in the driving seat. Mulligan fluffed a pass, Platini intercepted, and in a trice was through on goal. The Nantes prodigy had scored three goals in his first six internationals, and was bound for a fourth had not O'Leary's timely tackle diverted the ball for a corner.

For the final ten minutes the Irish were content to hoof the ball upfield or into the crowd. Central defender Patrick Rio was only playing because Trésor

Sheer magic! Liam Brady slides the ball past French keeper Andre Rey.

was recovering from a hernia operation. Now he and Daly were booked as tempers flared. Rocheteau and Platini couldn't capitalise on half-chances that came their way, and the final roar of the crowd told its own story.

Platini would play against Ireland four times in the World Cup. This was the one time he didn't score.

IRELAND   (1) 1   **FRANCE   (0)**
Brady 10

IRELAND: Kearns (WALSALL), Mulligan (WBA), O'Leary (ARSENAL), Martin (WBA), Holmes (SPURS), Daly (DERBY), Giles (WBA), Brady (ARSENAL), Heighway (LIVERPOOL), Treacy (WBA), Givens (QPR).
FRANCE: Rey, Janvion, Rio, Lopez, Tusseau, Bathenay, Platini, Synaeghel, Rocheteau, Lacombe, Rouyer.

BULGARIA v IRELAND
Wednesday, 1 June 1977   *Levski Stadium, Sofia – 50,000*

Ireland were alive and kicking. Those with their feet on the ground would remind Giles that goal-difference would be invoked in the event of a tie, so strictly speaking, Ireland were still adrift of the French. This would rebound against Ireland unless they could better France's results against Bulgaria. As France had drawn in Sofia, Ireland had to go for a win.

This was easier said than done. For all the lessons learned under Giles, Ireland's dismal away results had barely improved. In particular, their record behind the Iron Curtain was dire. This was Ireland's first trip to the Black Sea state. Bulgaria had done well to reach the last four World Cup finals, but having scaled the heights had died of oxygen failure almost at once. They had failed to win a single match in twelve attempts. Naturally enough, they fancied themselves to do better this time.

Bulgaria held a special place in the affections of Irish soccer historians. Ireland's first match under the FAI banner had been in the 1924 Olympics, in Paris, where Bulgaria were their first opponents and first victims. Then, it had been Bulgaria who played in green. Ireland wore blue. Paddy Duncan of St James's Gate scored the only goal.

The only subsequent footballing contact between the two countries had been in the European Cup-Winners' Cup, where – three times in the 1960s – Ireland's representatives had been sent packing.

To prepare for the present match, the FAI had invited Poland for the eighth friendly between the countries in nine years. Giles learned little from the goalless draw, either about Poland or communist tactics in general, though he did use the match to try out the promising Mark Lawrenson.

In Sofia, torrential rain presented a treacherous surface, but the arguments the match provoked had human, not elemental cause. Giles had reverted to his strongest eleven, which meant Frank Stapleton was back on board. Ireland were settling nicely when Heighway's intended pass to Mulligan was cut out by Tzvetkov. Milanov went past O'Leary, and Panov scored emphatically with his left foot. The damage might shortly have been yet worse, but no Bulgarian forward could supply the necessary touch to Panov's pass that flew across the face of the Irish goal.

The main talking points of the first half were two penalty claims that went unheeded. First, Martin appeared to handle in the box, but got away with it. Then, on the half-time whistle, Givens was barged over by Dimitrov in the act of heading into an empty goal. To Irish players and supporters alike, it was as clear-cut a penalty as one would wish to see, but Greek referee Zlatanos thought otherwise.

Fortunately for Irish morale, their frustration shortly turned to ecstasy. Two minutes after the interval Givens powered in Giles' corner-kick. It was a special moment for Givens, winning his thirty-ninth cap, in his third World Cup. He was at the time Ireland's all-time highest scorer, though, like Noel Cantwell before him, his goal-supply also evaporated in World Cup-ties. This was his third and last World Cup strike.

Givens was unfortunate in starting his career with Manchester United. Unfortunate in that, after that, the only way he could go was down. He had already scored four international goals by the time he was off-loaded to Luton for a measly £15,000. Those four goals were scored in just seven matches during the Republic's dog-days, when Ireland seldom scored at all.

Givens played the bulk of his international football while on the books of QPR. Pacy, commanding in the air, he scored twenty-three league goals in his first season with the London club, and in Ireland's colours forged a productive partnership with Ray Treacy. Treacy's international days were all but over, and it took time for Frank Stapleton to fill his shoes.

Stapleton would shortly feature in the game's flash-point, but for the moment he and Givens were intent on inflicting further damage on the Bulgarian defence. When Giles swept Daly's pull-back past Goranov, it seemed Ireland could start thinking about Argentina. The referee signalled a goal, then changed his mind on seeing a linesman's raised flag. It was impossible to detect who, if anyone, had been offside.

There are days when footballers just know the fates are against them. This was such a day for Ireland. Jimmy Holmes felt hard done by when pulled up for obstructing Borisov. Panov's free-kick clipped Giles on the head and deflected goalwards. The wrong-footed Kearns managed to keep the ball out, but succeeded only in directing it at Jeliazkov, who couldn't miss.

The Irish mood worsened when Aleksandrov, clearly offside, was allowed to run at Kearns, who saved at his feet. Noel Campbell replaced the limping Daly, and at once the game erupted. Tzvetkov's lunge at Stapleton sparked a touchline brawl that sucked in half the players from each side. When the dust finally settled, five minutes later, the referee sent off two players from each side, Mick Martin and Noel Campbell, from Ireland. The latter had only just come on, and had yet to touch the ball. A cap, a red card, and not a kick!

Ireland's last hope came when Givens raced onto O'Leary's through-ball but ballooned the chance. He would have been more mortified had he scored: the linesman had his flag up. No wonder the watching French manager, Michel Hidalgo, was moved to comment afterwards: 'I have no doubt that Ireland would have won without the referee.'

BULGARIA (1) 2   **IRELAND (0) 1**
Panov 13, Jeliazkov 76   Givens 47

BULGARIA: Goranov, Dimitrov, Ivkov, Arabov, Vasilev, Barzov (Jeliazkov), Borisov, Zdravkov (Aleksandrov), Panov, Milanov, Tzvetkov.
IRELAND: Kearns (WALSALL), Mulligan (WBA), O'Leary (ARSENAL), Martin (WBA), Holmes (SPURS), Daly (DERBY) (*sub* Campbell, FORTUNA COLOGNE), Giles (WBA), Brady (ARSENAL), Heighway (LIVERPOOL), Givens (QPR), Stapleton (ARSENAL).

IRELAND v BULGARIA
Wednesday, 12 October 1977   *Lansdowne Road – 25,000*

That sorry defeat left Ireland's hopes hanging by a thread. To stay alive they had to beat Bulgaria in Dublin by four goals, and then keep their fingers crossed that France and Bulgaria drew in Paris. For Bulgaria, two points from two matches would be enough.

Giles had, in the meantime, returned to Dublin as manager of Shamrock Rovers. One factor behind his success with Ireland was the way he kept faith with his players. Eight would be ever-present in this World Cup. It would have been ten, had Giles not decided the time was right to put Gerry Peyton in goal, and to put his trust in Mark Lawrenson in defence.

Both of them did their jobs, in the sense that Bulgaria didn't score. But Bulgaria didn't want to score, which took away much of the challenge. From the first whistle, when Bulgaria erected their defensive barricades, it was clear they were banking on two draws rather than gambling on one win.

In the first half, especially, Ireland squandered a litany of openings. Half the team took turns to shoot high, wide and handsome. The law of averages, if nothing else, suggested that sooner or later an Irish pot-shot would find the net, but Bulgaria tightened up appreciably as the match wore on. They even managed two shots themselves, both by Aleksandrov, the first saved at full-length by Peyton, the second skimming past a post. At the other end, Givens and Stapleton continued their profligacy, as Ireland slid anticlimactically from the World Cup.

At least the exit of Irish clubs from Europe was accompanied by the noise of swishing nets. Red Star Belgrade swished it six times against Sligo Rovers in the Champions' Cup. Newcastle United knocked four past Bohemians in the second leg of the UEFA Cup.

IRELAND (0) 0   **BULGARIA (0) 0**

IRELAND: Peyton (FULHAM), Mulligan (WBA), O'Leary (ARSENAL), Lawrenson (BRIGHTON), Holmes (SPURS), Daly (DERBY), Giles (SHAMROCK R), Brady (ARSENAL), Heighway (LIVERPOOL), Givens (QPR), Stapleton (ARSENAL).
BULGARIA: Staykov, Vasilev (Grantschanov), Angelov, Ivkov, Bonev, Kolev, Kostov, Arabov, Dvevizov, Panov, Tzvetkov (Aleksandrov).

Few Irish folk shed tears for Bulgaria when they went down 1-3 in Paris. France thereby claimed Group 5's nomination for Argentina, where they found themselves squeezed out in a group that contained both the hosts and Italy. England were once again absent, so were Wales, and so were Northern Ireland, who opened their qualifiers with a fine 2-2 draw in Holland, but tailed away after that, even losing to Iceland.

Argentina '78 was about juntas and tickertape, match-fixing and drugs, Ossie Ardiles and Ally MacLeod. Ardiles so impressed watching British managers that he was soon on his way. MacLeod was on his way, too, but for different reasons. Hogging the British limelight, MacLeod's Scotland became the laughing stock. Only Archie Gemmill, with the goal of the tournament, lifted the tartan gloom.

Argentina, with a nod here, a wink there, and doubtless backhanders to boot, survived on questionable merit one opponent after another to win the Cup from Holland.

Qualifying Group 5

	P	W	D	L	F	A	Pts
FRANCE	4	2	1	1	7	4	5
Bulgaria	4	1	2	1	5	6	4
Ireland	4	1	1	2	2	4	3

Other group results
Bulgaria v France   2-2   France v Bulgaria   3-1

Ireland appearances and goalscorers (substitute appearances in brackets)
World Cup qualifying rounds 1978

	Apps	Goals		Apps	Goals
Brady L	4	1	Kearns M	3	–
Daly G	4	–	Martin M *	3	–
Giles J *†‡§	4	–	Stapleton F	3	–
Givens D *†	4	1	Lawrenson M	1	–
Heighway S *	4	–	Peyton G	1	–
Holmes J *	4	–	Treacy R *†	1	–
Mulligan P *	4	–	Campbell N *	– (1)	–
O'Leary D	4	–	Walsh M	– (1)	–

---

* Appeared in 1974 World Cup.   *46 apps   2 goals*
† Appeared in 1970 World Cup.   *1 League of Ireland*
‡ Appeared in 1966 World Cup.   *44 English League*
§ Appeared in 1962 World Cup.   *1 German League*
16 players used

11

THE 1982 WORLD CUP

John Giles' Midas touch had the chance to make gold in the 1980 European Championship. What a mouth-watering draw Ireland received, pitched into the same group as Northern Ireland *and* England. Bulgaria and Denmark were included just to make up the numbers. Sadly, for the Republic, England ran away with the nomination, dropping just one point. That, as it happened, was the product of a 1-1 draw at Lansdowne Road, before a vast crowd of 50,000. Northern Ireland also claimed three points off the Republic, pushing them down into third place, with just two wins from eight matches.

In fact, it was looking as if the Giles revolution might peter out. In fifteen matches between the end of one World Cup and the beginning of the next, he manufactured just four wins – all of them at home. There is nothing so loud as the sigh of disenchantment, and Giles could hear the whispering.

At club level it was the same old story. Dinamo Dresden slammed six past Bohemians in East Germany, though the following season Dundalk achieved what had proved beyond all other LOI champions, surviving *two* rounds. Linfield of Northern Ireland and Hibernians of Malta were their victims. Dundalk were rewarded with a plum tie against Glasgow Celtic, going down by the odd goal. In the UEFA Cup, Finn Harps lost ten goals to Everton.

With ever more nations seeking affiliation to FIFA, and fancying a shot at the World Cup, group inflation was inevitable. The days of two or three opponents per group were consigned to history. FIFA was already pledged to increase the number of finalists in Spain '82 from sixteen to twenty-four, and although this was principally for the benefit of Third World nations, there were still enough extra berths to excite European aspirants.

Had the finals still accommodated sixteen teams, one shudders to think how many hopefuls would have been crammed into each European section. Ireland, we know, would be introduced to a *seven*-team group in 1994, so maybe the *five* named in 1982 was nothing to fret about – especially as two of the five would go through. Two from five was better than one from three.

Yet Ireland's lowly seeding predicted a bad hand. How true. Ireland's group was a stinker. While Cyprus should present little threat, Belgium,

Holland, and, yes, France again, looked far too strong. Ireland might finish as low as fourth. To take part in Spain they would need to oust not just one, but two of Europe's better sides.

Qualifying Group 2

CYPRUS v IRELAND
Wednesday, 26 March 1980   *Makarios Stadium, Nicosia – 10,000*

Ireland opened their series earlier than ever, twenty-seven months before the World Cup finals took place. Getting the trip to Cyprus out of the way made sense. The expected win would put Ireland on top of Group 2 until the qualifiers resumed in earnest in the autumn.

Ireland had never played Cyprus before. The strife-torn Mediterranean island was home to a team of international dogsbodies. They had first tried their luck in the World Cup in 1962, since when they had posted twenty-two defeats and one win, secured against Northern Ireland (1-0) in 1973 in this very stadium. Maybe Cyprus had the Indian sign on Irish footballers.

Among those losses were two at the hands of Scotland in 1968 and '69, who ran in a total of thirteen goals. Soccer on the Greek-Turkish divided island was amateur, and run by the Greek community. The better players were eagerly snapped up by clubs in Greece.

The Ireland national side had evolved since we last noted them in 1977. Giles had decided enough was enough and retired from international football, delegating Tony Grealish to take over his midfield duties, and Brady – FA Cup winner and English players' Player of the Year, 1979 – the captaincy. The vertebrae of the team was that nucleus of talent thrust to the fore in the previous World Cup – O'Leary and Lawrenson, the central pillars; Heighway, Daly, and Brady, the engine room; Stapleton the battering ram. Before the new campaign was over, Kevin Moran and Ronnie Whelan would climb aboard. It would take another ten years to complete, but two more pieces of the Irish jigsaw were slotted into place.

Cyprus's football pitches were a bit like jigsaws. They were among the worst in the world, bereft of grass, with what appeared to be a clay underlay. Cyprus were so used to defeat that they were not above the odd trick or two to waste time. Ball-boys, for example, were dispensed with. Better that opponents ate up vital seconds scampering after balls knocked out of play.

Even with ploys like this, visiting sides were on a hiding to nothing. Paul McGee's eighth-minute goal was therefore especially welcome. McGee was one of the few Sligo-born footballers to have made the grade. He served his apprenticeship, briefly with Hereford United, and, more unusually, in Canada for three summers, while helping Sligo Rovers to the championship in 1976-

77. When Johnny Giles called him into his squad, McGee was thrust into the shop window, and it was London club QPR which quickly agreed terms. For two seasons everything seemed to go right for McGee. He hit his share of goals for his club and more or less held a regular place in the Ireland side. But when QPR were relegated in 1979 he found himself off-loaded to Preston North End – then a second division club, but one headed for the third.

A bubbly, confident character, renowned for his speed off the mark, McGee had only a couple of matches left in Ireland green. But this would be the game he'd cherish most. Brady initiated the move for McGee's first goal with a forty-yard pass to Stapleton, whose knock-back was smashed into goal off defender Lyssandrou. McGee was vocal in claiming the goal for himself. Lyssandrou was happy to oblige.

Ireland's second goal was a peach. It was begun and finished by Lawrenson, who ventured upfield from deep inside his own half, slipped the ball to Brady, took the return and walloped it past Stylianou.

Two goals up, with a quarter of the match gone. Ireland might have set a target of six or seven. But football rarely runs like clockwork. In the lee of Lawrenson's goal Cyprus bagged one themselves. Lawrenson got his body in the way of Kissonergis's shot, but the rebound dropped for Pantziaras.

Jerry Murphy's effort would have restored the two-goal margin, had the referee not ruled him offside. Paul McGee was more fortunate, capitalising on O'Leary's knock-down. It was his fourth, and last, international goal.

Midway through the second half Ireland still led 3-1. First Daly, then Murphy took turns to batter a Cypriot goalpost. It might have been 5-1. In the blink of an eye it was 3-2. Heighway and Murphy had both limped off by the time O'Leary questionably fouled Kaiafas, who took the spot-kick himself.

Ireland hung on, a little inelegantly, to record their first away win in the World Cup since Denmark in 1957. They handed Cyprus a 'first', too – their first World Cup 'double'.

'The points are all that matter,' said Giles beforehand. He couldn't have been more wrong.

CYPRUS (1) 2   **IRELAND (3) 3**
Pantziaras 27, Kaiafas 74 pen   McGee 8, 37, Lawrenson 23

CYPRUS: Stylianou, Papacostas, Lyssandrou, Pantziaros, Papadopoulos, Neofitou, Mauroudis, Kissonergis, Demetriou (Tsingis), Kaiafas, Kanaris (Theofanos).
IRELAND: Peyton (FULHAM), Grealish (LUTON), O'Leary (ARSENAL), Lawrenson (BRIGHTON), Grimes (MAN U), Daly (DERBY), Brady (ARSENAL), Murphy (PALACE) (*sub* O'Brien, PHILADELPHIA FURIES), Heighway (LIVERPOOL) (*sub* Ryan, BRIGHTON), McGee (PRESTON), Stapleton (ARSENAL).

IRELAND v HOLLAND
Wednesday, 10 September 1980   *Lansdowne Road – 30,000*

Three weeks later Johnny Giles resigned. The public were told only that he wished to devote his energies to Shamrock Rovers. Inevitably, other factors intruded, though they remain speculative. Although Giles had turned Dublin into a footballing fortress – just two defeats in seventeen games – seven years in the hot-seat is long enough for anyone, especially when grenades lobbed by the press and public are starting to land too close for comfort.

Maybe Irish expectations were becoming too high. Having been greeted as a saviour, some critics said Giles was now holding the team back. One or two complained that his taste for slow, methodical, possession football was alienating fans, many of whom yearned for good old blood and thunder.

Whatever, no one needed to tell Giles when his time was up. He would jump rather than be pushed. With onerous fixtures against Holland, Belgium and France looming, perhaps Giles, ever the realist, looked into his crystal ball and sensed it was time to go.

Giles' number two, veteran goalkeeper Alan Kelly, took charge for one match, at home to Switzerland (2-0), before accepting that he could not serve two masters. His duties to Preston North End must come first. He stepped down and Eoin Hand – appointed as Kelly's assistant – stepped up. The FAI was nothing if not consistent. Each of its managers was an ex-Ireland international and (Kelly excepted) not yet into his forties.

At thirty-four, Hand was among the youngest national managers in the world. He had won his twenty caps while playing for Portsmouth. Returning to Ireland to try his hand at player-management, he had, in his first season, guided Limerick to their first title in twenty years. For this he was voted by journalists Ireland's 'Soccer Personality of the Year'. When Giles resigned, Hand found himself in the shop window at the most opportune time.

Hand had actually played under Giles during a brief spell with Shamrock Rovers, so knew the Leeds wizard both as team-mate and manager. Like Giles, he was more familiar with the game across the Irish Sea than at home. Unlike Giles, Hand had never played in the English first division. He seemed to be caught between the devil and the deep blue sea, intimate neither with Irish soccer nor top-class English.

Hand's first game in charge, while the FAI were still deliberating whether to offer him the job on a permanent basis, was in May 1980 against world champions Argentina, Maradona and all. Hand's appointment was confirmed after the match, which Ireland lost 0-1.

This was, it should be remembered, still the age of part-time management. Hand stayed in charge of Limerick, plotting the downfall of Real Madrid in the European Cup.

Ireland's next fixture was not till September, enabling Hand to find his feet, so to speak, and to prepare the first of those weighty dossiers on the opposition that would be a hallmark of his tenure. The World Cup-tie against Holland exposed Ireland to both the 1978 Finalists, one after the other. To many observers, Holland were simply the best team in the World. The Dutch had lost two World Cup Finals, on both occasions to the tournament hosts, and on both occasions having played the better football. In the absence of the real thing, Holland assumed the tag 'people's champions'. When one recalls that Dutch football was totally amateur until 1954, one can see the immensity of her progress. And for one small nation to go so far inevitably stimulated the aspirations of others, such as Ireland.

There being no prizes for runners-up, Holland had once again to fight their way through the qualifiers. Their ageing team appeared to be undergoing the strains of rebuilding. Holland failed to make the semi-finals of the 1980 European Championship, which only hastened the team's dissolution. Of the side defeated by Argentina, only Ernie Brandts remained, though Willy van de Kerkhof would take the field as a substitute. This amounted to wholesale execution of a great team, and no matter how promising the newcomers they would take time to gel. This transitional Dutch side was home-based, with one or two exceptions. Frans Thijssen was instrumental in Ipswich Town's assault on the English championship.

As such he was well known to Ireland's Anglos. There were nine of them, buttressed by the inclusion of Liam Brady, who had signed for Juventus, and David O'Leary's brother, Pierce, of Shamrock Rovers. To Pierce O'Leary would fall the distinction of being the last LOI player to start a World Cup match for Ireland. The two other newcomers to World Cup football were David Langan and Chris Hughton, both winning their fifth caps.

From the first minute of his first World Cup match, it was clear that Eoin Hand's tactics were culled from a different manual from Giles'. No more 'one step forward, two steps back'; no more probing here and prodding there. Hand instructed his men to get forward, to attack with pace and in numbers. He may, of course, have been persuaded to play direct football by weighing the conditions, high wind, plus rutted pitch and grass for cows. What suited rugby did not suit soccer, but beggars can't be choosers, and Eoin Hand did not have the clout of Jack Charlton.

Ireland were almost rewarded with an instant goal. Stapleton's first shot was blocked, his second smacked against a post. Holland soon cancelled out Ireland's moral advantage, Thijssen hitting the crossbar.

For most of the half the Dutch were forced back. Another referee another day might have given penalties for tackles on will-o'-the-wisp Daly (who had transferred to Coventry City) and Frank Stapleton. Hiele saved well from Brady, and Lawrenson – prominent in midfield – miscued from close in.

A dressing room pep talk put the Dutch on their toes in the second half. Three times Peyton came to the rescue before Holland scored the goal they had been promising. It might have been merited; it was no less messy for that. Toine van Mierlo skirted two flimsy challenges, but lost control of the ball. Peyton came to collect, failed to gather it, and allowed Van Mierlo to poke it to the unmarked Simon Tahamata.

Instead of settling the Dutch, the goal lit the fuse of an Irish onslaught. As the game entered its final eleven minutes Ireland must have thought their sweat would go unrewarded, but then Tony Grealish played a one-two with Stapleton. The Dutch raced out to catch Grealish offside, but he switched the ball inside to Gerry Daly, who kept his head to beat Joop Hiele.

Daly was also instrumental in Ireland's winner, five minutes later. He was fouled thirty yards out by Johnny Metgod, later to play for Nottingham Forest. Brady chipped the free-kick wide of the wall for Mark Lawrenson to connect with a horizontal header.

Ireland somehow survived the Dutch riposte. Ireland's worst moment came when Peters lunged in the goalmouth. Lawrenson hoofed the ball away.

Ireland's were the only matches in Group 2 to date. They therefore found themselves in pole position with four points.

IRELAND (0) 2   **HOLLAND (0) 1**
Daly 79, Lawrenson 84   Tahamata 57

IRELAND: Peyton (FULHAM), Langan (BIRMINGHAM), D O'Leary (ARSENAL), P O'Leary (SHAMROCK R), Hughton (SPURS), Daly (COVENTRY), Lawrenson (BRIGHTON), Grealish (LUTON), Brady (JUVENTUS), Stapleton (ARSENAL), Givens (BIRMINGHAM).
HOLLAND: Hiele, Wijnstekers, Vander Korput (Metgod), Spelbos, Brandts, Schoenaker (W van de Kerkhof), Peters, Thijssen, Van Diesen, Van Mierlo, Tahamata.

IRELAND v BELGIUM
Wednesday, 15 October 1980   *Lansdowne Road – 40,000*

France's 7-0 victory in Cyprus put Ireland's squeaky win into perspective. Points were *not* all that mattered. France had opened up a six-goal advantage that Ireland would never recoup. Cyprus were not the only ones to be hit by seven goals: Hand's Limerick had surrendered that number (over two legs) to Real Madrid, who would go on to meet, and lose to, Liverpool in the Final.

1934 was the last occasion Ireland had faced Holland and Belgium in the World Cup. The Dutch defeat had been avenged. Now for Belgium. In that earlier match Paddy Moore had scored all Ireland's goals in a 4-4 draw.

Since 1945 Belgium had held the whip hand, beating Ireland three times out of four. Belgium still struggled to make any impact in World Cups, being overshadowed by their Dutch neighbours. Belgium had qualified just twice since the war, and not since 1970, when they had won their only finals match (against El Salvador) in nine attempts.

But Belgium were another small European nation whose star would rise. Indeed, it was high in the sky already. Shrewdly tutored by Guy Thys, they had beaten Scotland home and away on their way to the finals of Euro '80. There, they survived a 1-1 draw with England to reach the Final, which they lost 1-2 to West Germany. Belgium, in other words, took the field against Ireland as number two in Europe.

Whereas a great Dutch side had been dismembered, seven of Belgium's European silver medallists – almost all of whom played in Belgium – turned out at Lansdowne Road. These included curly-haired gypsy goalkeeper, Jean-Marie Pfaff; iron defender Eric Gerets; and the leggy, goalscoring midfielder, Jan Ceulemans of Bruges. Both Gerets and Ceulemans would be propping up the Belgian side in Italia '90, aged thirty-six and thirty-three respectively.

Having observed how young Kevin Moran coped against Switzerland and Argentina, Eoin Hand confidently fielded him in the absence of the injured O'Leary. Ireland enjoyed the luxury, even then, of being blessed with a surfeit of top-drawer central defenders, some of whom – when all were fit – were shunted forward into midfield. Moran was the first player to play in, and win, a GAA All-Ireland Final and play in the World Cup for Ireland.

Having looked on in admiration as Ireland overcame the Dutch, Belgium set out to smother Irish attacks by means of a hard-working midfield and a blanket offside trap. To counter this, Hand called up Steve Heighway to provide added width. Their defensive tactics did not prevent Belgium launching numerous virile raids of their own.

From one such raid the visitors took the lead. Hughton and Lawrenson were caught square near the half-way line. Wilfred van Moer, thirty-five and balding, headed on to Cluytens, who outpaced Hughton, went wide of Peyton, and tucked the ball in from a narrow angle. Hughton had resisted the temptation to bring down Cluytens in full flight. If he were to do so today, he would be sent off for a professional foul; had he done so then he would probably have got away with it and prevented a goal.

For all Ireland's efforts, Belgium called the tune. Peyton kicked away one shot from Vandenberg, and when the eye-catching Ceulemans (who scored against England in Italy) was put clear, he miscued badly. Ireland could have trailed 0-3, but raised their spirits with a flying header from Daly, athletically turned over by Pfaff.

It was Belgium's offside trap that was their undoing. With Brady in full flow, their back four dashed upfield. Brady's pass struck a defender *en route* wide to Grealish. The linesman waved his flag, the referee from Luxembourg ignored him, and Grealish took the ball round Pfaff to level.

Liam Brady looks to be giving his Belgian opponent a hand.

For some reason Belgium shut up shop in the second half. The best chance fell to Ireland. Daly had time and space but Pfaff saved bravely at his feet.

IRELAND (1) 1   **BELGIUM (1) 1**
Grealish 42   Cluytens 13

IRELAND: Peyton (FULHAM), Langan (BIRMINGHAM), Lawrenson (BRIGHTON), Moran (MAN U), Hughton (SPURS), Daly (COVENTRY), Grealish (LUTON), Brady (JUVENTUS), Heighway (LIVERPOOL), Givens (BIRMINGHAM) (*sub* McGee, PRESTON), Stapleton (ARSENAL).
BELGIUM: Pfaff, Gerets, Millecamps (de Wolf), Meeuws, Renquin, Van Moer (Heyligen), Vandereycken, Coeck, Cluytens, Vandenberg, Ceulemans.

FRANCE v IRELAND
Tuesday, 28 October 1980   *Parc des Princes, Paris – 46,300*

With five points in the bank, maybe Ireland were a mite complacent in the closing minutes. But aspirants to World Cups must win their home games, and when the dust had settled, that lost point would make all the difference.

This was the fourth time, and the third in succession, that France had been thrown into Ireland's World Cup group. The roll of the dice in World and

European eliminators ensures that some pairings crop up with dreary familiarity. In Scotland's case, her constant bedfellow used to be Czechoslovakia. In England's, her *bête noire* is Poland, and more recently Turkey, Holland, and Ireland herself.

France had been teetering on the brink of success for several seasons. They had deserved better than early elimination from Argentina '78. Their hopes of qualifying for Euro '80 were dashed by Czechoslovakia, who went on to take third place. All this left French football wondering if the breakthrough would ever come. No one knew how near or how far they were to having a fine, perhaps very fine, side. France had set the ball rolling in the 1982 World Cup with that 7-0 stuffing of Cyprus.

But more pieces of the French jigsaw were fitting together. Patrick Battiston and Max Bossis had come into the side, plus that wafer-thin nugget Jean Tigana, who would outshine Brady on the day. For Ireland, in place of the indisposed Gerry Daly, Hand recalled veteran Mick Martin, now playing in his third World Cup.

The match would be remembered as much for its pre-match controversy as its on-field drama. Determined that Ireland be permitted to field her strongest side, the FAI compelled FIFA to intervene on its behalf. A clutch of English clubs engaged in midweek Milk Cup action was refusing to release players. Tottenham and Arsenal, for example, had four players Hand needed. The English clubs were obliged to back down, the Spurs v Arsenal cup-tie was postponed, and the FAI appeared to have won a famous victory. It could rebound against them, however, if English clubs, in future, cussedly blocked the release of Irish players for non-competitive internationals.

On top of this were the circumstances of Michael Robinson's inclusion in the side. The one-time boot-boy for Ray Treacy, Robinson was still only twenty-two, but had attracted an astronomical fee when signing for Manchester City from Preston. The move hadn't worked out and he had quickly moved on, cut-price, to Brighton. Now he let it be known that he hankered to play for Ireland. His grandmother had been born there, but in 1980 these were insufficient grounds for eligibility. FIFA permitted the birthplace of a parent to count in a player's favour, but not a grandparent. Whereupon *mère* Robinson, citing her own mother, took out Irish citizenship. Hey presto, Robinson had the means of obtaining an Irish passport and was therefore eligible. A loophole had been found and exploited, and the FAI was taken to task for appearing to acquiesce. Robinson duly won his first cap, in place of the venerable Don Givens, and set the precedent for what later became derided as the 'granny-passport' ticket for Ireland.

Robinson was making headlines for the wrong reasons, yet he tried to knuckle down. France started the match as though they were still playing Cyprus. Bernard Lacombe and Didier Six both squandered early openings, prior to Tigana's swirling cross being 'killed' by Platini, who scored with ease.

Ireland hit back. The French keeper had the unfortunate name of Dropsey, but he showed no signs of water-retention, dealing capably with efforts from Grealish, Robinson, and, early in the second half, Chris Hughton.

Ireland's big chance came when Robinson blasted home a knock-down by Moran, only for the referee to penalise the Manchester United defender. Whether for offside or handball was impossible to say, though photographs clearly show the referee blowing *before* the ball hit the net. Lawrenson then came within inches of an own-goal, his attempted pass-back bouncing off a post, but a second French strike was only postponed. Ireland had players upfield in numbers when Zimako cut out Moran's pass and the stranded Mick Martin was overwhelmed. Six loaded the gun; Zimako – of New Caledonia – pulled the trigger.

Near the end Robinson forced another save from Dropsey, who at least proved fallible. In the dying moments he dropped a Lawrenson cross, but Ryan could only hit a post.

FRANCE (1) 2   IRELAND (0) 0
Platini 10, Zimako 77

FRANCE: Dropsey, Battiston, Specht, Lopez, Bossis, Larios, Tigana, Platini (Petit), Rocheteau, Lacombe (Zimako), Six.
IRELAND: Peyton (FULHAM), Langan (BIRMINGHAM), Lawrenson (BRIGHTON), Moran (MAN U), Hughton (SPURS), Martin (NEWCASTLE) (*sub* Ryan, BRIGHTON), Grealish (LUTON), Brady (JUVENTUS), Heighway (LIVERPOOL), Stapleton (ARSENAL), Robinson (BRIGHTON).

IRELAND v CYPRUS
Wednesday, 19 November 1980   *Lansdowne Road – 22,000*

Ireland were midway through their programme, having faced each of their opponents once. They had five points to show. Another five points from the return fixtures might be enough. Or it might not. Six would surely do.

Two more points should be garnered from Cyprus in November. Bearing in mind the punishment France had meted out, there would be no excuses for any pip-squeak victory. Cyprus had to be put in their place.

Not all the Cypriot players were strangers to Dublin. A few had been over recently in European club competition. Nevertheless, familiarity did not breed success. Ireland won by six a match they might even have won by twelve. An early penalty settled their nerves. Kalotheou took Robinson's legs from behind. The Cypriot thought he had dived, and was booked for arguing. Daly was one of those penalty experts who rarely missed. Nor did he now.

The goal put the skids under Cyprus, who had come to defend and who had no contingencies for restoring parity. Three more goals in a five-minute spell condemned them still further. Lyssandrou mistimed his intervention and permitted Daly his second; Grealish hit back a clearance on the drop for number three; and Robinson's volley registered his first and Ireland's fourth of the match.

Seconds after the changearound Frank Stapleton curled the ball past Constantino from Robinson's knock-on, and suddenly minds turned to record scores. Ireland had only twice gone nap in their history (v Germany and Luxembourg, both in 1936) and never managed six. That tally was reached midway through the second half, when full-back Chris Hughton capped a run that took him past four lunging tackles.

Robinson and Daly had already struck the crossbar, and Heighway soon suffered the same fate.

When Cyprus made a substitution, the player pulled off came to the touchline, sat himself down and lit up a fag. His team-mates out on the pitch threatened Ireland only at the close, when Peyton twice denied Mavroudis.

IRELAND   (4) 6   **CYPRUS   (0) 0**
Daly 11 pen, 24, 25, Robinson 29,
Stapleton 46, Hughton 65

IRELAND: Peyton (FULHAM), Langan (BIRMINGHAM), Lawrenson (BRIGHTON), Moran (MAN U), Hughton (SPURS), Daly (COVENTRY), Grealish (LUTON), Brady (JUVENTUS), Heighway (LIVERPOOL), Stapleton (ARSENAL), Robinson (BRIGHTON) (*sub* Givens, BIRMINGHAM).
CYPRUS: Constantino, Loucia, Lyssandrou, Pantziaras, Erotokritou, Kalotheou, Theofanous, Miamiliotis (Mavroudis), Yiagoudakis, Kaiafas (Kovis), Tsingis.

BELGIUM v IRELAND
Wednesday, 25 March 1981   *Heysel Stadium, Brussels – 47,000*

On the same day Belgium beat Holland 1-0, handing the Dutch their second defeat and jeopardising their prospects. Ireland's seven-point haul from five games was a fair return, but her rivals had games in hand. By the time Ireland journeyed to Brussels, the Belgians and Dutch had made up some leeway, but both had struggled to take full points from Cyprus, and Belgium's razor-thin 3-2 home win suggested Ireland might pull the rug from under them.

Belgium showed two changes from the side that performed ably in Dublin. One of these was in goal, where the evergreen Pfaff made room for another goalkeeper set to hog the position. Michel Preud'homme would still be first choice goalkeeper in USA '94, where for a time he seemed to be heading for an appointment with Ireland in the second round.

In February, Ireland had experimented with two or three players in a friendly with Wales at Tolka Park, the first full international staged in the stadium. Ireland lost 1-3, but Everton goalkeeper Seamus McDonagh retained his place for the trip to Brussels. Hand was bothered by the loss of the injured Lawrenson, which was exacerbated before kick-off when David O'Leary failed a fitness test.

Given the shape of Group 2, and the fact that Belgium had shared the spoils in Dublin, it was essential Ireland fare no worse in the return. In the event, they were outplayed, but that was small consolation for the manner of defeat.

Ireland took the field determined to hold what they had. The best that Belgium managed in a first half played in driving rain was a Ceulemans header nodded off the line by Hughton. The interval was seconds away when Ireland took their first body blow. Belgium's offside trap was no less adept in Brussels than it had been in Dublin. In such circumstances, set-pieces became that much more important. In a well-rehearsed Arsenal routine, Brady chipped a free-kick to the near post to coincide with Stapleton's run, and turned away in delight as Stapleton fired into the net.

Horror of horrors. Portuguese referee Nazarre disallowed the goal. No explanation was given, no linesman's flag was raised, and the Belgian player prostrate on the grass appeared to have been knocked over by the referee himself. The story went round afterwards that Nazarre had inadvertently impeded Preud'homme, and blew up to avoid a Belgian riot. Photographs of the goal show Belgian defenders with their arms raised in appeal.

The second half – which at one stage was lucky to be completed when a storm left the pitch sodden – repeated the pattern of the first; few chances, most of them to the home side, but Ireland occasionally breaking out.

With hindsight, had Ireland held out for a goalless draw they would have qualified for Spain. The clock showed just three minutes to play when the wily Gerets threw himself to the ground outside the box and won a free-kick. Vandereycken's kick dipped over the wall and bounced vertically into the air off the top of the crossbar. When the ball dropped, Ceulemans leaped highest to nod it over the line. Gerets' vital contribution to the goal provoked a heated war of words. At the final whistle Eoin Hand eyeballed Nazarre angrily and delivered expletives he would later regret. Mickey Walsh spoke some Portuguese, and he chipped in too.

Hand had to stew for six months before Ireland had the chance to make amends in Rotterdam.

BELGIUM (0) 1   **IRELAND (0) 0**
Ceulemans 87

BELGIUM: Preud'homme, Gerets, Millecamps, Meeuws, Renquin, Coeck (Wellens), Vandereycken, Mommens (Vercauteren), Cluytens, Vandenberg, Ceulemans.
IRELAND: McDonagh (EVERTON), Langan (BIRMINGHAM), Martin (NEWCASTLE), Moran (MAN U), Hughton (SPURS), Daly (COVENTRY), Grealish (LUTON), Brady (JUVENTUS), Heighway (LIVERPOOL), Stapleton (ARSENAL) (*sub* Walsh, PORTO), Robinson (BRIGHTON).

HOLLAND v IRELAND
Wednesday, 9 September 1981   Feyenoord Stadium, Rotterdam – 50,000

While Ireland were going down in Brussels, the Dutch were simultaneously sinking France by the same score. Group 2 was heading for a blanket finish. Belgium – played 6, points 9; Ireland 6-7, France 4-6; Holland 5-6, Cyprus 7-0. Belgium were clear in front, but with France and Holland having games in hand, both were poised to overtake Ireland. Ceulemans' late sickener in Belgium meant Ireland had to win both their last two matches. Anything less was liable to see them pipped at the post.

Eoin Hand had filled the World Cup's six-month hiatus with friendlies – beating Czechoslovakia (3-1) at home, but losing badly, 0-3, in Poland and in Bremen, the latter to West Germany's 'B' team.

Gerry Daly's booking in Brussels, added to that against Cyprus, meant he would sit out the match in Rotterdam. Otherwise, Hand packed his side with tried and tested faces, unlikely to fail through want of nerve. Three players had changed clubs in the summer. Frank Stapleton had swapped the red of Highbury for that of Old Trafford. The other transfers involved Liverpool. Mark Lawrenson was ushered in, Steve Heighway ushered out, across the Atlantic to Minnesota Kicks.

The Dutch side paraded three ghosts from the past – Ruud Krol, Johnny Rep, and, on the bench, René van de Kerkhof. All three had collected losers medals after the 1974 Final. Holland also included both jewels from Ipswich Town, Frans Thijssen and Arnold Muhren, who had recently earned UEFA Cup-winners medals at the expense of Dutch side AZ 67 Alkmaar. Clearly, Holland were turning in their hour of need to proven players, and in the case of Muhren and Thijssen, to players intimate with the physical nature of the British game.

To describe this match as critical is to understate. Defeat for either side spelled almost certain elimination. A draw would stack the cards against them. Not surprisingly, that was the result craved by supporters of Belgium and France. The prospect of both sides going for goals ensured that this would be a match to live in the memory.

Mick Robinson might have scored within seconds, but, sliding in, he made poor contact with John Devine's cross. The Dutch soon asserted themselves, however, bombarding the Irish goal and scoring after eleven minutes.

Heighway copped much of the flak for giving the ball away to Thijssen, who exchanged passes with Van Kooten and scored emphatically.

Despite trailing for much of the half, Ireland recovered. Heighway atoned for his error with an exquisite cross that Robinson volleyed past Schrijvers.

Still the momentum remained with Holland. They threatened to reclaim the lead time and again before they actually did so, midway through the second half. Gerry Ryan had just come off the bench for Heighway when Johnny Rep hoodwinked David Langan on the edge of the box and the full-back took him down from behind. To add insult, McDonagh got a touch to Muhren's penalty.

Forced onto the offensive, Ireland swiftly equalised. Lawrenson skipped past Muhren and Brandts and crossed to the far post. It was bread and butter for Stapleton, whose header was down and true. Hand then made a second substitution, giving young Ronnie Whelan the chance to make a name for himself. Ireland's only opportunity of stealing both points fell to Robinson, but his header was high.

Holland had had the chances to win, but manager Kees Rijvers graciously conceded Ireland their worth.

HOLLAND   (1) 2   **IRELAND   (1) 2**
Thijssen 11, Muhren 65 pen   Robinson 40, Stapleton 71

HOLLAND: Schrijvers, Wijnstekers, Brandts, Vander Korput, Krol, Muhren, Thijssen, La Ling (R Van de Kerkhof), Van Kooten, Geeles (Peters), Rep.
IRELAND: McDonagh (BOLTON), Langan (BIRM'HAM), O'Leary (ARSENAL), Lawrenson (L'POOL), Devine (ARSENAL), Martin (NEWC) (sub Whelan, L'POOL), Grealish (BRIGHTON), Brady (JUVENTUS), Heighway (MINNESOTA KICKS) (sub Ryan, BRIGHTON), Stapleton (MAN U), Robinson (BRIGHTON).

IRELAND v FRANCE
Wednesday, 14 October 1981   *Lansdowne Road – 53,000*

In other circumstances that draw would have been acclaimed, especially as Ireland had taken three points off the powerful Dutch. The downside was that Ireland had taken just one from three matches off Belgium and France, and that could still seal their World Cup fate. Belgium's win over France had guaranteed the Belgians a place in Spain. Ireland, Holland and France were contesting second place. Even if Ireland won in Dublin, their fate was in the hands of others. The French or Dutch could still leapfrog above them.

France were handicapped by injuries to Dominique Rocheteau (Achilles tendon) and Jean Tigana, who had eclipsed Brady in Paris.

The side that Eoin Hand now fielded was probably the strongest in Ireland's history. Defenders O'Leary, Moran and Lawrenson, midfielders

Brady and Whelan, target-man Stapleton – here were six players who would challenge for places in any all-Britain line-up.

The knife-edged nature of Ireland's quest encouraged supporters to pack Lansdowne Road in their thousands. Ireland stood poised on the brink of the World Cup finals, and the gate – over 53,000 – may never be exceeded, at least not while Ireland play their soccer at Lansdowne.

The multitudes witnessed an extraordinary start to an extraordinary first half. Hand had decided that the best way to unnerve France was to attack them with a sledgehammer. Seamus McDonagh was instructed to use the ball like a mortar, to be pummelled downfield like a missile from the sky. The tactic paid quick dividends when Robinson's low cross was steered into his own net by Mahut, under pressure from Stapleton breathing down his neck.

But before Ireland could stabilise, France pulled back to 1-1. A thrilling attack down the left enabled Bellone to turn on a sixpence and rifle past McDonagh from twenty yards.

It was, in the vernacular, end to end stuff. O'Leary had the chance to shoot for goal, but with defenders converging he squared to Stapleton, whose shot sailed into the top corner. 2-1. When Whelan, a minute later, sent a shot smacking against the crossbar, France began to reel. McDonagh pumped another drop-kick downfield. Larios, in a whirl, directed his back-pass hopelessly adrift of his intended target, Mahut, allowing Robinson to blast a shot that Castaneda touched but couldn't save.

Two up by half-time, Ireland might have pressed to double that advantage, and thereby seek to erase France's superior goal-difference. But these are the idle thoughts of armchair enthusiasts. To the men on the ground, victory was all-important, especially as France had no thoughts of throwing in the towel. Indeed, France had the better of the second period. Michel Platini three times threatened a goal, but was frustrated each time with a save or a block. Yet the French captain was not to be denied. With eight minutes left, Hughton could only half-clear Janvion's cross, and Platini was on it in a flash.

To eat up precious seconds, Hand sent on Don Givens for the exhausted Stapleton. Driven from the English game by the boo-boys of Birmingham City, Givens had transferred to Swiss side Neuchatel Xamax, where he was exhibiting a new lease of life. There were plenty of goals in him still. Givens was now allotted three minutes in which to seal Ireland's victory. He would never play for Ireland again.

In injury time France might have reduced Ireland to tears, but McDonagh was equal to Didier Six's desperate shot, leaping to palm the ball behind.

Ireland won, but Brady lost. A second-half booking was his second of the competition. That meant he would be banned from Ireland's first match in Spain. But would Ireland be there?

IRELAND (3) 3
Mahut 5 (o.g.), Stapleton 25,
Robinson 39

FRANCE (1) 2
Bellone 8, Platini 82

IRELAND: McDonagh (BOLTON), Langan (BIRMINGHAM), O'Leary (ARSENAL), Moran (MAN U), Hughton (SPURS), Whelan (LIVERPOOL), Martin (NEWCASTLE), Lawrenson (LIVERPOOL), Brady (JUVENTUS), Stapleton (MAN U) (*sub* Givens, NEUCHATEL XAMAX), Robinson (BRIGHTON).
FRANCE: Castaneda, Bossis, Mahut (Bracci), Lopez, Janvion, Girand, Larios, Christophe, Platini, Couriol, Bellone (Six).

Meanwhile, Belgium were sliding to a 0-3 defeat in Rotterdam. That was the worst possible result for Ireland. Belgium had already qualified, and their unmotivated side had thrown the Dutch a lifeline. Now, Ireland's only salvation would be a Dutch draw in Paris. If Holland won, they were through. If France won, they would need only to beat Cyprus in Paris. Alas, France beat Holland 2-0, on the same night that Northern Ireland beat Israel to qualify. The Republic wept, while Ulster cheered. In due course France swept Cyprus aside, leaving Ireland out in the cold once more.

The completed Group 2 table reveals the extent to which the home teams dominated. The two teams to qualify both showed 100% home records. Did Ireland lose out by failing to bury Cyprus, by losing cruelly in Brussels, or by failing to beat Belgium in Dublin? The arguments lasted long.

Both Belgium and France prospered in Spain. The Belgians shocked champions Argentina in the opening match, in an atmosphere overshadowed by the Falklands War. Belgium reached the second phase, before their goal-shy attack paid the price against Poland and the Soviet Union. France went even further, surviving defeat by England to overpower Northern Ireland 4-1 in the second phase. France frittered a two-goal advantage over West Germany in the semi-final, in a match marred by goalkeeper Schumacher's beastly assault on Patrick Battiston. Italy beat the Germans 3-1 in the Final.

Eoin Hand was there in Spain to look, learn, and plan the future. The FAI viewed the trip as extravagant, washed their hands of it and allowed Hand to fend for himself. Such things still besmirched the name of Irish soccer.

Qualifying Group 2

	P	W	D	L	F	A	W	D	L	F	A	Pts
			Home					Away				
BELGIUM	8	4	0	0	7	2	1	1	2	5	7	11
FRANCE	8	4	0	0	11	2	1	0	3	9	6	10
Ireland	8	3	1	0	12	4	1	1	2	5	7	10
Holland	8	3	1	0	9	2	1	0	3	2	5	9
Cyprus	8	0	0	4	2	13	0	0	4	2	16	0

Other group results

Cyprus v France	0-7
Belgium v Holland	1-0
Cyprus v Belgium	0-2
Belgium v Cyprus	3-2
Holland v Cyprus	3-0
Holland v France	1-0

France v Belgium	3-2
Cyprus v Holland	0-1
Belgium v France	2-0
Holland v Belgium	3-0
France v Holland	2-0
France v Cyprus	4-0

Ireland appearances and goalscorers (substitute appearances in brackets)
World Cup qualifying rounds 1982

	Apps	Goals		Apps	Goals
Brady L *	8	–	O'Leary D *	4	–
Stapleton F *	8	3	McDonagh S	3	–
Grealish A	7	2	Givens D *†‡	2 (2)	–
Langan D	7	–	McGee P	1 (1)	2
Lawrenson M *	7	2	Whelan R	1 (1)	–
Heighway S *†	6	–	Devine J	1	–
Hughton C	6	1	Grimes A	1	–
Daly G *	5	3	Murphy J	1	–
Moran K	5	–	O'Leary P	1	–
Peyton G *	5	–	Ryan G	– (3)	–
Robinson M	5	3	O'Brien F	– (1)	–
Martin M *†	4	–	Walsh M *	– (1)	–
			(own-goals)		1

* Appeared in 1978 World Cup.
† Appeared in 1974 World Cup.
‡ Appeared in 1970 World Cup.

97 apps   17 goals
1 League of Ireland
85 English League
7 Italian League
2 US League
1 Portuguese League
1 Swiss League

24 players used

12

THE 1986 WORLD CUP

The hair's breadth that separated Eoin Hand's team from Spain '82 kept the snipers at bay, for the time being. Dwarfing all other considerations was Northern Ireland's achievement, firstly, reaching the finals, secondly, beating the hosts to reach the second phase. This heaped greater expectation on the Republic. If Northern Ireland could scale such heights, so could the South.

In the wake of Ireland's elimination, and before the finals started, Hand took his players on an ill-conceived and badly-arranged tour of South America, where they lost three out of three. It was hard to know which was the more painful, the seven goals they lost to a Brazilian team about to woo the footballing world, or defeat by the rag-tag team of Trinidad and Tobago.

Come the new season, Ireland embarked on the long road to Euro '84. With just eight finalists, it is considerably harder to qualify for the Euros than for the finals of the World Cup. Ireland needed to stave off the challenge of Malta, Iceland, Spain and – Holland, again. Although Ireland rounded off their programme with a record win, 8-0 against Malta, two earlier defeats by Holland, and three points dropped against Spain, left Ireland off the pace from the start.

It was following defeat in Spain that Irish supporters began to turn against the manager. Public disenchantment would cloud his remaining years in the job. Hand was a courteous man, but many doubted his ability to impose himself on the big names under his command. Losing at home to the Dutch, in Ireland's first competitive home reverse in eleven years, brought even more boo-boys into the open. They had witnessed Ireland's two-goal lead overturned by strikes from a youthful Ruud Gullit (two) and Van Basten.

Meanwhile, Northern Ireland had beaten West Germany *twice* in the Euro qualifiers. That fanned the flames of Irish discord, and one wonders to what extent Hand was plagued by the fallout of Northern Ireland's success. When Ireland were sunk 0-3 in Israel the knives were out. Liverpool manager Bob Paisley, according to reports, was ready to take over, but Hand – who had lost his job at Limerick, and taken another at St Patrick's Athletic – somehow hung on. He would be the first manager to guide Ireland's fortunes in two

World Cups. By this time, support had fallen away alarmingly. When Ireland entertained Mexico in August 1984, for a dreary goalless draw, just 5,000 turned up, an all-time low. Morale was as low as in the pre-Giles era. The clock appeared to have been turned back a dozen years.

Nor was there any ray of sunshine in the European Cup. LOI clubs kept tumbling at the first hurdle, more often than not by embarrassing margins. Liverpool went home from Dundalk with four goals under their belt; the following season Standard Liege crashed eleven goals past Athlone Town. If the LOI standard-bearers continued to wilt in the face of the European storm, greater responsibility was inevitably heaped on the Ireland national side. No one doubted that the coming World Cup would be Hand's last chance.

Five-team groups were now par for the course, though FIFA invited two teams from each to join the fun. From Ireland's point of view, the opposition was at least fresh. No France, no Holland. Instead, Denmark, Norway, Switzerland and the Soviet Union stood between them and Mexico '86.

Hand had been instrumental in doing away with the long-standing use of the Gresham Hotel as the team's pre-match headquarters. These were now switched to the Dublin Airport Hotel, more convenient for players flying in from England, and it was there that Hand and his men schemed the downfall of the Soviet Union.

Qualifying Group 6

IRELAND v SOVIET UNION
Wednesday, 12 September 1984   *Lansdowne Road – 28,000*

Having to start with the Soviet Union was a tough nut to crack. Ireland had set the 1974 qualifiers in train by losing to the same opponents, having their hopes dashed, and shortly ushering in Johnny Giles.

The 1970s had not been kind to the Soviets. They had, it will be recalled, refused to play-off in Chile and been barred from the '74 finals. Four years later they had been pipped by Hungary. Spain '82, therefore, marked their first appearance in the finals for twelve years. There, they had held off a challenge from Scotland and been denied a semi-final place on goal-difference. The Soviets had also finished third in the 1980 Olympics.

In preparing for Dublin, manager Eduard Malofeyev – a member of the Soviet team in England '66 – masterminded a 2-0 win over England at Wembley, and kept faith with seven of the team who had outmanoeuvred Scotland in Spain. Dinamo Kiev players formed the nucleus of his side. In a country where goalkeeper Lev Yashin was legend, it says much for Rinat Dasaev (Spartak Moscow) – tall, lean, agile – that he should invite comparison. The defence was marshalled by the moustachioed Alexander

Chivadze (Dinamo Tbilisi). In attack, a star of yesterday – Oleg Blokhin (Dinamo Kiev) – paid a welcome return visit to Dublin. He would spend much of the match in heated exchanges with the bench.

Ireland's new captain, Frank Stapleton, was recuperating from surgery on a leg injury. Tony Grealish had skippered the side before, and he did so now. Liam Brady had moved on to Internazionale, and was winning his forty-sixth cap. In fact, the whole side bristled with experience, the only player introduced since the previous World Cup being Tony Galvin. Even he had five caps under his belt.

To protect his central defenders against the mobile Soviet front men, Hand asked O'Leary to act as sweeper. To the extent that the visitors failed to score, the tactic could be said to have worked. But most neutrals in the crowd would have given the Soviets the benefit of the doubt, eleven minutes into the second half, when Aleinikov's shot hit Whelan and flew to Olganesian. Whelan seemed to have played the Soviet player onside, but the linesman's flag went up as Olganesian netted.

Robinson and Walsh had earlier missed promising openings, but the Soviets grew in confidence the longer the match progressed. It was therefore against the tide of play when Whelan interrupted a Soviet attack and set Robinson free on the right. Robinson hared away from Aleinikov and crossed low for Mickey Walsh to thrash a first-timer into the net.

The Soviets had twenty-six minutes to save the match. The time must have seemed endless to Irish supporters, who watched their team driven back, almost into the Liffey. McDonagh saved at Blokhin's feet, Rodionov headed wide, and two minutes from time the same player smashed a shot against the crossbar. The ball flew back to Litovchenko, who promptly rattled a post in its base. Three minutes' injury time whittled down many an Irish fingernail.

IRELAND   (0) 1   **SOVIET UNION   (0) 0**
Walsh 64

IRELAND: McDonagh (NOTTS CO), Devine (NORWICH), O'Leary (ARSENAL), Lawrenson (LIVERPOOL), Hughton (SPURS), Whelan (LIVERPOOL), Grealish (WBA), Brady (INTERNAZIONALE), Galvin (SPURS), Walsh (PORTO) (sub O'Keefe, PORT VALE), Robinson (LIVERPOOL).
USSR: Dasaev, Sulakvelidze, Baltacha, Chivadze, Aleinikov, Demianenko, Bessanov (Zygmantovich), Litovchenko, Olganesian (Gotsmanov), Blokhin, Rodionov.

NORWAY v IRELAND
Wednesday, 17 October 1984   *Ullevaal Stadium, Oslo – 12,468*

Ireland had suffered so much ill-fortune in the previous World Cup that they could afford to be magnanimous this time. The gods had smiled on them, and on Eoin Hand, who might otherwise have been driven from office after just one game.

By the time Ireland flew to Oslo, the Republic had suffered another slap in the face. All Ireland had been captivated when the name of Shamrock Rovers was pulled out of the hat to play Linfield in the European Cup. In keeping with Northern Ireland's recent ascendancy, Linfield won through – on away goals. That setback obliterated gutsy performances in the other European tournaments. University College Dublin did well to hold Everton to 0-1 on aggregate, while Bohemians lost to Glasgow Rangers 3-4 over two legs.

Norway seemed there for the taking. They had picked up just one point from three matches, at home to the Soviets. They had lost in Denmark and at home to Switzerland, and had no chance of qualifying from Group 6. With nothing to play for, they were expected to surrender precious points to the Irish. Norway could also atone for knocking Ireland out of the 1938 World Cup. The sides had met often enough since, and Ireland had never lost.

But Norway could pack a punch. In 1981 they had rocked the footballing world by beating England. Much later they would defeat England a second time, preparatory to facing Ireland in USA '94. But in 1984 there were few signs of this Norwegian bloom. They had slumped in the European qualifiers, surrendering three points to Wales. Since 1945 they had never come close to qualifying for a major tournament. Knowing their own limitations, Norway habitually played with a massed defence.

Their first buds were present in young goalkeeper Erik Thorstvedt, later to transfer to Tottenham Hotspur, and Age Hareide, who had already played for Manchester City and Norwich. These were just the beginnings of Norway's soccer exodus.

Hand welcomed back a semi-fit Frank Stapleton. Otherwise the team was unchanged. Ireland tried to stretch their opponents by playing wide, and, indeed, saw enough of the ball, with Galvin projecting teasing crosses at Stapleton and Robinson. Had Stapleton or Whelan capitalised on golden opportunities – Thorstvedt stopped the former's weak header with his knee – Ireland might have been spared the embarrassment that followed. Three minutes before half-time Jakobsen played a one-two with Larsen-Okland. Jakobsen's shot struck the diving keeper's legs and bobbled into the net.

To further stretch Norway's eight-man defence, Hand sent on Kevin O'Callaghan and Mickey Walsh. But Ireland couldn't recapture their earlier control. Brady came nearest with a shot deflected into the side-netting, and a diving header near the end. Norway had few chances, but twice might have increased their lead. Lawrenson headed one effort off the line, McDonagh saved another with his legs.

In twelve attempts Norway had beaten Ireland just twice. Both were in the World Cup. That's what hurt the most.

Norwegian manager Tor Roste Fossen admitted to being surprised that Ireland had played so poorly. Only Tony Galvin had caused his players any worries.

'Beaten by complacency?' reporters demanded of Eoin Hand. But Hand would have none of it. Nor would he admit that he had bowed to player-power in picking Stapleton, who had spluttered throughout the match. His captain had yet to force his way back into Manchester United's first team, and lacked match-fitness. But who could Hand have picked in his place? The only alternative was Mickey Walsh, and he wasn't match-fit either.

NORWAY (1) 1   **IRELAND (0) 0**
Jakobsen 42

NORWAY: Thorstvedt, Fjaelberg (Davidsen), Hareide, Kojedal, Mordt, Soler, Ahlsen, Thoresen, Herlovsen, Okland, Jakobsen (Henriksen).
IRELAND: McDonagh (BIRMINGHAM), Devine (NORWICH), O'Leary (ARSENAL), Lawrenson (LIVERPOOL), Hughton (SPURS), Whelan (LIVERPOOL) (*sub* O'Callaghan, IPSWICH), Grealish (WBA), Brady (INTER), Galvin (SPURS), Stapleton (MAN U), Robinson (LIVERPOOL) (*sub* Walsh, PORTO).

DENMARK v IRELAND
Wednesday, 14 November 1984   *Idraetspark, Copenhagen – 45,300*

Defeat in Oslo was catastrophic. Norway couldn't qualify themselves, but they had done their best to make sure that Ireland wouldn't either. The defeat needed to be undone by victory in Copenhagen.

Only two or three years earlier, Ireland would have viewed a trip to the Danish capital as gleefully as they would to Oslo. But in a metamorphosis of Kafkaesque proportions, Denmark had thrown off their timeless timidity and presented a titan to the world.

The transformation had begun at Wembley in the European qualifiers. The result said merely England 0 Denmark 1, but it could not begin to illustrate the ineptitude of the English or the magnificence of the Danes. Denmark had stormed the European finals, drawn 1-1 with Spain in the semis, and to the dismay of all neutrals were put out in a penalty shoot-out. Denmark now appeared to be galloping towards their first World Cup finals. There were some prepared to go on record as rating them the best team in Europe.

The genesis of this dramatic flowering was twofold. A diaspora of skilful players had learned their trade with the great clubs of Europe. As Denmark was traditionally one of soccer's backwaters, several players had in the past exhibited indifference to playing for their country. But German manager Sepp Piontek had wooed them with a dashing, devil-take-the-hindmost style that emphasised attack with almost foolhardy disregard for defence.

Denmark's football was cavalier, it was joyous, and, most importantly, it won matches.

Hand had to prepare accordingly. Three players were given their World Cup spurs. Two of them, Mick McCarthy and Kevin Sheedy, would hang around for many years to come. The third, Jim Beglin, might have done so too, but for breaking a leg.

Bolstered by these weapons of the future, Ireland were still no match for an exuberant Denmark. Indeed, Ireland were grateful only that Denmark declined the turn the screw following a third goal shortly after half-time. Ireland's best chance of a one-sided first half came when Frank Stapleton headed goalwards, but John Sivebaek was on hand to clear. For the most part, Ireland were on the back foot, trailing from the moment Elkjaer seized on Grealish's wayward pass, outpaced McCarthy and blazed past McDonagh.

The second half was just forty-eight seconds old when Denmark sealed the result. Ireland were caught cold by a slick move that sped from one end of the pitch to the other. Veteran Danish captain Morten Olsen switched play to Sivebaek, who in turn fed Michael Laudrup. Elkjaer befuddled O'Leary – no mean feat – in the act of scoring. And when Sören Lerby – who had scored against Ireland six years earlier in the Euros – switched passes with Laudrup and squeezed the ball past McDonagh, Ireland knew the game was up. Elkjaer later spurned an easy chance for his hat-trick.

Ireland had been let off lightly, and Eoin Hand was man enough to admit it. 'Denmark's display against us was one of the best I have ever seen in international football.' This did not prevent him being hauled before the FAI to account for Ireland's malaise.

DENMARK (1) 3   **IRELAND (0) 0**
  Elkjaer 29, 46, Lerby 54

DENMARK: Qvist, Sivebaek, Nielsen, Olsen, Busk, Bertelsen (Mölby), Lerby, Arnesen, Berggren, Elkjaer (Brylle), Laudrup.
IRELAND: McDonagh (NOTTS CO), Lawrenson (LIVERPOOL), O'Leary (ARSENAL), McCarthy (MAN C), Beglin (LIVERPOOL), Brady (INTER), Grealish (WBA), Sheedy (EVERTON), Galvin (SPURS) (sub O'Callaghan, IPSWICH), Stapleton (MAN U), Walsh (PORTO).

IRELAND v NORWAY
Wednesday, 1 May 1985   *Lansdowne Road – 15,000*

Two points out of six. Ireland would be lucky to recover from that, and anyway, they had to wait six months before attempting to pick up the pieces. They filled the hiatus with three friendlies. Two of these were big 'uns, against the world champions, Italy, and England. Ireland lost them both 1-2.

Paulo Rossi and Altobelli – scorers in the World Cup Final – scored in Dublin, while Gary Lineker netted at Wembley, his first England goal in his first full international. Ireland's other match resulted in a goalless draw in Tel Aviv. Since crashing eight past Malta, Ireland were now in the grip of an acute goal drought, just four goals in ten games.

For all their ability to topple England and Ireland in Oslo, nothing as yet suggested Norway could inflict comparable damage on opponents' grounds. A feeble crowd endured an awful match, from which the only Irish player to escape censure was Pat Bonner. Packie had been making the odd appearance, here and there, for four years, but never before in the World Cup.

Even without Hughton and Sheedy, Hand could find no excuses – other than in Ireland's ugly yellow-hooped shirts – for what he later described as 'perhaps the worst display of any Irish team I had managed'. Even Liam Brady, for so long Ireland's great white hope, had a stinker, and was pulled off in favour of Whelan.

Brady had come nearest to breaking the stalemate when firing against the crossbar. Stapleton headed the rebound into the net, but a linesman was busy flag-waving. Robinson was the culprit. At the other end, Norway twice broke away to leave Okland one on one with Pat Bonner. Both times Bonner saved.

Another first. Seven minutes from the end Paul McGrath trotted on for his first World Cup match. He could do little to prevent Norway repeating their 1938 trick, taking three points off Ireland.

After such a feeble show, which dealt a heavy blow to Ireland's hopes of qualification, Eoin Hand had to run the gauntlet of irate fans. So did some of his players, especially the experienced ones – including Brady and Stapleton – who, some supporters sneered, had barely gone through the motions.

In the privacy of the changing room Hand told his players he intended to quit. They dissuaded him – for the time being.

IRELAND   (0) 0   **NORWAY   (0) 0**

IRELAND: Bonner (CELTIC), Langan (OXFORD) (*sub* McGrath, MAN U), Lawrenson (LIVERPOOL), O'Leary (ARSENAL), Beglin (LIVERPOOL), Daly (BIRMINGHAM), Brady (INTER) (*sub* Whelan, LIVERPOOL), Waddock (QPR), Galvin (SPURS), Stapleton (MAN U), Robinson (QPR).
NORWAY: Thorstvedt, Fjaelberg, Kojedal, Hareide, Henriksen, Herlovsen (Erlandsen), Ahlsen, Thoresen, Soler, Okland, Moen (Jakobsen).

IRELAND v SWITZERLAND
Sunday, 2 June 1985   *Lansdowne Road – 17,300*

A 0-0 draw with Spain in Cork later in May lengthened Ireland's goalscoring fatigue to four from twelve matches. June was hardly the time for World Cup action, with players tired in mind and body and anxious to pack their bags for their holidays. These disadvantages were offset by having most of the players together for ten days, something almost unheard of in the past. They could, for once, prepare and train as a team. The Manchester United contingent flew in later, from their Caribbean tour, while the Liverpool players arrived heavy-eyed after the trauma of Heysel.

Swiss football had peaked before and after World War II, since when their fortunes had tailed away. Switzerland were now just another small European nation struggling to make an impact either at club or international level. Not for twenty years had the Swiss competed in a World Cup finals, though they, like Norway, had been in England's group last time round – and beaten them.

Past results showed eight wins to Ireland, three to Switzerland. This was the first occasion their paths had crossed in the World Cup, though they had shared one win apiece in the 1976 European qualifiers. Switzerland had recently deprived Scotland of three points in attempting to reach Euro '84. The Swiss had, moreover, made a promising start on the road to Mexico. Five points from their first three matches had put them in with a shout, though they had collapsed 0-4 in their fourth, to the Soviets. All the Swiss played for Swiss clubs, with the exception of Andre Egli, who represented Borussia Dortmund in West Germany.

Hand felt buoyed up for this match. Another sparse crowd witnessed Ireland's biggest score in nearly two years. Frank Stapleton had a clause in his contract that even released him for friendlies, never mind World Cup-ties. He had graduated to soccer from Gaelic football, and his height, strength, ability in the air, and above all his equable temperament made him an ideal target-man. Manchester United and Arsenal were both after him as a boy. He trialled with the former, didn't get a peep, so signed for the latter. When United realised the enormity of their mistake, it cost them almost £1,000,000 to buy him back. Stapleton had already appeared in three FA Cup Finals and been voted Arsenal's Player of the Year.

First called up for Ireland in 1976, by Giles, Stapleton had scored three minutes into his international debut, against Turkey. He was now a month short of his thirtieth birthday, and knew perfectly well that if he didn't see Mexico '86 he was unlikely to be around for Italia '90.

Never as comfortable on the ground as in the air, Stapleton had to live with criticism that he didn't score the number of goals expected of a No. 9. But then there was always more to his game than that. Besides, he was destined in the fullness of time to overtake Don Givens as Ireland's all-time top goalscorer.

It took him just seven minutes against Switzerland to notch his thirteenth Ireland goal. A free-kick was headed back by Langan to Stapleton lurking at the far post. He looked offside, but duly tucked it in.

Swiss defenders appeal against Frank Stapleton's headed opener.

Switzerland suffered a further setback midway through the half. Goalkeeper Engel (of Xamax) had distinguished himself with a save from Sheedy when he collided with Grealish and was unable to continue. Engel's deputy, Burgener (Servette), was powerless to prevent Ireland's second goal. Daly centred, and Grealish's back-header bounced against a post and in.

Whelan replaced the limping Daly at half-time and might have scored with his first kick. Burgener saved. Ireland's third goal followed McDonagh's massive punt downfield, allowing Sheedy to sprint clear of the offside trap. With the game safe, Hand sent on Paul McGrath to stretch his legs.

Ireland had five points from five games, and might yet spring a surprise.

IRELAND (2) 3   **SWITZERLAND (0) 0**
Stapleton 7, Grealish 33,
Grealish 57

IRELAND: McDonagh (GILLINGHAM), Langan (OXFORD), O'Leary (ARSENAL), McCarthy (MAN C), Beglin (LIVERPOOL), Daly (BIRMINGHAM) (*sub* Whelan, LIVERPOOL), Grealish (WBA) (*sub* McGrath, MAN U), Brady (INTERNAZIONALE), Sheedy (EVERTON), Stapleton (MAN U), Robinson (QPR).
SWITZERLAND: Engel (Burgener), Geiger, Ludi, Wehrli, In-Albon, Egli, Barberis (Bregy), Hermann, Descastel, Matthey, Braschler.

SWITZERLAND v IRELAND

Wednesday, 11 September 1985   *Wankdorf Stadium, Berne – 24,000*

Football was in the dock. The tragedies of Heysel and Bradford City invited much introspection on the causes of footballs ills. Football was not more important than life and death, no matter what the late Bill Shankly would have us believe.

For reasons quite unrelated, Ireland's manager, players and administrators passed a miserable summer. This Ireland side was going nowhere, and changes could not be postponed for much longer. Not that the Swiss were riding on the crest of a wave. Heavy defeats in Moscow and Dublin had derailed their hopes, and they badly needed a win to get back on track.

Yet the state of Group 6 showed everyone had cause for hope. Denmark were out in front with six points from four matches, but it was nip and tuck behind them. Switzerland and Ireland had five points from five games, the Soviet Union and Norway four from five. It might take five more points to do so, but Ireland could still make it. One thing was clear: the losers in Berne could forget about Mexico.

The Ireland side that marched out in the Wankdorf Stadium, home of Young Boys Berne, and venue for the 1954 World Cup Final, was full of tried and trusted names. Even though Hand was deprived of Whelan and Langan, seven players had more than twenty caps and only one had fewer than six. He was Gillingham's Tony Cascarino, winning his first in place of Michael Robinson.

When one considers Ireland's losing run, either the players were at fault or the system was. But eight of the starting eleven, plus Paul McGrath on the bench, would be in the squad for Italia '90. Nine, if one overlooks Jim Beglin's misfortune. Ireland's World Cup giants were, in other words, out there on the pitch already, five years before they came of age. All they lacked was Jack Charlton. And he was coming.

Anyone watching this match would have seen that these were two teams short of confidence. Switzerland strung five players across midfield, forcing Hand to withdraw Brady from his advanced position to match the Swiss in numbers. Inevitably, the match deteriorated into a midfield quagmire. Passes went here, there, and everywhere. Shots likewise. Switzerland had the more of them, and more of the wild misses. It was the same story in the second half, except this time the roles were reversed. Ireland did more of the shooting and more of the missing. The only time the ball nestled in the net was in the last minute, but the referee had already blown for offside against Stapleton.

The match was punctuated by fifty-two fouls, which at least showed that the players were trying. Not that Irish fans were in a mood to believe it.

SWITZERLAND   (0) 0   IRELAND   (0) 0

SWITZERLAND: Engel, Geiger, In-Albon, Hermann, Egli, Schällibaum (Brigger), Perret, Bregy, Koller, Lüthi, Matthey.

IRELAND: McDonagh (SUNDERLAND), Hughton (SPURS), O'Leary (ARSENAL), McCarthy (MAN C), Beglin (LIVERP'L), Daly (BIRM'HAM) (*sub* McGrath, MAN U), Brady (INTER), Lawrenson (LIVERP'L), Sheedy (EVERTON) (*sub* O'Callaghan, PORTSMOUTH), Stapleton (MAN U), Cascarino (GILLINGHAM).

SOVIET UNION v IRELAND
Wednesday, 16 October 1985   *Lenin Stadium, Moscow – 103,000*

Come October, Ireland's three clubs in Europe were as usual out for the count. Shamrock Rovers had been dumped by Honved, Galway United by the Danes of Lyngby, and Bohemians by Dundee United in the UEFA Cup. The Bohs' 2-5 first-leg defeat at Dalymount was hard to stomach. That margin of defeat ought to be the prerogative of Maltese or Cypriot clubs, not Irish ones.

Though the Kremlin had replaced deceased presidents Andropov and Chernenko with the smiling Gorbachev, the Soviet Union's footballers were in no mood for smiles. They had started Group 6 with a whimper, losing in Dublin and Copenhagen, drawing in Oslo and Berne. These setbacks were offset by boasting the most phenomenal home record of any nation in the World Cup. On the eve of Ireland's visit it read: Played 19, Won 19, For 53, Against 5. A 100% record, no less, with no opposition having scored since 1965, when Wales went down 1-2. Since that time the Soviets had not conceded a home goals in thirteen World Cup-ties. The figures, daunting in themselves, had to be further measured against Ireland's dreadful away record.

This was make or break for Eoin Hand. If Ireland could overturn history and win in Moscow, that would set them up for a show-down with the Danes in Dublin, with everything to play for. Realists, or pessimists, however they called themselves, pooh-poohed the prospect. Their numbers even included the toffs in Merrion Square, who threw up one obstacle after another when Hand demanded they take this fixture as seriously as any other, no matter the financial costs involved.

Eventually, he got his way – up to a point. He flew out to watch the Soviets play Denmark, learned at first hand the bureaucratic thorns likely to confront him, and came back to demand that the FAI take along food for the players and a chef to cook it. Such requests are second nature to the English or Scottish FA's, and would be to the FAI under Jack Charlton. But Merrion Square was not yet geared for demands of this nature. They dolefully agreed to provide the food, but balked over a chef. At which point Mrs Hand volunteered, and duly donned her apron to cook meals for two dozen players and coaching staff.

Eoin Hand may have had his limitations as a manager, but few can doubt that he operated within an administration that got little back because it put so little in.

For all his groundwork, Hand had to fly out without the injured Paul McGrath. The Soviet strength was in midfield, which Hand sought to counter by playing 3-5-2. Though lacking penetration up front, Ireland held their own for an hour. Indeed, had Italian referee Casarin seen fit to blow for a penalty when Chivadze upended Beglin, one wonders how the Soviets would have responded to being behind. But that is hypothetical.

As time went on, Ireland found the Soviet goal an ever-receding target. Nine minutes into the second half Blokhin exploded a shot from thirty yards that McDonagh repulsed with difficulty, requiring Lawrenson to clear up the pieces. With an hour gone, Protasov escaped from Lawrenson and crossed for the unmarked Cherenkov to shoot past McDonagh.

The Soviets were now happy to trade space in midfield. Substitute Whelan had no sooner come on than he obliged Dasaev to turn his snap-shot behind. Then Stapleton failed to make decisive contact with Brady's free-kick. With seconds to play Gotsmanov took the ball round McDonagh, and Protasov met the cross with a diving header that clipped McCarthy *en route* to goal.

The curtain had come down on Ireland and on Eoin Hand. This time, his decision was irrevocable. He would go after the match with Denmark.

SOVIET UNION   (0) 2   **IRELAND   (0) 0**
Cherenkov 60, Protasov 89

USSR: Dasaev, Morozov, Demianenko, Chivadze, Bubnov, Aleinikov, Gotsmanov, Zavarov (Bessanov), Cherenkov, Protasov, Blokhin (Kondratiev).
IRELAND: McDonagh (NOTTS CO), Hughton (SPURS), O'Leary (ARSENAL), Lawrenson (LIVERP'L), McCarthy (MAN C), Beglin (LIVERP'L) (*sub* O'Callaghan, PORTSMOUTH), Waddock (QPR), Grealish (WBA) (*sub* Whelan, LIVERPOOL), Brady (INTER), Stapleton (MAN U), Cascarino (GILLINGHAM).

IRELAND v DENMARK
Wednesday, 13 November 1985   *Lansdowne Road – 15,154*

This match saw the *au revoir* for two Irishmen. It marked the end for long-serving keeper Seamus McDonagh. A statisticians' nightmare, he had been farmed out, while officially on the books of Notts County, to one club after another. He ended up guesting for Wichita Wings across the Atlantic. He features in this book with seven clubs, five in the current campaign. When he retired from club football in 1988, he had represented *eleven* English clubs.

Denmark's Jan Mölby tries to get away from Ireland's David O'Leary.

It was also the end for Eoin Hand. For reasons that can be debated, his players had not responded as he had wished. He had had five years in the job, but his record was infinitely poorer than Giles'. Under Giles, Ireland won as many as they lost; under Hand they lost twice as many as they won. It is curious, but Ireland's away records under both managers were equally dismal. The difference was that Giles had learned the knack of winning at home, so important for spectators. Hand had lost that knack and the FAI had finally lost patience.

To all intents Group 6 was settled. Denmark and the Soviet Union were booked for Mexico, but if Ireland lost today and Norway won in Switzerland, Ireland might yet be saddled with the wooden spoon.

It was all the fault of England that Denmark wore the robes of princes. Had Bobby Robson's team averted an injury-time equaliser in Copenhagen in the Euro '84 qualifiers, or Phil Neal not given away a penalty at Wembley in the return, Denmark would not have qualified or proceeded to make hay. With their all-action, attacking style, Denmark were poised to emulate the great Dutch side, who rose from nowhere to flourish in the World Cups of the 1970s.

The match in Dublin took on the air of a massive farewell – to Ireland, back to the drawing board; to Eoin Hand, out of football; and to Denmark, off to Mexico. Nowadays, to flip through that rampant Danish side is to find names sliding off the tongue like honey.

For starters, they had Johnny Sivebaek, shortly to join Manchester United, in defence. In midfield there was Sören Lerby (Bayern Münich), Jan Mölby (Liverpool), Klaus Berggren (Pisa) and Frank Arnesen (PSV Eindhoven). Hunting for goals were Jesper Olsen (Manchester United), Michael Laudrup (Juventus) and Preben Elkjaer (Verona).

These were the mainstays of a side overflowing with talent. Most of the squad attended the best finishing schools in Italy, Germany, Holland, England. Laudrup, for example, showed astonishing maturity for someone of just twenty-one. He had blossomed early. His striking partner, Elkjaer, blossomed late, overcoming a head-down, awkward gait to become a master dribbler with searing pace.

Elkjaer, scorer of over thirty goals in over fifty internationals and dubbed 'Golkjaer' by supporters of Verona, described the Danish style as 'playing by memory, football mixed like a cocktail, counter-attacking at full speed.'

Sponsored by the brewery, Carlsberg, and coached since 1979 by the former West German international, Sepp Piontek, the side had risen almost overnight, aided by funds to entice Denmark's legionnaires home for internationals, coupled with a philosophy of all-out attack. The downside was that several Danes were past their sell-by date, and one sensed that the team would need to strike while the iron was hot.

Looking ahead, Denmark would fail to qualify both for Italia '90 and Euro '92. There, in Sweden, profiting from a wild card entry, following the demise of Yugoslavia, Denmark would overturn predictions by lifting the European title. But who is to say another gate-crasher might not have done likewise?

A Dublin crowd of just 15,000 (of whom a quarter were Danes) was unworthy of Ireland's illustrious visitors, though those who stayed away may have had a sixth sense about the torture to be inflicted. Ireland's defeat would be the worst under Eoin Hand and their worst at home since 1971, when Austria matched the score. Yet the match started so darkly for the Danes, trailing after just six minutes to a vintage Stapleton header.

But Denmark levelled within seconds, Elkjaer thrashing Sivebaek's cross past McDonagh. Three minutes later Lawrenson tackled Berggren in the box from behind as the Dane was in shooting stride. The sparse crowd sucked in its breath, but the referee waved play on.

It was even-Steven after forty-five minutes; game, set and match to the Danes after ninety. Laudrup shook off O'Leary to convert Elkjaer's flick-on. Ten minutes later Sivebaek played a one-two with Laudrup, cut inside on full throttle, skirted past Moran and Beglin, and chipped a wonder goal that must have inflated the fee Ron Atkinson was set to splash out to bring Sivebaek to Old Trafford.

Denmark had one more goal to offer, another classic. Sivebaek was again instrumental. Berggren steered his cross into the path of Elkjaer, lurking at an impossible angle, but who nevertheless found the top corner. With the final whistle Denmark had wrecked Ireland's thirteen-year unbeaten home record in competitive internationals.

'The Danes destroyed us,' confessed Eoin Hand. But few were listening. They were tuned to Wembley, where that wily campaigner, Billy Bingham, had guided his charges to their second World Cup finals.

IRELAND (1) **1**   **DENMARK** (1) **4**
Stapleton 6   Elkjaer 7, 76, Laudrup 49,
                               Sivebaek 59

IRELAND; McDonagh (WICHITA WINGS), Moran (MAN U), Lawrenson (LIVERPOOL), O'Leary (ARSENAL), Beglin (LIVERPOOL), McGrath (MAN U), Grealish (WBA) (*sub* Byrne, SHAMROCK R), Brady (INTER), Sheedy (EVERTON) (*sub* Robinson, QPR), Stapleton (MAN U), Cascarino (GILL'HAM). DENMARK: Rasmussen, Sivebaek, Busk, M Olsen (Arnesen), Nielsen, Mölby, Lerby (Bertelsen), J Olsen, Berggren, Laudrup, Elkjaer.

Denmark and the Soviet Union both topped their sections in Mexico, though both tumbled spectacularly at the next hurdle. Having beaten Scotland, West Germany and Uruguay (6-1), the unseeded Danes collapsed like a punctured balloon (1-5) against Spain. The Soviets, six-goal slaughterers of Hungary, fell 3-4 to Belgium in an extra-time classic.

England were put out in the quarter-finals by Argentina's Diego Maradona and the Hand of God. In the semis, Argentina proved too strong for Belgium, in the Final too strong for West Germany.

The greatest impact on Irish football, however, came from the achievement of Northern Ireland. They didn't fare so well second time round, losing twice and taking just one point, from Algeria. But just to be there threw down the gauntlet to the Republic.

But for Billy Bingham, there might have been no Jack Charlton.

Qualifying Group 6

		Home					Away					
	P	W	D	L	F	A	W	D	L	F	A	Pts
DENMARK	8	3	1	0	8	2	2	0	2	9	4	11
SOVIET UNION	8	4	0	0	8	0	0	2	2	5	8	10
Switzerland	8	1	3	0	4	3	1	1	2	1	7	8
Ireland	8	2	1	1	5	4	0	1	3	0	6	6
Norway	8	1	1	2	3	7	0	2	2	1	3	5

Other group results

Norway v Switzerland	0-1	Denmark v Soviet Union	4-2
Denmark v Norway	1-0	Soviet Union v Denmark	1-0
Norway v Soviet Union	1-1	Denmark v Switzerland	0-0
Switzerland v Denmark	1-0	Norway v Denmark	1-5
Switzerland v Soviet Union	2-2	Soviet Union v Norway	1-0
Soviet Union v Switzerland	4-0	Switzerland v Norway	1-1

Ireland appearances and goalscorers (substitute appearances in brackets)
World Cup qualifying rounds 1986

	Apps	Goals		Apps	Goals
Brady L *†	8	–	Daly G *†	3	–
O'Leary D *†	8	–	Whelan R *	2 (3)	–
Lawrenson M *†	7	–	Walsh M *†	2 (1)	1
McDonagh S *	7	–	Devine J *	2	–
Stapleton F *†	7	2	Langan D *	2	–
Beglin J	6	–	Waddock G	2	–
Grealish A *	6	1	McGrath P	1 (3)	–
Robinson M *	4 (1)	–	Bonner P	1	–
Galvin A	4	–	Moran K *	1	–
Hughton C *	4	–	O'Callaghan K	– (4)	–
McCarthy M	4	–	Byrne P	– (1)	–
Sheedy K	4	1	O'Keefe E	– (1)	
Cascarino A	3	–			

* Appeared in 1982 World Cup.
† Appeared in 1978 World Cup.

102 apps   5 goals
1 League of Ireland
88 English League
8 Italian League
3 Portuguese League
1 US League
1 Scottish League

25 players used

13

THE 1990 WORLD CUP

How Eoin Hand must have secretly cursed the magic of Billy Bingham. Overshadowing all Hand's endeavours was the simple, inescapable fact that his tenure coincided with that of Bingham, and, by extension, a golden age of Ulster football. Without the impetus provided by Northern Ireland's World Cup triumphs – from the FAI's vantage-point both laudable and humiliating – one wonders whether the powers that be in Merrion Square would ever have been driven to set in train the extraordinary events that followed.

Neither Hand's predecessor, Giles, nor his successor, Charlton, had to weigh the Ulster factor. If timing is of the essence, then poor Eoin Hand was simply the wrong man at the wrong time. In any walk of life, to be left behind by one's neighbour can sow the seeds of discord.

The story of Jack Charlton's appointment has been told many times. Among the nominees were former Ireland managers Liam Tuohy and Johnny Giles, and – heretically – non-Irishmen, among them Billy McNeill, a Scot, and Jack Charlton. Behind the scenes, a coup was hoping to install Bob Paisley, just retired at Anfield. Through various leaks we know that, back in 1980, Eoin Hand had been appointed on a split vote. The same thing happened now. Amid the shenanigans, the nods and winks, Charlton swept past Paisley on the second ballot. What might have happened had one member of the FAI council not switched his vote remains one of football's abiding mysteries. Could anyone else have done what Jack was about to do?

Worse than a triumphant neighbour is having a triumphant kid brother. That was the fate of Jack Charlton, who grew up wistful of the admiring glances cast at young Bobby. The talent displayed by 'our kid' was enough to have him sealed and delivered to Old Trafford at a time when Big Jack must have feared ending up back down the mines.

All things are relative, of course. Jack might be no Bobby, but he was a mean enough centre-half to warrant a place with second division Leeds United. He first pulled on the blue and gold of Leeds in the home draw with Doncaster Rovers in April 1953, at a time when Johnny Carey and Tommy Eglington were still pulling on the green jerseys.

Never an aesthetically pleasing player, with sloping shoulders and a craning neck, Jack might have gone the way of scores of other big, hard stoppers. But in 1961 Don Revie was promoted internally by Leeds from player to manager. Revie had big plans, aiming to turn the club into the Real Madrid of English football. He changed Leeds' strip to all-white in imitation of the Spanish giants, and began the policy of nurturing almost familial bonds of loyalty and commitment among players. Once a Leeds man, always a Leeds man, even when that man moved on to pastures new.

Jack Charlton, maverick by temperament, forward with his opinions, did not always see eye to eye with the new broom sweeping through the club. For a while it was touch and go whether he would remain part of the new set-up. It is to the good fortune of the player, the club, the England national side and that of the Republic of Ireland that Charlton stayed put. In the years that followed, and under Revie's tutelage, he transformed from competent stopper to worthy international defender.

The Leeds mud didn't stick to Charlton as much as to Giles, Bremner, and Hunter, though his early forays to the opposition goal-lines at corner-kicks, for the purpose of obstructing the goalkeeper, were widely thought to be against the spirit, if not the letter, of the game.

Leeds were promoted in 1964. A year later they were denied the championship by Manchester United on goal-difference. It was now, when Charlton was pushing thirty, that Alf Ramsey finally took notice of him. Jack's late international beckoning was partly down to his own consistent form, helped by anchoring a strong team, but partly, too, due to good timing. Ramsey was short of top-class stoppers, and Charlton was plucked from a barren field. Maurice Norman had retired, Ron Flowers was essentially understudy to Bobby Moore, and Brian Labone held back till Mexico '70.

All this meant that, in two summers, Charlton swept from second division football to the World Cup Final. No rise could be swifter or more complete. A career that seemed to have run out of steam was now crowned with gold.

Nor was it over. In 1967 Jack was voted Footballer of the Year, and three years later played his part in England's attempts to retain their title. Mexico '70 ended the international careers of both Charlton brothers.

Big Jack played the last of his record 628 league matches for Leeds in 1973. A door in his life had closed. As he himself cheerfully admits, Charlton knows nothing but football, and it was evident he would stay in the game, passing on what he knew, which was much. To prepare for this day he had taken FA coaching qualifications while still young.

Charlton returned to his north-east roots, dipping into the second division with Middlesbrough. His managerial reward was instant and spectacular. Middlesbrough ran away with the second division title by a record fifteen-point margin.

Charlton's success at Ayresome Park assured him of future employment in football. The question was, did he want it? When Middlesbrough did no more than tread water in the top flight he opted to dip into the third with Sheffield Wednesday. In six seasons, though able to climb one division, he was unable to climb two. It was while at Hillsborough that Charlton's link-up with his future Ireland assistant, Maurice Setters, was forged.

Rumours of a return to Leeds, now languishing in the second division, never materialised. After a period out of the game, Jack's final managerial stop took him 'home' to Newcastle United, newly promoted to the top flight.

Managing a football club, whether in high division or low, brings hassle that can drive the toughest skinned men to seek more tranquil environments. Charlton always made clear his disdain of the daily grind of club management. When fans on Tyneside started to make a noisy nuisance of themselves, Charlton walked out. The season was barely under way.

He found solace in his beloved fishing, retaining his high public profile through TV punditry, where his pithy, entertaining and enlightening comments found an appreciative audience. He had for many years been a star turn on the sportsmen's dinner circuit.

Charlton had been angling contentedly for six months when Eoin Hand's position with the FAI became vacant. Some years previously Charlton had famously applied for the England job, and been outspoken in his anger at not receiving even the courtesy of an acknowledgement. From the mere fact that an alien was considered for the Ireland post, it is clear the FAI was prepared to change course, to think big. Northern Ireland's success (and perhaps Denmark's), coupled with the impatience of Irish supporters, compelled the FAI to expand its horizons in ways never previously entertained.

For one thing, Ireland managers up to and including Eoin Hand had been part-time postings. Hand had even kept playing for a few years, for Limerick. In appointing Charlton, this bits-and-pieces philosophy was consigned to the bin. Likewise, the penny-pinching amateurishness, which bedevilled Hand and those before him. The FAI was accustomed to employing just one full-time official, the general secretary. They now appointed a chief executive and launched a money-making commercial section. This administrative shake-up would prove crucial to Charlton's shake-up on the pitch.

Given the choice, Charlton would have preferred his first challenge to be the World Cup rather than the European Championship, with its premium on qualifying places. Scotland, for example, would reach five successive World Cups without once qualifying for any intervening Euro finals.

Charlton's reign started quietly, as all good reigns should. He even lost his first match, a friendly at home to Wales, though as he allowed the team to be picked by others and merely observed from the side-lines, he was quick to dissociate himself from the result.

As it turned out, that match had consequences far beyond what Charlton expected. Welsh goalkeeper Neville Southall fell awkwardly on the uneven surface and broke an ankle. The injury provided Charlton with ammunition with which to berate the rugby authorities about the state of the pitch.

Charlton could not realistically have expected to qualify for Euro '88, not after Ireland's first five matches harvested just five points. But two of these had been at Hampden Park, which raised eyebrows in one or two places.

It is as well Ireland did not take their foot off the gas. By winning their remaining matches – one of which, a squeaky victory over Luxembourg, saw Ireland's players jeered off the pitch – they gave themselves a glimmer of hope. But they needed help from others if they were to make it. Scotland, who could not qualify themselves, owed Jack Charlton no favours. Quite the contrary, he was English, dammit. And it was his Ireland team that had scuppered their own hopes. Gary Mackay evidently hadn't read the script, for his late winner in Sofia caused Bulgarians to clutch their heads and Ireland to scream for the champagne.

'You can never trust the Scots,' said Charlton, afterwards, adding, with a diplomatic touch, 'and I mean that in the nicest possible way.'

The question is hypothetical, but inescapable. Would Ireland have flourished in two World Cups without that kiss from Lady Fortune? This is not to doubt the merits of Ireland's qualification. Their eleven points exceeded their rivals' tally, and established an Irish record. Nevertheless, had Mackay fluffed his shot Ireland would have missed out on Euro '88, missed out on shaming England, missed out on their rapturous homecoming. Not least, they would have missed out on the experience gained and confidence boosted. These were the priceless weapons with which Ireland now assaulted the World Cup. Football managers may manage, but fortune ultimately determines which teams prosper and which ones drown.

One wonders, what would Johnny Giles or Eoin Hand not have given for third-party intervention, à la Mackay, during their own years in charge? On such razor-edges are destinies shaped and histories written. Managers are wont to say that good sides make their own luck, but that applies to what their *own* are doing, not others half a continent away. Jack Charlton was big, he was brave, he was good, but most of all – to a people bountifully superstitious – he enjoyed the rub of the green. He was lucky and, what's more, he stayed lucky. No wonder Ireland loved him.

If Ireland could scale one mountain, there was little reason to think they could not scale another, especially when it was only half as high. Second-place was good enough in World Cup qualifiers, and for that reason Irish ears wagged joyously when the draw was announced.

Spain, Hungary, Malta and Northern Ireland came out of the hat with the Republic. Aside from the nuisance factor attending matches with the North, this was otherwise a welcome assortment of the rich and poor, near and far. The big wigs were undoubtedly Spain. Hungary hadn't asserted themselves for a generation or more, while Malta were there to be trodden on. It might come down to whoever stamped on them hardest. In terms of recent World Cup performance, Spain and Northern Ireland were clearly the front runners.

Qualifying Group 6

NORTHERN IRELAND v IRELAND
Wednesday, 14 September 1988   *Windsor Park, Belfast – 24,000*

Arranging to start by visiting the three toughest teams was a high-risk policy. It was Jack's policy, and he took a mighty gamble. True, in the worst scenario, three defeats could be cancelled out by three home wins. But unless Ireland came back with some reward they were likely to find themselves knocked off the pace, with much leeway to make up.

Opening up in Belfast was especially tricky – notwithstanding the political aspect, which meant that, for security reasons, Jack's Army of fans would be unable to lend their massive support. The Republic had lost, in 1979, on their one previous visit to Windsor Park. Northern Ireland had two World Cup points already stowed away, courtesy of Malta. It didn't take a wise man to realise that Big Jack, while hoping for a win, wished fervently to avoid losing this one, and would, in that hackneyed phrase, set out his stall accordingly.

As for Northern Ireland, they were embarked on a voyage they hoped would lead to their third straight finals. In Billy Bingham they had found exactly the right man to captain the ship. It is no simplification to say that he was to the North what Jack would become to the South. Two towering leaders, inspiring crew of whom some were gifted, others journeymen, but welding the whole into a formidable alloy.

Bingham had been at the helm since 1980 and had enjoyed eight years' unprecedented success. His team had claimed the last British Championship, in 1983-84, winning it outright for the second time in five seasons. In reaching two World Cups, Bingham's teams had played 16 games, scored 14 goals, conceded 8. Less than a goal a game, but he had twice come up trumps. Indeed, eight away fixtures yielded just two goals. These were mean figures, and one did not need to know football's ins and outs to appreciate where Northern Ireland's strength lay.

That the match had 'goalless draw' stamped all over it was little in doubt. What was open to question was whether Bingham's unit was running out of steam. It was certainly running out of manpower. Pat Jennings had gone. So had Jimmy Nicholl, Martin O'Neill and Sammy McIlroy. Of the current team, only Mal Donaghy, Alan McDonald, Nigel Worthington, Steven

Penney, and Colin Clarke had seen action in Mexico. Norman Whiteside would have been added to their number, but he was victim to chronic injury. The newcomers did not look a patch on the old. And Bingham knew it.

Just three of Charlton's players were not inherited from Eoin Hand. Two of these – John Aldridge and Ray Houghton – had shared Charlton's baptism, against Wales. The other, full-back Chris Morris, had slotted into the jigsaw later, but well in time for Euro '88. With Bonner convalescing after surgery on his back, Gerry Peyton stepped confidently into the breach. He had been doing much the same for a dozen years. Charlton's team, in other words, was both experienced and battle-hardened.

Not all Hand's players were to his taste. McDonagh, for example, along with Langan, Robinson, and Tony Grealish, who had bedded the midfield since Giles' retirement. None of these had a future under the new regime. Age had caught up with some, as it had with Frank Stapleton, Ireland's trusty captain. His armband had passed to Kevin Moran, now improving his Spanish with Sporting Gijon.

It was as well that Charlton was spoiled for choice in defence, for he had lost two Liverpool king-pins prematurely. Losing Jim Beglin with a horribly fractured leg was bad enough; to be deprived of Mark Lawrenson, as well, could have driven a lesser manager to reach for the valium. Lawrenson was exactly what Charlton liked in a central defender, someone with vision, plus the ability to anchor midfield when necessary. The only consolation was that, having lost Lawrenson, Charlton could summon McGrath to do the same job.

The match was no prettier in fact than in prospect, two bruising teams, the ball nailed to the sky, a diet of crunching tackles. Yet Ireland so nearly snatched a third-minute lead. Alan McKnight, in Northern Ireland's goal, had made his league debut for West Ham on the Saturday, recording a shut-out against Wimbledon. Now he clung on to a Cascarino header that flew off a post along the goal-line. The goalkeeper was clearly behind the line, the ball not quite, though Aldridge turned away, arms raised in premature glee.

McKnight's next feat was to save with his legs as Cascarino burst into the box. Come the second half, the keeper experienced the pleasure of saving from Houghton, the alarm of seeing the same player dragging the rebound wide, and the relief of seeing O'Neill block Houghton's second attempt.

Lest the impression be given that the game was one-sided, headers from Jimmy Quinn and Colin Clarke threatened Peyton's goal. By the final whistle McDonald had been booked for the North, Whelan for the South, and the corner count was: Northern Ireland 3; the Republic 9.

'A sloppy game,' sighed the *Irish Independent,* who adjudged McKnight man of the match, and Kingsley Black and Steven Penney the duffers.

'I am happy with the result, but if we had taken our chances we would have won it,' said Jack Charlton, articulating the thoughts of everyone.

NORTHERN IRELAND   (0) 0   IRELAND   (0) 0

N IRELAND: McKnight (WEST HAM), Donaghy (LUTON) (*sub* Rogan, CELTIC), McClelland (WATFORD), McDonald (QPR), Worthington (SHEFF W), Penney (BRIGHTON), Wilson (LUTON), O'Neill (NEWCASTLE), Black (LUTON), Quinn (LEICESTER), Clarke (SOUTHAMPTON).

IRELAND: Peyton (BOURNEMOUTH), Morris (CELTIC), McCarthy (CELTIC), Moran (SPORTING GIJON), Hughton (SPURS), Houghton (LIVERPOOL), McGrath (MAN U), Whelan (LIVERPOOL), Sheedy (EVERTON), Aldridge (LIVERPOOL), Cascarino (MILLWALL).

SPAIN v IRELAND
Wednesday, 16 November 1988   Benito Villamarín Stadium, Seville – 50,000

Spain were one of those countries owing Ireland a debt or two, not least for agreeing to stage a World Cup play-off in Paris in 1965, and for Ireland's win in Prague two years later that sent Spain sailing through to Euro '68.

Though Spain's World Cup path had crossed Ireland's only once, they had provided frequent opposition in the European Championship. Ireland's was a sorry record, no wins, two draws, four defeats. Overall, in fifteen matches since 1948, Ireland had won just once, through Iribar's own-goal in 1965.

Spain were still not in the habit of setting the World Cup alight. Since we last encountered them, they had failed to qualify in 1970 and '74 and been sent home after the group phase in 1978. Even with home advantage in 1982 they achieved just one win in five (losing memorably to Northern Ireland). Spain had saved their best for Mexico '86, taking revenge on Northern Ireland (2-1) and advancing to the last eight, where they were put out in a penalty shoot-out by Belgium.

Spain had done better in the Euros, taking gold in 1964, silver in 1984, but it was her club sides that kept the flag flying. Real Madrid and Barcelona still regularly contested European finals.

As with Italy, Spain's better players see no incentive to migrate. The Spanish league is big enough and strong enough to accommodate native and foreign talent. The present national side, like most of its predecessors, was home based and extracted from the usual select clubs. Barcelona provided two players – including the capable goalkeeper, Zubizarreta – and Real Madrid four, among them the captain, Emilio Butragueno, the quicksilver striker who had been the scourge of goalkeepers for as long as most people could remember. In Mexico '86 Butragueno, with five, had been second top scorer to Gary Lineker, with six.

Ireland had squeezed in a friendly since drawing in Belfast, a testimonial for long-serving FAI general secretary Peadar O'Driscoll. Tunisia were offered as sacrificial lambs, beaten 4-0 in a match that introduced Steve Staunton to international ways and John Aldridge into the ways of international goalscoring. It was his twentieth match, and after 1,738 minutes of endeavour he tapped in from three yards. Never could a goal have tasted sweeter.

In keeping with their custom of spreading home internationals around, the Spanish FA selected Seville as the venue, not the Sánchez Pizjuán Stadium, where Spain had vanquished Ireland in 1965, but the city's other, Benito Villamarín arena. It was there that Brazil had flayed Scotland 4-1 in 1982.

Charlton's squad was decimated by injuries, especially his midfield, where Sheedy, Whelan, and McGrath were all on the treatment table, and Brady was playing on borrowed time. Charlton kept faith with young Staunton, restored Pat Bonner to goal, and Tony Galvin to add width, and summoned John Sheridan for his first World Cup action. Moran was pushed into midfield, to the displeasure of McCarthy, who felt more at ease with Moran alongside him. The injury crisis prompted a surprise recall for David O'Leary, out in the international wilderness for two years.

It took Staunton just fifty-six seconds to earn his corn, clearing Manolo's header off the line. The effort was to typify the action, which was so one-way as to detach Aldridge and Cascarino from the play. Ireland lacked cohesion, and it showed.

On the evidence of the first half, a draw would be a famous result. Seven minutes into the second half, debut-boy Manuel Manolo scored from Martin Vazquez's pass. Bonner parried Manolo's first effort but was powerless with the second. A second Manolo 'goal' was annulled for offside, but Spain did not have to wait long to seal the points. Quique beat Staunton to the ball, crossed, and Butragueno treated his fans to one of his famous volleys.

Ireland had few chances – the best being Quinn's header that was cleared for a corner – and fewer complaints. Johnny Giles, writing in the Dublin *Evening Herald*, awarded just four marks out of ten to Houghton, Aldridge and Cascarino.

'Outclassed! Spanish sparkle in Benito cauldron,' screamed the *Irish Press*.

'It could have been 4-0 or 5-0,' confessed McCarthy.

'I can't see anyone taking a point from them here,' said Jack.

SPAIN (0) 2   IRELAND (0) 0
Manolo 52, Butragueno 65

SPAIN: Zubizarreta, Quique (Solana), Gorriz, Sanchis, Andrinua, Jiminez, Michel, Roberto, Martin Vazquez, Butragueno, Manolo (Ramon).
IRELAND: Bonner (CELTIC), Morris (CELTIC), McCarthy (CELTIC), O'Leary (ARSENAL), Staunton (LIVERP'L) (*sub* O'Brien, NEWCASTLE), Houghton (LIVERPOOL), Moran (SPORTING GIJON), Sheridan (LEEDS), Galvin (SHEFF W), Cascarino (MILLWALL), Aldridge (LIVERPOOL) (*sub* Quinn, ARSENAL).

HUNGARY v IRELAND
Wednesday, 8 March 1989   *Nep Stadium, Budapest – 33,966*

Not for twenty years had Ireland exchanged hellos with Hungary. The two nations had faced each other regularly in the 1930s. This was followed by a thirty-year lull before Hungary did the double in the 1970 qualifiers. Ireland were still looking for their first win.

Hungary had reached all finals from 1978 onwards, but in each case failed to survive the group phase. Goalkeeper Laszlo Disztl, defenders Zoltan Bognár and Ervin Kovács, forward players Lajos Détári and Joszef Kiprich were all veterans of Mexico '86.

But Hungarian football had been shamed by allegations of match-rigging, which had eaten into the very core of the national side. They had changed their manager yet again, and half a dozen players had been banned.

Group 6 was shaping up nicely. Northern Ireland had lost twice to Spain and once to Hungary. Those reverses seemed to put Bingham's boys out of contention, leaving Hungary as the Republic's main rivals in pursuit of Spain. But Hungary had themselves amazingly dropped a point in Malta.

Needing to keep his players on their toes, Charlton had arranged a home friendly with France. Though the match was dull and goalless, it provided Andy Townsend with a first cap. Townsend might have been required in Budapest, except for the return to fitness of McGrath, Whelan, and Sheedy.

Hungary showed most of the skills, yet paradoxically Ireland did most of the attacking in a cold and windy Nep Stadium. Hungary's one-touch football and lightning break-outs threatened more than once to carve open the Irish defence. Bonner saved one shot with his legs, and later raced out of his box to clear. But most of the game's few goalmouth incidents were at the Hungarian end. The most spectacular effort belonged to McGrath, but his bicycle kick was comfortably tipped over.

Hungary saw more of the ball in the second half. Kiprich shot wide when clean through, and Kovacs headed over. Towards the end the match appeared to fizzle out, neither side wanting to lose what they had.

Ireland's territorial dominance was reflected in the number of corner-kicks – 6-0 in their favour.

'Hungary had the skills, but at times you would have thought Ireland was the home side,' opined Kevin Moran.

'You've got to say it was a terrific result for us. Yet in the dressing room the general feeling was that the players were disappointed not to have cinched it,' added John Aldridge.

'I am nit-picking if I try to find fault with that performance' – Big Jack.

HUNGARY (0) 0   **IRELAND (0) 0**

HUNGARY: P Disztl, Kozma, Bognár, L Disztl, Kovács, Sass, Gregor (Boda), Détári, Hajszan, Mészáros (Bognár), Kiprich.
IRELAND: Bonner (CELTIC), Morris (CELTIC), McCarthy (CELTIC), Moran (GIJON), Hughton (SPURS), Houghton (LIVERPOOL), McGrath (MAN U), Whelan (LIVERPOOL), Sheedy (EVERTON), Cascarino (MILLWALL) (*sub* Quinn, ARSENAL), Aldridge (LIVERPOOL) (*sub* Brady, WEST HAM).

IRELAND v SPAIN
Wednesday, 26 April 1989   *Lansdowne Road – 49,600*

Hungary would rue their complacency. The following month they would drop yet another point to Malta, and thunder clouds were mounting. By late April the table read – Spain played 5, points 10; Hungary 4-5; N Ireland 5-3; Ireland 3-2; Malta 5-2. Spain appeared to be over the horizon, but Hungary had run out of easy games, and still had to travel to Spain and both Irelands.

This was the moment of truth for Charlton. His team had yet to score in the campaign, but no way could they gloss over failure to do so now.

Although Charlton had just one physical injury to consider – Chris Morris recuperating from surgery – the recent Hillsborough tragedy had inflicted deep psychological scars. The Ireland side was crammed with Liverpool players. Of these, John Aldridge appeared so stunned by the disaster that he briefly contemplated retirement. Charlton granted him compassionate leave, allowing Frank Stapleton to take over. Houghton, Staunton, and Whelan all did their best to put on a brave face. In a separate move, Charlton switched the captaincy from Moran to McCarthy.

An enormous crowd was held in check by unprecedented safety measures. They roared their support as, on a heavy pitch, Ireland set about breaking Charlton's World Cup duck. Ireland employed pressure tactics to the ultimate degree, bombarding the Spanish goalmouth with lobs, punts, crosses, anything to get the ball where it hurts as often as possible, and to knock the opposition out of their pretty stride.

Bookmakers would have given long odds against Spain losing consecutive World Cup-ties in Dublin by the same score, 0-1, and to an own-goal. But that is precisely what happened. In 1965, it was the goalkeeper who fluffed: this time it was Michel. Houghton's cross was touched on by Whelan to Stapleton. Michel got there first, and the deflection deceived Zubizarreta.

An early strike by the home side often stirs up a rich cocktail, as opponents are obliged to venture forth. As might be expected, no quarter was asked, or given. On forty-one minutes McCarthy was booked for a dreadful foul on Manolo (the thirteenth to be committed on a Spanish player) which, were it committed today, would surely have merited a red card rather than yellow. Michel touched the free-kick to Martin Vazquez, whose low drive was blocked for a corner by Bonner. This was some achievement by Spain: it

Michel diverts the ball past keeper Zubizarreta to give Ireland a vital win.

amounted to their only shot on target during the whole match. On the half-time whistle Houghton's 'goal' was ruled offside.

Spain upped the tempo after the break. Manolo wriggled past Moran but forgot where the target was. Midway through the half Charlton buttressed his midfield by sending on Andy Townsend. Ireland were now playing 4-5-1, a formation Charlton would return to in times to come.

Ireland continued to fashion chances, and finished on the up. Sheedy's header was saved, and a McGrath 'goal' annulled for Cascarino's push.

Spain had dropped their first points of the campaign, and few would deny Ireland's right to them. Although Spain outscored Ireland on corners 9-2, Ireland managed seven goal-attempts on target to Spain's one.

The *Irish Independent* had no doubt as to who was the architect of victory. Ray Houghton received top marks, ten out of ten.

On the same day Northern Ireland won 2-0 in Malta. Two weeks later Zubizarreta and his Barcelona team-mates were smiling again. The Catalan club lifted the European Cup-Winners' Cup.

IRELAND (1) 1   **SPAIN   (0) 0**
Michel 15 (o.g.)

IRELAND: Bonner (CELTIC), Hughton (SPURS), McCarthy (CELTIC), Moran (SPORTING GIJON), Staunton (LIVERPOOL), Houghton (LIVERPOOL), McGrath (MAN U), Whelan (LIVERPOOL), Sheedy (EVERTON), Stapleton (LE HAVRE) (*sub* Townsend, NORWICH), Cascarino (MILLWALL).
SPAIN: Zubizarreta, Quique (Eusebio), Gorriz, Sanchis, Serna, Jiminez, Michel, Roberto, Martin Vazquez, Manolo, Butragueno (Salinas).

IRELAND v MALTA
Sunday, 28 May 1989   *Lansdowne Road – 48,928*

Victory over Spain had been of incalculable importance. With the domestic season over, Ireland now geared themselves for the back-to-back visits of Malta and Hungary.

It says much for the enthusiasm generated by Jack Charlton and the lads that Lansdowne Road could command nearly 49,000 spectators for the visit of a team like Malta. Six years previously Ireland had run up their record win, 8-0, against these very opponents.

What pleasure the Maltese derived from seeing their team regularly butchered must lie in the recesses of masochism. Malta had first dipped their toes into the World Cup in 1970, and their record since then showed no wins, one draw, and twenty-three defeats. Rather, that was their record prior to the present campaign, since when they had trebled their points tally through two draws with Hungary. The Hungarians must be smarting.

Those two draws were both a godsend and a warning. While pulling the rug from under Hungary's feet, they underlined Malta's capacity to cause upsets. Their German manager, Horst Heese, had made the players more professional in outlook, and results over the past year or two had improved.

Charlton would have to do without McCarthy (knee) and Sheridan (hamstring), and trust that his four-man Liverpool contingent could cope with having to play four matches in nine days. Their third, a championship decider at Anfield, had seen Arsenal snatch a dramatic injury-time winner.

From the first whistle Ireland saw more of the ball than was decent, and flowed towards the Maltese goal as if the pitch was tilted towards it. Indeed, the most intimidating thing about the visitors was the sight of the Maltese cross stamped large across their red shirts.

For all their gravitational pressure, Ireland seldom created much, and when thirty minutes had elapsed without a goal, everyone grew edgy. Cascarino was the player with most shots and most misses. Cluett saved one, one went wide, another over. Ireland weren't helped by losing Stapleton's battering ram. Hurt during an attack, he had to be replaced by Aldridge. Malta defended their goal so desperately that three players were booked in the first half, among them their goalkeeper.

It was Ray Houghton who made the breakthrough. Moran's high ball,

Cascarino's knock down, Houghton's firm shot.

Ireland's first corner of the second half fashioned their second goal. Everybody seemed to have been picked up at Sheedy's corner, but decoy runs by others enabled Kevin Moran a clear header.

Not for Malta the kamikaze tactics of seeking to rescue the match. If anything, they summoned even more defenders back. The days of Maltese thrashings were past. When the dust had settled on Group 6 they would have conceded barely two goals a game, and only once more than three.

The frustration was too much for Ronnie Whelan, booked a second time (following that in Belfast) and out of the match against Hungary.

Only in the final ten minutes, when Malta were reassured that they were not going to be dished to the crows, did they venture out of their cocoon. Carmel Busuttil had the nerve to try to score from the touchline. He won a corner, from which John Buttigieg, of English club Brentford, fired wide.

Tony Cascarino did not score, but he was announced Opel (Ireland's sponsors) man of the match. The crowd went away muttering. Ireland hadn't dominated Malta like they'd hoped.

IRELAND   (1) 2   **MALTA   (0) 0**
Houghton 32, Moran 54

IRELAND: Bonner (CELTIC), Hughton (SPURS), O'Leary (ARSENAL), Moran (GIJON), Staunton (LIVERP'L), Houghton (LIVRP'L) (*sub* Townsend, NORWICH), McGrath (MAN U), Whelan (LIVERP'L), Sheedy (EVERTON), Stapleton (LE HAVRE) (*sub* Aldridge, LIVERPOOL), Cascarino (MILLWALL).
MALTA: Cluett, Galea, Buttigieg, S Vella, Azzopardi (Carabott), Camilleri, Gregory, Busuttil, R Vella, Degiorgio, Scerri.

IRELAND v HUNGARY
Sunday, 4 June 1989   *Lansdowne Road – 49,600*

Ireland showed five points from five games, and were banking on a strong finish to carry them though, as it had in Euro '88.

For both Ireland and Hungary this match was tantamount to a cup final. Ireland had their noses in front. Barring improbable results elsewhere, only Hungary stood between them and their first World Cup. But history weighed heavily against the Irish, in the shape of ten failed attempts to beat Hungary. Aldridge for Cascarino was Charlton's only change.

For the second successive Sunday, Lansdowne Road crackled with the nervous energy of almost 50,000 expectant fans. Both sides set off at a rush, searching for a quick goal. Hungary came closest to finding it when Laszlo Disztl's effort was wonderfully stopped by Bonner. The other Disztl, goalkeeper Peter, saved with his legs to deny Houghton. Aldridge threatened twice before Ireland took a merited lead, just after the half-hour. Fitos headed out Staunton's cross, but only to McGrath lurking on the eighteen yard line. His sweet volley was unstoppable.

Moran nearly increased the lead early in the second half, but Disztl saved on the line. Once again Charlton dabbled with 4-5-1, taking off Aldridge and bringing on the forgotten man of Irish football, Liam Brady. Imre Garaba – veteran of Spain '82 – responded with a ferocious, long-range drive which Bonner, who saw it late, fingertipped against a post.

Morris took over from the limping McGrath, and Ireland scored again. With Hungary camped upfield, Houghton dispossessed Garaba with what some considered to be a push. He burrowed along the by-line and his cross was deflected by Laszlo Disztl over the head of his goalkeeper brother. Cascarino had the easiest of jobs to head home, but was almost decapitated by a defender's boot in the process.

Everyone concurred that Bonner's saves, especially that from Garaba, had won the day, but the man-of-the-match award went to Andy Townsend.

Ireland got drunk and partied till dawn.

IRELAND (1) 2   **HUNGARY   (0) 0**
McGrath 33, Cascarino 80

IRELAND: Bonner (CELTIC), Hughton (SPURS), O'Leary (ARSENAL), Moran (GIJON), Staunton (LIVERPOOL), Houghton (LIVERPOOL), McGrath (MAN U) (*sub* Morris, CELTIC), Townsend (NORWICH), Sheedy (EVERTON), Aldridge (LIVERPOOL) (*sub* Brady, W HAM), Cascarino (MILLWALL). HUNGARY: P Disztl, Kozma, Bognár, L Disztl, Garaba, Keller, Détári, Fitos, Csehi (Bognár), Mészáros (Vincze), Boda.

IRELAND v NORTHERN IRELAND
Wednesday, 11 October 1989   *Lansdowne Road – 46,800*

Football hibernated for the summer, leaving Ireland with one foot and three toes over the line to Italy. The table read – Spain played 6, points 10; Ireland 6-8; Hungary 5-5; N Ireland 6-5, Malta 7-2.

Having no qualifier in September, Ireland fixed up a gentle friendly with West Germany, which finished 1-1 before another huge Lansdowne crowd.

That same day Northern Ireland lost at home to Hungary. Bingham's boys were now out of the running. Hungary could still amass eleven points, but to do so they would have to beat Spain twice. But if they did, Spain would stay on ten points themselves. Eleven was therefore the target to aim for. Three more points was all Ireland needed. They could even afford to draw with Northern Ireland, provided they won in Malta. But no one wanted to drag it out that long.

Tony Cascarino leads the conga after he puts Ireland 2-0 up against Northern Ireland.

It was a shame Northern Ireland hadn't beaten Hungary, not only because of brotherly goodwill, but because both Irelands would then have gone at each other hammer and tongs. They still would, of course, but Northern Ireland could no longer help themselves, only hurt others, and that undermined the balance of the contest.

So did the fact that Bingham was inevitably looking to the future. His line-up was not necessarily that which he would have chosen had he been chasing points. George Dunlop of Linfield would play in goal, having spent three years in the international wilderness. Norman Whiteside, a teenage sensation in Spain '82, now pulled on a Northern Ireland shirt for the last time. Injury would force him out of football, a has-been in his mid-twenties.

John Aldridge had joined Kevin Moran in signing for a Spanish club, in his case Real Sociedad, and although both played at the weekend they came through. Moran was nursing his back, but, typically, would play through the pain. Mick McCarthy, restored as captain, was also on his travels, with French club Olympique Lyon. David O'Leary dropped down to accommodate him. McGrath was in the squad, but he wasn't fit.

This was as big a game as the Republic had ever known. The economy was under threat if, as some feared, the whole nation became 'non-runners', absconding from work to watch the action on television.

Though both teams were equally hyped up, the Ulstermen were first out of the traps. It took Whiteside less than two minutes to be yellow-carded for a crude lunge at Houghton. Midway through the first half Michael O'Neill lost McCarthy, but Bonner beat out his shot. McCarthy cleared up the pieces. Within seconds Ireland's captain charged to the rescue a second time. Bonner had flapped at O'Neill's cross and presented Robbie Dennison with a fleeting chance that he was not quick enough to exploit.

The let-off was vital. Even a transitional Northern Ireland team knew all about protecting leads. 0-1 at that stage could have been it.

The Republic had accomplished little, and on the balance of play it was more than they deserved when they scored. Staunton's cross, Dunlop's punch, Whelan's low shot through a phalanx of legs, including the keeper's. Dunlop had strayed too far from his line.

Despite the goal, Charlton roasted his players at half-time. His words sunk in, and two minutes after the changearound the contest was effectively settled. Dennison was still cursing the team-mate who deflected his shot over Bonner's crossbar, when Ireland were awarded a corner-kick at the other end. It wasn't properly cleared. Sheedy flicked the ball back in, and Cascarino leapt in front of Fleming to leave Dunlop helpless.

Everything was happening too fast to take in. A bewitching Irish move from one end to the other deserved a goal, but ended with Aldridge heading wide. His next header, from Sheedy's corner, bruised an upright.

Houghton capped the Republic's onslaught with a dazzling third goal. Sheedy set him up, Houghton skirted Mal Donaghy and fired into the corner.

Thereafter it was back to the John Aldridge catalogue of misses. A couple of hat-tricks went a-begging, but he was man enough to take it on the chin. It was all in good cause, and what the hell, Ireland had won.

The physical nature of the contest saw Nigel Worthington join Whiteside in the referee's book, along with Chris Morris and the luckless Aldridge.

There were any number of heroes on the pitch and any number of men of the match. Pick of the votes went to Ray Houghton.

IRELAND (1) 3   **NORTHERN IRELAND (0) 0**
Whelan 42, Cascarino 47,
Houghton 56

IRELAND: Bonner (CELTIC), Morris (CELTIC), McCarthy (OLYMPIQUE LYON), Moran (GIJON), Staunton (LIVERPOOL) (*sub* O'Leary, ARSENAL), Houghton (LIVERPOOL), Whelan (LIVERPOOL), Townsend (NORWICH), Sheedy (EVERTON), Aldridge (REAL SOCIEDAD), Cascarino (MILLWALL).
N IRELAND: Dunlop (LINFIELD), Fleming (MAN C), McDonald (QPR), Donaghy (MAN U), Worthington (SHEFF W), D Wilson (LUTON), McCreery (HEARTS) (*sub* C O'Neill, MOTHERWELL), Whiteside (EVERTON), M O'Neill (DUN U) (*sub* K Wilson CHEL), Clarke (QPR), Dennison (WOLVES).

MALTA v IRELAND
Wednesday, 15 November 1989   *Ta'Qali Stadium, Valetta – 25,000*

While all Ireland stopped still for ninety minutes to examine its navel, a topsy turvy match later that day in Budapest saw Hungary snatch a late leveller. If only Spain had held on, Ireland would have qualified and Dublin would have thrown a party like no other. Now they had to wait five endless weeks to guarantee their place by taking a point in Malta. In all probability they wouldn't need it. Hungary were two points behind, with a vastly inferior goal-difference, and had to try to make up the points and the deficit in Seville of all places. But football always likes to throw up the unexpected.

As D-Day loomed Ireland almost found themselves managerless. Charlton had found himself compromised by a sponsorship wrangle that threatened briefly to detach him from his players. Mercifully, it all blew over, and the squad flew out with Moran clutching his Irish Player of the Year award.

Come the day, McCarthy was injured and Charlton reshuffled his defence, O'Leary returning, McGrath switching to right-back in place of Morris, Whelan borrowing the captain's armband.

Malta were handicapped by the suspension of two of their better players, David Cluett, in goal, and Raymond Vella.

Some 6,000 Irish supporters escaped the Dublin fog to descend upon the unsuspecting Mediterranean island, bringing their own special brand of good cheer and their own unique tales of how they got there.

The soothsayers among them were probably hoping to recoup their outlay by predicting the time of the first goal. Ireland had made a recent habit of going ahead in the quarter-hour before half-time. Right on cue they extended their sequence. Houghton's corner, O'Leary's back flick, Aldridge's far post header. After three years, Aldridge had broken his competitive duck. Twenty-eight caps, and now *two* goals.

Malta had few chances to hit back, fewer once Townsend had his legs whipped from under him in the second half by David Carabott, and Aldridge smote the penalty past Cini. If Ireland were on cloud nine, what number must Aldridge have been on?

Not that it mattered any more, but Spain were happily battering Hungary into submission. Spain couldn't afford to take it easy. Seeding for the finals might take heed of group positions, and Spain wanted top spot.

Long before the final whistle Ireland knew they'd done it. It had taken thirteen attempts, but – lucky thirteen – Ireland were set for the World Cup.

MALTA   (0) 0   **IRELAND   (1) 2**
                                     Aldridge 30, 67 pen

MALTA: Cini, Vella, Buttigieg, Galea, Assopardi (Suda), Zerefa (Zarb), Scerri, Degiorgio, Gregory, Carabott, Busuttil.
IRELAND: Bonner (CELTIC), McGrath (VILLA), O'Leary (ARSENAL), Moran (SPORTING GIJON) (*sub* Morris, CELTIC), Staunton (LIVERPOOL), Houghton (LIVERPOOL), Whelan (LIVERPOOL), Townsend (NORWICH), Sheedy (EVERTON), Aldridge (REAL SOCIEDAD), Cascarino (MILLWALL).

Qualifying Group 6

| | | | Home | | | | Away | | | | |
	P	W	D	L	F	A	W	D	L	F	A	Pts
SPAIN	8	4	0	0	14	0	2	1	1	6	3	13
IRELAND	8	4	0	0	8	0	1	2	1	2	2	12
Hungary	8	1	3	0	4	3	1	1	2	4	9	8
Northern Ireland	8	1	1	2	4	4	1	0	3	2	8	5
Malta	8	0	1	3	2	8	0	1	3	1	10	2

Other group results

N Ireland v Malta	3-0	Spain v Malta	4-0
Hungary v N Ireland	1-0	Hungary v Malta	1-1
Malta v Hungary	2-2	Malta v N Ireland	0-2
Spain v N Ireland	4-0	N Ireland v Hungary	1-2
Malta v Spain	0-2	Hungary v Spain	2-2
N Ireland v Spain	0-2	Spain v Hungary	4-0

World Cup finals – ITALY   **June-July 1990**

Even if Jack Charlton had quit there and then, he would have achieved what no other Ireland manager had. Johnny Giles had performed half the trick, and turned Lansdowne Road into a fortress, but he hadn't found any magic spell to prevent Ireland crumbling on opponents' grounds.

Charlton had done just that. One of Europe's most travel-shy teams was now one of its most feared. In eight away qualifiers – in Euro '88 and World Cup '90 – Ireland had lost just twice and kept five clean sheets. That, in a nutshell, was the measure of Charlton's achievement. Nothing breathes confidence into the lungs of footballers so much as the knowledge that their arrival in some far off city is greeted with fear.

If the chests of Ireland's footballers were thrust out just that little bit more, who could blame them? They were the first of their countrymen ever to be accorded such respect. It was a new feeling, and a mighty pleasant one. If Ireland had qualified for Euro '88 by a coat of paint, this time they had the luxury of an oceanic four-point margin. There could be no talk of fluke this time. Ireland deserved to be in Italy, and none could, or dared, dispute it.

Victory in Valetta ignited a surge of joy that – hard-line unionists aside – convulsed the Irish nation. As a bonus, the finals were scheduled not for some far off field in some far off continent, but in warm, hospitable, nearby Italy. When the time came, Ireland might find herself severely depopulated, as thousands upon thousands of fans decamped for the Mediterranean, tickets in hand and hope in their hearts. It was, cracked one wag, a good time for English bachelors to nip over to Dublin in search of a Molly Malone.

Much of Ireland tuned in for the World Cup draw, staged in December 1989, and debased by irrelevant contributions from Sofia Loren and Luciano Pavarotti. The twenty-four qualifying nations would be divided by the organisers into four tiers, with six in each. The likes of Costa Rica and the United States found themselves among the bottom, fourth seeds. Italy, West Germany, Argentina, Brazil, Belgium, and England were creamed off into the top tier. Ireland were listed among the third rank. No shame in that. After all, in 1986 Denmark had been dumped in the fourth! Nations competing in their first finals couldn't expect star billing. What it all meant in practice was that Ireland would be grouped with two tigers and one rabbit.

It is curious how chance sometimes conspires with collusion. With Ireland having faced England and Holland in Euro '88, FIFA's lottery now threw up the same two opponents, with England once again the aperitif and Holland the dessert. The only change was the main course. In the Euros, that had been the Soviet Union. Now, Ireland would take on Egypt, surely a gentler foe.

In the European Championship, the top two progressed to the next round. In the World Cup, four third-placed teams would also survive. This practice had first been introduced in Mexico '86, when – as it turned out – all teams with three points had gone through, and even some with two.

Charlton's boys had earned three points, unavailingly, in Germany. Their immediate task now was to dredge up the same number. If all went well, two would be plucked from Egypt, which left just one to be secured from either the English or the Dutch.

England would be seeded, dubiously, on account of reaching the quarter-finals in 1986. So had Spain, but her claim was overturned on grounds of security. England's hooligan following needed to be caged up somewhere. Seeded nations had their venues settled in advance, and arrangements behind the scenes determined that England's group would be quarantined to the Mediterranean islands of Sardinia and Sicily. England would play her matches in Sardinia; her opponents, the remainder of theirs in Sicily.

The substitution of the Soviets by the Pharaohs, and the life-saver thrown to teams finishing third, meant the draw was kinder than in the Euros. For these reasons, it might have brought a smile to Jack's face. It did not.

Bloody hell! he exploded. For reasons not all to do with football, he viewed the draw as catastrophic. Variety is the spice of life. No one wanted to play England *and* Holland again. The Dutch were European champions, while England were less likely to be caught out a second time. Added to which, the Mediterranean venues were too hot (for players), too far and too expensive (for supporters), and – in view of the lunatic fringe coat-tailing the Dutch and English – too scary (for everyone). With Holland's thugs enjoying a reputation scarcely less malign than England's, the wretched citizens of Cagliari and Palermo were advised to bolt their doors.

The six months between Valetta and Cagliari must have seemed a lifetime as Ireland's manager, players, and supporters planned and prayed for the trials ahead. Would Ireland sink or soar, or even, as Ally MacLeod once infamously predicted for Scotland, go all the way?

Charlton used the time to prepare and select his squad of twenty-two. Its composition did not attract endless speculation, for there was no bottomless pool from which to choose. One of Ireland's strengths was its finite reservoir of talent. Besides, Charlton was not one to reach out and grab unknowns who had not previously done the business under his critical eye.

Seeking to unnerve opponents with Ireland's unbeaten record, it made sense for Charlton to keep his powder dry. He didn't want his side losing matches, and credibility, by inviting top-drawer opponents for warm-ups. Wales were overcome 1-0 in Dublin, an under-strength Soviet Union – in what should have been Ireland's one serious test – likewise.

Ireland did, however, need a late leveller at home to Finland to preserve their unbeaten record. A goalless, thrill-less draw in Turkey could have taught Charlton little he did not already know. Ireland's final-warm up, in Malta, where the squad were acclimatising, was presumed by Charlton to be little more than a semi-serious kickabout. The FAI had to remind him that caps would be awarded. Ireland did not trip up, winning 3-0. Chris Hughton won his fiftieth cap, Alan McLoughlin his first, and Frank Stapleton notched his record twentieth Ireland goal. His international career had extended over fourteen years, but, as with Brady, the World Cup came four years too late for Stapleton. He would not see action in Italy.

Following the match with Malta, Charlton confirmed his twenty-two:

No	Name	Position	Club	Age	Caps	Goals
1	Pat Bonner	Goalkeeper	Celtic	30	38	–
2	Chris Morris	Full-back	Celtic	26	21	–
3	Steve Staunton	Full-back	Liverpool	21	13	1
4	Mick McCarthy (c)	Central defence	Millwall	31	42	1
5	Kevin Moran	Central defence	Blackburn	34	50	6
6	Ronnie Whelan	Midfield	Liverpool	28	38	3
7	Paul McGrath	Central defence	Aston Villa	30	36	4
8	Ray Houghton	Midfield	Liverpool	28	29	3
9	John Aldridge	Forward	Real Sociedad	31	30	3

10	Tony Cascarino	Forward	Aston Villa	27	21	5
11	Kevin Sheedy	Midfield	Everton	30	28	5
12	David O'Leary	Central defence	Arsenal	32	51	–
13	Andy Townsend	Midfield	Norwich	26	12	1
14	Chris Hughton	Full-back	Tottenham	31	50	1
15	Bernie Slaven	Midfield	Middlesbrough	29	4	1
16	John Sheridan	Midfield	Sheffield Wed	25	8	1
17	Niall Quinn	Forward	Manchester C	23	15	2
18	Frank Stapleton	Forward	Blackburn	33	71	20
19	David Kelly	Forward	Leicester	24	6	4
20	John Byrne	Forward	Le Havre	29	19	1
21	Alan McLoughlin	Midfield	Swindon	23	1	–
22	Gerry Peyton	Goalkeeper	Bournemouth	34	28	–
			Averages	*28.4*	*27.2*	

Most squads had three goalkeepers. Ireland's was restricted to two.

Charlton allocated his ideal first team with shirts 1-11. Nineteen of the squad were retained from the European Championship. They had not been spring chickens then – now, with an average age of 28½, and ten players in their thirties, Ireland's would be the oldest squad in Italy.

They would also, to listen to some critics, be the most cosmopolitan, or, to put it less charitably, the most mercenary. Human nature being what it is, there are always those wanting to criticise, and to see fault where others find praise. Debate over Jack Charlton's tactics was one expression of that criticism, a legitimate one; questioning the elastic nationality credentials of certain players, quite another, and one that sorely touches Irish sensibilities.

'I own an Irish wolfhound, please can I play for Ireland?' Jibes of that kind are sure to get up Irish noses, as do suggestions that London accents outnumber Dublin ones among the players.

The question of who is and who is not eligible to play for Ireland has always excited opinion. Back in the last century, protests accompanied the selection of players who, though Irish through and through, dared to earn their shilling in England.

Judging from the way 'granny passport' players are clutched to present-day Irish bosoms, opinion has turned turtle, and those former critics would receive scant sympathy today. Long before the arrival of Jack Charlton, the FAI (mischievously dubbed in some quarters 'Find An Irishman') were happily picking players with ever looser Irish connections.

In this, they were at one with moves within FIFA. In the early 1960s, football's governing body enabled players to switch allegiance, permitting them to play for countries in which they were commonly resident, as opposed to those in which they were born.

This ruling, for example, permitted Ferenc Puskás to play for his native Hungary in the 1954 World Cup and for his adopted Spain in 1962.

Such legislation could, if unchecked, pave the way for absurd abuses. Faced with protests from the international football fraternity, FIFA rewrote the rule-book. Thereafter, players could play in official competition for one country only, and once the decision was taken it was irrevocable. Even to pull on a youth-team international shirt in a competitive match would cement that player to that country for ever more.

In the British context, this led to a number of hasty, and later (privately) regretted decisions by young players in a rush to play international football. They might be born in England, for example, of Scottish father and Welsh mother. In which case, the player may in theory choose to represent any one of three countries. Multi-eligibility, in other words, is at the heart of the problem, and it affects 'British' players more than any other.

The fact that England is by far the most populous British nation means, inevitably, that selection for the English national side is that much harder to attain. For that reason, many a player has pledged himself elsewhere when – with a bit of patience and a lot of skill – the England summons might have arrived. These are just facts of footballing life, and the reader knows the names of those involved without being told.

From time to time anomalies occur. Pat van den Hauwe, of Belgian father and English mother, suddenly found himself playing for Wales. Scotland's lamentable failure over the years to find goalkeepers up to English standard, encouraged them to pluck goalies from down south – Bob Wilson of Arsenal, David Harvey of Leeds. Both players were as 'English' as Jack Charlton, except for the coincidence of having a parent born north of Hadrian's Wall. Bruce Rioch, another outwardly 'English' player, rose (or, rather, had the misfortune) to captain Scotland in the 1978 World Cup.

Critics of the FAI's policy – and they are not wholly to be found outside Ireland – note that cases of 'adoption' by England, Scotland, and Wales are comparatively rare and, more importantly, that players seldom do themselves any favours by taking the easy option. Wilson and Rioch, for example, were never taken to Scottish supporters' hearts, precisely because it takes more than the accident of a parent's birth to make a man a Scot. Wilson and Rioch did not speak, did not think, did not behave like Scotsmen. Many Scottish fans confessed to preferring a truly Scottish goalkeeper to a questionably more gifted English one.

We might call this 'transplant rejection'. It is less likely today that an English-raised, English-accented player could ever be chosen for Scotland merely on the grounds of paternal links.

With regard to England, notwithstanding the case of John Barnes and one or two others, the sense of nationality is equally strong. Examples are best drawn from outside soccer. Tony Greig and Alan Lamb have both captained England's cricket teams. Though both satisfied the regulations that they were naturalised English, many cricket lovers have never seen them as anything other than South African.

These examples contradict the Irish experience. In Ireland, there appears to be no question of transplant rejection. Quite the contrary. This is the more surprising because the FAI may pick players not merely with parental ties, but with even more extended grand-parental ones. Anyone may take out Irish citizenship upon proof that a grandparent was born within the island of Ireland. Hence, such a person may play soccer for the Republic.

Though within FIFA rules, this widens the net one generation beyond that cast by British nations, and self-evidently dilutes the blood-line still further. If one-quarter Irish is good enough, why not one-eighth, or one-sixteenth? If taken to extremes, the Irish might come to regard themselves like the Jews, for whom a trace of ancestry, no matter how small, labels the person 'Jewish'. Indeed, one hears of young players rummaging among parchment birth certificates – some dating back to the nineteenth century – of their grand-folks in the hope of unearthing Irish credentials.

Eoin Hand has written: 'Unequivocally, my opinion is that qualification [to play for the Republic] should be allowed only if the player's father or mother was born in Ireland.' Though Hand exploited the granny rule to try to strengthen his team, he reminds us that it was those very players who bore the brunt of criticism for alleged 'lack of commitment' whenever Ireland lost. National sentiment being the most fickle of animals, one wonders whether Jack's 'foreign element', for want of a better phrase, enjoy the cheers and the back-slapping only so long as the team is winning.

The solution to this conundrum exists in the psyche of the Irish people. It cannot be further explored in the pages of the present book, other than to observe that Scotland, whose history parallels that of Ireland in so many respects, even to the extent of enduring mass-migrations abroad, responds so differently to the question of who is 'one of us'.

John Aldridge, Tony Cascarino and Andy Townsend are among those whose selection arouses most doubts among sceptics, for these are the most prominent players to invoke the third generation, granny rule. Had the ancestral links of these players been Scottish or Welsh, one wonders whether the football authorities in Glasgow and Cardiff would have contemplated selecting them. And if not, why not?

The bottom line, one suspects, is that players stand a better chance of being successfully integrated only if they are transparently better than what is otherwise available, and if they contribute to a winning side.

The fact that the entire Ireland team is expatriate might also play a part. No man is a hero to his valet, so they say. By the same token, no matter their parentage, players whom most Irish folk have seen only through their television screens tend to adopt larger-than-life, Hollywood-type attributes. That is human nature.

Aldridge and Cascarino also underscored one of the biggest handicaps of trying to manage a small country with finite resources. While England have abundant players to cover for all positions, she finds it more difficult to instil the notion of a 'team'. Charlton's problems are in reverse. He could fashion a team easily enough, whose members bonded together for common cause, but was unlikely to find his talent spread equally over all positions.

In Ireland's case, their principal riches were in central defence. Charlton boasted so many imposing No. 5s – Moran, O'Leary, McGrath, McCarthy, the luckless Lawrenson – that his left-overs would be eyed wistfully by other managers. Charlton was able to capitalise on this surfeit by employing one of them in midfield, in front of the back four, ready to help out whenever a central defender was forced wide to cover the full-back.

The downside was Charlton's dearth of 'native' strikers. Without Aldridge and Cascarino, one shudders to think how Ireland would have fared.

All managers stamp their clubs with their own personal playing style. Kevin Keegan, an adventurous forward, has fashioned a gung-ho Newcastle team playing in his image. Johnny Giles, a thoughtful midfielder, got his teams to play diligently through the middle. Jack Charlton was a master defender in a negative Leeds team and a negative English one. That was his education. His two tutors were Don Revie and Alf Ramsey. His managerial priorities, it should surprise no one, is a consequence of that education, his emphasis being on preventing goals rather than scoring them.

Middlesbrough and Sheffield Wednesday under Charlton were renowned as defensively-minded teams, that neutrals could admire but few could enjoy. Beauty being in the eye of the beholder, the drabbest of goalless draws can inspire paeans of praise from coaches, even as the terraces are being drained of spectators. There was never any doubt that an Irish team fashioned by Jack Charlton would see its share of nil-nils, and hold these up triumphantly. Besides, nil-nil was better than the defeats Irish fans were accustomed to.

Charlton, moreover, is nothing if not his own man. If playing bread and butter football brings jam to the Irish people, so be it. Managers live or die by results, not aesthetics, and Charlton would expect to be no different. In football, winning is more potent than beauty – but winning is beautiful.

Knowing the limitations of his players, Charlton devised a masterplan. The ball should not be worked through midfield, but over the top, cutting out the risk of dispossession, and driving opposing defenders backwards towards the corner flags. As he knew for himself, defenders hate having to face their own goal and turn under pressure. Therefore, that is how his team would play. His midfielders would pursue and hustle, deny the opposition room, and welcome passes not from their own defenders, but from their own forwards laying the ball back. Those forwards would not spend their time goal-hanging, but chasing and harrying defenders from one touchline to the other. Charlton had players who could turn on the style, but they were only given licence to do so in the last third of the pitch.

The consequences of these tactics were clear. His players must be fitter than most, for they had more running to do. While his team would not easily concede goals, they were unlikely to plunder many themselves. This was, partly, because his strikers had other duties to perform, partly, because it was in that area of operations that the talent available was most thin.

In saying this, one is aware that John Aldridge is a prolific goalscorer. He is a natural predator, one who keeps himself in such trim that even in his mid-thirties he is the bane of opposing goalkeepers. Unfortunately, Aldridge suffered a block every time he pulled on the green.

By USA '94, that block would be swept away, and Aldridge would enjoy a monsoon of goals for Ireland. But between 1986 and 1990 he couldn't hit a barn door. Publicly, Charlton rushed to his defence, insisting that Aldridge's running role for Ireland lessened the chances that came his way. This was true. The trouble was that when they did, he missed them.

This gave rise to a torrent of jokes. 'I see Aldridge kept a clean sheet again.' When the Guildford Four were released after seventeen years in prison, they demanded to know 'has Aldridge scored a goal yet?'

If Aldridge wasn't scoring, who was? Under Charlton's system, the midfield had to bag their share. And to their credit, they did. Otherwise, it was down to Aldridge's sidekick, Tony Cascarino.

Cascarino was a trooper, a straightforward target-man much in demand in club football, so much so that no sooner had he signed for one than he was on his way to another. He had risen through the ranks from Gillingham to Aston Villa, via Millwall. It was during his time at the Den, during an effervescent period in Millwall's history, that he formed a feared partnership with Teddy Sheringham. This brought him to the attention of Jack Charlton and to Aston Villa, whose £1.5 million fee in March 1990 was a record both for the club and for an Irish international.

Upon Cascarino fell much of the flak concerning Ireland's granny rule. He was born near London and speaks like a Cockney. His name – shrink-wrapped by Big Jack to 'the Ice Cream Man' – told of an Italian father. His mother was English. It was her mother who provided the Irish link.

Doubts over Cascarino's eligibility were matched by those over his talent. At first, even Charlton shook his head. When Italia '90 was over, first Villa, then Glasgow Celtic and Chelsea would quickly offload the player. Many judges were of the opinion that, honest trier that he was, Cascarino was simply not international calibre.

Added to Cascarino's burdens was the fact of Aldridge's goal-drought. That increased the responsibility on him. He had netted twice in the qualifiers, but scoring was always going to be a trial, for Cascarino, for Aldridge, and for everyone else. The only striker to have netted more than five international goals was Frank Stapleton, and he was mothballed.

Things looked brighter in defence. Packie Bonner was in his prime, a sound keeper and eminently likeable man, who had been custodian of Celtic goalmouths throughout the 1980s. A veteran of Celtic's numerous assaults on Europe, Bonner was just the man to stabilise Ireland's back four, though he took time to adapt to the goalie-cum-sweeper role Charlton demanded.

Captaining the side would be Mick McCarthy, an uncomplicated central defender who never pretended to be anything else. He was less elegant on the ball than David O'Leary, but less inclined to dwell on it. As such he suited Charlton's ideas to the tee, though purists took exception to the manager's preference for the one over the other.

At thirty-four, Kevin Moran never thought he would see a World Cup. Not the tallest of centre-backs, he was certainly one of the bravest. His blood-stained, bandaged head is an icon of his years at Old Trafford. The only player to have been sent off in a Wembley FA Cup Final, Moran had ended his long association with Old Trafford to play out his days in Spain with Sporting Gijon. That is, until Kenny Dalglish's predecessor, Don Mackay, got in touch from second division Blackburn Rovers and brought him back.

One particular player touched the affections of the Irish people as perhaps no other. Paul McGrath was not the first black player to appear for the Republic. That distinction went to Chris Hughton. But, whether in the back four or just in front of them, McGrath performed with such distinction that it was evident Ireland were in possession of an exceptional player.

Great talent often brings conceit in its wake. Not with McGrath, whose off-field shyness is as legendary as his on-field steel. McGrath would not be the first great Irish player with personal difficulties to turn to drink for solace. One thinks immediately of Paddy Moore and George Best. But they were washed up before their time. Perhaps Alex Ferguson thought McGrath would be too, for he transferred him to Aston Villa. Yet McGrath would still be a titan come USA '94.

Buttressed by able full-backs, Ireland boasted a defence that feared no one. Fully-manned, the midfield might have been equally formidable, but injuries and retirements invited Charlton to think long and hard.

The announcement of the final squad was a bitter pill for Millwall's Gary Waddock. Just days earlier he had been named in the provisional twenty-two. But lingering doubts over the fitness of Ronnie Whelan and Ray Houghton prompted a late change. If one or other didn't make it, Charlton doubted Waddock could carry the burden himself. The manager would have liked to experiment with the Swindon player, Alan McLoughlin, but the trials and tribulations of the English play-offs had given Charlton no opportunity. At the eleventh hour he gambled, contradicting his previous assertion that no untried players could be included. McLoughlin was in; Waddock was out.

If only Liam Brady were a few years younger. History is littered with memories of great players who blossomed at the wrong time. Northern Ireland reached two World Cups in the 1980s, long after George Best had addled his brain with drink. Eric Cantona missed out on two World Cups when his peak failed to coincide with that of France.

A World Cup would have been the perfect stage for Brady, especially in Italy, whose teams he graced for seven years, and where his talent shone like a beacon. Not since John Charles in the 1950s had an import from British football created such a stir in Italy. Brady was rarely prone to injury or suspension, but fell foul of both in his latter years, suffering the frustration of missing Euro '88 when he still had much to offer. Two years later, injury and age conspired to keep him out of the theatre of dreams.

Superficially, Brady's cultured style seemed ill-suited to Charlton's hard-running game, though Brady reckoned he played his best football for Ireland under the Englishman. In the event, it took Charlton barely half an hour, against West Germany in September 1989, to realise that Brady's patched up knee and general decline would not carry him through a World Cup. Charlton hauled him off there and then. That, Brady's 71st, might have been his last international. Hours afterwards the player declared it had been. But as an unprecedented tribute, the FAI decreed that Brady's testimonial should not be a razzamatazz outing against some All-Star XI, but a full, official international. Finland obliged. Brady donated much of the proceeds to help alleviate Dublin's drug problem.

Having sorted out his squad, Charlton had to ponder FIFA's instructions to referees. Ireland had a poor disciplinary record in the qualifiers – ten bookings, and Houghton and Whelan had already served suspensions for picking up two apiece. Now FIFA were telling referees to get tough. Players would be fined for cautions and sendings off. Charlton feared that Ireland had had their card marked and that referees might stifle their natural, chasing game. His players agreed beforehand to club together to pay all fines.

Now they had to pay their dues to their adoring fans. Ireland rolled into Italy on the back of an unbeaten run stretching back thirteen games with the loss of just two goals. The squad arrived wearing the grin of urchins set on causing mischief at an upper-crust tea party, and no one had any doubts they could topple an apple-cart or two.

ENGLAND v IRELAND

Monday, 11 June 1990   *Sant'Elia Stadium, Cagliari – 35,238*

The opening matches of Italia '90 had set the tone. Cameroon, with two players sent off, sensationally beat defending champions Argentina. Less sensationally, perhaps, Costa Rica toppled Scotland.

Two positions troubled Jack Charlton as he prepared his players for the biggest day of their professional lives. He counselled McCarthy on who best to partner him in defence. David O'Leary was more cultured and more fleet of foot than Moran, but Moran and McCarthy were old hands who knew each other's game. Despite aggravating an Achilles tendon, Moran got the nod.

More worrisome was what to do about Ronnie Whelan, under normal circumstances the player around whom Charlton would build his side. Losing Whelan *and* Brady might have crippled lesser sides. Whelan had broken a bone in his foot in April. At the time, it hadn't seemed like a break, and weeks were lost before it was diagnosed. He was now racing against the clock. Whelan hadn't kicked a ball for two months and was sure to be ring rusty. Had Houghton's mystery back spasms not suddenly cleared, Charlton might have had no choice but to risk Whelan. Now he could trust his better judgment and leave him out.

The prospect of Ireland versus England in the finals of the World Cup was enough to make the Irish people go wobbly at the knees. If England's visit to Dalymount in the 1958 qualifiers was billed as titanic, what price this one?

England were one of six countries to have lifted the World Cup, though the only ones not to have won it on foreign soil. Their home triumph in 1966 was ambiguously received, ecstatically on patriotic grounds, dubiously on footballing ones. Ramsey's wingless wonders might be efficient; they were hardly fun.

Many thought the England team better in 1970, though it did not survive the quarter-finals. That was some feat compared with what was to follow. Twice in the 1970s England failed to qualify at all. Since those dark days they were on the mend, finishing unbeaten in Spain '82, and beaten by the Hand of God in Mexico '86. They had qualified for Italia '90 by what seemed a mile, but what was in fact a whisker. Though finishing unbeaten, without the loss of a goal, in a group with Sweden, Poland and Albania, they survived a last-minute piledriver against Peter Shilton's crossbar in their final match, in Katowice. Had it gone in, England would have been out. On the eve of the finals, Uruguay ended England's seventeen-match unbeaten run.

Manager Bobby Robson was an old sparring partner of Jack's. He'd played in the 1958 World Cup, and earned his crack at bossing England after transforming Ipswich Town from provincial also-rans into a consistently successful, and attractive, outfit.

He had taken the top job after the 1982 World Cup, but in view of England's subsequent failings was considered to be fortunate still to have it. Denmark had put paid to Euro '84, Diego Maradona to Mexico '86, and, er, Ireland to Euro '88. After eight years in the hot seat, during which the tabloids had treated him shamelessly, he was now bowing out, having agreed to minister to PSV Eindhoven once the tournament was over.

To previous Irish generations, the Matthews and Finneys, Mannions and Milburns, were household heroes. Irish players looked up at their English counterparts with stars in their eyes.

Not any more. Ireland's win in Stuttgart – only their second in ten matches against the English – meant Jack Charlton's crew could take the field in Cagliari with a spring in their step.

England took to Italy their share of competent players and one or two outstanding ones. Peter Shilton, Terry Butcher and Bryan Robson all belonged to the latter category in 1986, but age was no ally to any of them. John Barnes and Chris Waddle were prodigiously gifted, but you wouldn't think so to watch them in international action, when too often they flattered to deceive. Indubitably of top class was Gary Lineker, the leading scorer in Mexico, the most rapacious goalscorer in English football of his generation.

Each manager retained seven of the side from Stuttgart. No surprise in that. The two teams knew each other intimately. Robson's choice of young Paul Gascoigne, however, did bring a smile to Big Jack, as did the retention of Bryan Robson. The one, Charlton felt, was too maverick, the other too battle-weary. At least, that's what he *said*; what he inwardly felt we shall never know. Few neutral commentators, however, thought Ireland would beat England a second time. England would surely have learned their lesson. Ireland would no longer enjoy the element of surprise, and the passing of two years had not strengthened Charlton's ageing team. But did England have enough to beat Ireland? A draw was always on the cards.

The match was ugly, the ball always in the sky, two sides equipped for little more than attrition. Even the conditions were familiar – squally, cloudy, cool. But England, playing against the wind, were favoured with an early goal. Sheedy loitered, expecting the ball to pass out for a throw. It didn't, and Waddle's one dangerous cross of the night lured Bonner from his goal-line. Lineker thrust back his shoulders and chested the ball past him, pursued by McCarthy and Morris, who were unable to prevent him shepherding it over the line. The scorer thereby matched Geoff Hurst's achievement of '66 and '70, scoring his team's last goal in one World Cup, and its first in the next.

The goal was Ireland's collective fault, but Lineker was McCarthy's responsibility, and he bravely took the can.

As an attacking force that goal was the last seen of England, as ball and limbs were whacked indiscriminately with all the grace of a street fight. For

England, it was now a case of guarding that precious lead. It might have been doubled when Waddle skipped past Staunton and Townsend but was earthed by Moran. The German referee shook his head. No penalty.

An electrical storm during the interval provided more thrills than the action that preceded it. The wind then died and the rain fell. Two substitutions saved Ireland's day. Charlton introduced Alan McLoughlin to press forward from midfield. Tit-for-tat, Robson promptly sent on Steve McMahon. Both teams were now playing 4-5-1. Almost McMahon's first act was to fumble the ball on the eighteen-yard line, and it bobbled to the Irishman best equipped to exploit the error. Kevin Sheedy's drive was low, true, and wide of Shilton's straining left hand.

'I sent him on to win us the game,' bleated Bobby Robson afterwards. 'Instead, he cost us it.'

Jack Charlton pooh-poohed the idea that England had been unlucky.

'They never had the game safe,' he snorted. 'Nor was it a penalty when Waddle tumbled.'

Clearly, neither manager was disheartened by the result, the first draw of the tournament. Those most unhappy were the neutrals – wondering how the Irish and British could endure, nay enjoy, such fare – and Greenpeace, intending to protest that the ball had damaged the ozone layer. It was later confirmed that it had been in play for just forty-seven minutes out of ninety.

ENGLAND   (1) 1   **IRELAND   (0) 1**
   Lineker 8   Sheedy 73

ENGLAND: Shilton (DERBY), Stevens (RANGERS), Pearce (FOREST), Gascoigne (SPURS), Walker (FOREST), Butcher (RANGERS), Waddle (MARSEILLE), Robson (MAN U), Beardsley (LIVERPOOL) (*sub* McMahon, LIVERPOOL), Lineker (SPURS) (*sub* Bull, WOLVES), Barnes (LIVERPOOL).
IRELAND: Bonner, Morris, Staunton, McCarthy, Moran, McGrath, Houghton, Townsend, Aldridge (McLoughlin), Cascarino, Sheedy.

EGYPT v IRELAND

Sunday, 17 June 1990   *Della Favorita Stadium, Palermo – 33,288*

Despite orders not to overdo it, the Ireland players celebrated deep into the night, and once they had arrived in Sicily next day were in no shape to train. Ireland's hotel was remote to the point of being monastic, and lacked mod-cons such as air conditioning. The whirring fans in their rooms were as loud as helicopters. The food was under-cooked, over-greased, and insubstantial.

Against Egypt, Charlton saw no reason to change his team or his substitutes, which meant no role for Ronnie Whelan. Whelan did not take kindly to his omission. Nor did Anfield team-mate Steve McMahon, who,

Steve McMahon looks up in horror as Kevin Sheedy equalises against England.

before long, left Bobby Robson in no doubt what he thought about being left out of the England eleven. Maybe Liverpool players considered themselves indispensable. After all, they usually were.

Anyway, a win over Egypt would take Ireland – barring improbable results elsewhere – through to the second round. Charlton knew his team *ought* to win, but Egypt had humiliated Scotland 3-1 in Aberdeen three months before the finals. And against Holland, Egypt overturned predictions with a 1-1 draw that left onlookers breathless with the virility of their play.

British colonists had introduced soccer to the Nile-land early this century. Egypt's best achievement to date had been fourth place in the 1964 Tokyo Olympics. Their manager, Mahmoud El Gohary, had succeeded Mike Smith, the in-and-out manager of Wales. Gohary was a former army colonel, though Egyptian football managers were dubbed 'captains'.

Sadly, Ireland contributed to their second wretched match of the tournament. They hoped to stop others playing by closing down space: this objective was countered by opponents who allowed Ireland even less space themselves. In a dramatic switch of emphasis, Egypt rarely ventured across the halfway line, packing their half with bodies in the knowledge that Ireland hadn't a Platini or a Brady – or a fit Whelan – to unpick their defence. Egypt time-wasted blatantly, for which goalkeeper Shobeir was belatedly booked.

Their substitutes dallied in coming on, and exchanged kisses as well as handshakes when they did so.

Ireland's crosses went anywhere except where they ought, and their half-chances could be counted on one hand. Cascarino's volley was saved, Sheedy's likewise. Staunton shot through the legs of Ibrahim Hassan, and wide, and Houghton, finding himself clear, drove to the near post when he might have squared. Ireland reacted to the final whistle as if they'd lost 0-6.

Charlton could not contain himself. He refused to shake hands with Egyptian players and delivered inflammatory words to a press-conference, where he slated Egypt's negativity. There was some irony in this: the rest of the world was busy slagging Ireland. Here was the pot calling the kettle black. Charlton's bluntness upset diplomats no less than footballers. His words were taken as an insult to the Egyptian nation. It is as well Ireland had not been playing Iran, for the mullahs might have slapped a *fatwa* upon him. In criticising Egypt for not creating a single goalscoring chance, Charlton was reminded that his own club, Leeds, had been of the same ilk, and had specialised in cynicism. El Gohary said:

'Ireland are like a very strong horse, very difficult to hold,' and an Egyptian spokesman elaborated:

'Charlton failed to show British courtesy and sense of fair play. We understand what psychological warfare is all about. The Pharaohs started it. What Charlton should have done was have a cup of tea and a nice piece of cake, watch TV, go to bed, sleep on it, discuss it with the players, and then speak. The bad performance by England was decided by the type of football Ireland play, which forces an unentertaining game on the opposition. It is a puzzle like football has never had to solve before. We don't have the stamina to contain the war of attrition Ireland conducted against us.'

'Jack-Ass' sneered the English press. Charlton was rightly angered, but it was reaction from one particular quarter in Ireland that most upset him.

English football has never known a dissenting journalist or ex-player with the clout to eyeball the manager of the day. The nearest was perhaps Brian Glanville of *The Sunday Times*, who for years carried on a one-man crusade against Bobby Robson. But Glanville was speaking for himself, not the public, far less Fleet St. Other hacks were busy launching their own attacks.

In Ireland, however, in a land where Jack Charlton was close to being sanctified, Eamon Dunphy continued to wage a high-profile war of words. Capped twenty-three times, Dunphy's eloquent, if acid, pen had provided the *Sunday Independent* with a much read and much vilified heretic. Dunphy's face was everywhere, his criticisms of Charlton's style, and some of his players, familiar to every Irish fan. In essence, Dunphy argued that Ireland were prospering in spite of Charlton rather than because of him. This was not a view with which the Irish public concurred. It says much for Charlton's place in Irish esteem that, while he was dubbed 'Our Jack', Dunphy, though doubtless sincere and selling lots of newspapers, was widely ostracised.

The source of Jack's anger? Dunphy had slated Ireland's lack of ambition. Charlton's only weapon had been to try to bully Egypt into submission.

EGYPT (0) 0   **IRELAND (0) 0**

EGYPT: Shobeir (AL AHLY), I Hassan (AL AHLY), Yassein (AL AHLY), H Ramzy (AL AHLY), Yakan (ZAMALEK), Tolba (PAOK, GREECE) (*sub* Abouzeid, AL AHLY), Youssef (ZAMALEK), Abdou (Z'LEK) (*sub* Abdelhamid, Z'LEK), Abdelghani (BEIRA MAR, PORT'), H Hassan (AL AHLY), Oraby (AL AHLY).
IRELAND: Bonner, Morris, McCarthy, Moran, Staunton, Houghton, McGrath, Townsend, Sheedy, Aldridge (McLoughlin), Cascarino (Quinn).

HOLLAND v IRELAND
Thursday, 21 June 1990   *Della Favorita Stadium, Palermo – 33,288*

Having got his rage off his chest, Charlton devoted himself to scheming the downfall of Holland, whose goalless draw with England left all four sides with identical records: two games, two draws, two points, one goal. But Ireland had Holland to play, and were up against it. The Dutch were one of only two teams to have beaten Ireland in a competitive international in two years. Ireland had to avoid defeat this time, but even that might not be enough. Should England and Egypt also draw, by the same score, all four nations would have unprecedented identical records. The only solution would be to draw lots. Three teams were sure to go through, but one would not.

As for Holland, they'd been more daisies than tulips. They hadn't qualified in 1982 and '86, and were renowned for snatching victories and defeats they did not deserve. If they suffered cruel luck in the World Cup Finals of 1974 and '78, their European triumph in 1988 was born of indubitable style married to prodigious good fortune. Thumped by the Soviet Union in their first match, Holland survived two dented goalposts in their second, against England, another against the Irish, and only qualified from their group by virtue of a late, offside goal against Jack Charlton's side. West Germany were overcome in the semi-final with the aid of a nonsensical penalty. The Soviets even missed a penalty in the Final. As they say, if your name is on the Cup, no mere footballers can wipe it off.

True, Dutch football had some magical players. Frank Rijkaard and Ruud Gullit (European Footballer of the Year, '87) were dreadlocked Surinamese, able to sparkle in any position, while Marco van Basten (European Footballer of the Year, '88 and '89) had some claim to be even better than Gary Lineker. This trio had recently helped AC Milan retain the European Cup, against Benfica, ensuring that Italian sympathies would be vested in Holland.

In the debit column, blond sweeper Ronald Koeman, never fleet of foot, was now finding himself outpaced so often that he increasingly resorted to holding on. Coloured cards were likely to come his way.

Tactically, the Dutch were ready for anything: they could match Ireland for muscle, if necessary, and outplay them for skill, for sure. Equally, they had the air of a team which knew their time had come, continuing to forge results not always merited by their performances. Egypt had shown that it might take more than just a superior team to beat them.

If Dutch fortunes had changed for the better, their ill-tempered squabblings had not. When had a Dutch squad not been riven by bickerings over money or player-power? This one was no more insouciant than its predecessors. The coach who guided Holland to the finals, Thijs Libregts, had been ousted by a mutiny of star players – Gullit prominent – but they were denied the replacement they demanded, Johann Cruyff. Rinus Michels, grand vizier of Dutch football, appointed Leo Beenhakker for the arduous task of healing the rifts and extracting the best.

England had earned a moral victory against the Dutch by springing a tactical surprise. Abandoning his previous instincts, Bobby Robson played a sweeper, and it had worked a treat. The Irish players were bemused to find Charlton briefly toying with the idea himself. But sweepers were completely alien; the experiment did not last long.

Charlton did make one change. Though not prepared to risk Whelan, except on the bench, he replaced the out of sorts Cascarino with Niall Quinn.

The stadium was awash with face-painted, flag-waving supporters of both sides who witnessed a match that – in terms of goals – was a near replica of Ireland's v England. After ten minutes Ireland were trailing. Ronald Koeman tapped a free-kick to Gullit, who played a one-two with Wim Kieft. Gullit speared between two defenders to score. He was enjoying a free role in midfield, and no Irish player had picked him up. But then could anyone?

Ireland were now in trouble. But the virility of their response was such as to banish memories of their earlier matches. Ireland fought for their lives, and as the game progressed the Dutch found themselves under the kind of pressure they rarely encountered. True, Gullit might have scored a second, heading over, and Ronald Koeman's shot from thirty yards kept Bonner on his toes, but the pressure was building at the other end. Aldridge 'scored' but was offside. At last, Ireland started to get their crosses in, and the pace of the game left some Dutch players panting for breath.

Just after the hour Charlton made a double switch, replacing the spent Aldridge with the extra bulk of Cascarino, and giving Whelan his wings and asking him to fly. Within ten minutes Ireland were level, though neither sub played a part. Another booming punt by Bonner landed deep in the Dutch half. Van Aerle, stretching to reach the ball, toe-poked it diagonally across goal. It bounced awkwardly, and Van Breukelen, who should have claimed it, didn't. The ball broke from his body and Niall Quinn tucked it into the net.

As with Sheedy's goal against England, Ireland had squeezed the opposition until the rivets popped. Off the pitch, all ears now tuned into Cagliari, where England were heading Egypt 1-0. Perfect. If both scores stayed the same, both Ireland and Holland would live on. When Houghton was treated for an injury, the England score buzzed among the players. Gullit was seen chatting to McCarthy, and when play resumed the Dutchman all but turned his back on the game. The match fizzled out, the score threatened only by players who did not know or did not care about happenings elsewhere. The referee thought the cease-fire so blatant that he had words with both captains. Truce or no, Jack Charlton described those concluding minutes as the longest of his managerial life. Had Egypt not missed a late chance against England, it would have been even longer.

At one stage it appeared that all four teams in Group F were headed for lots. Now it was just two. Ireland and Holland had both qualified, but one would play Romania, the other West Germany. Not much doubt about the easier option. The lottery placed Ireland second, Holland third. The luck of the Irish had staved off the luck of the Dutch.

HOLLAND (1) 1   **IRELAND (0) 1**
Gullit 10   Quinn 71

HOLLAND: Van Breukelen (PSV), Van Aerle (PSV), Rijkaard (MILAN), R Koeman (BARCELONA), Van Tiggelen (ANDERLECHT), Witschge (AJAX) (*sub* Fräser, R KERKRADE), Wouters (AJAX), Gullit (MILAN), Kieft (PSV) (*sub* Van Loen, R KERKRADE), Van Basten (MILAN), Gillhaus (ABERDEEN).
IRELAND: Bonner, Morris, McCarthy, Moran, Staunton, Houghton, McGrath, Townsend, Sheedy (Whelan), Quinn, Aldridge (Cascarino).

Final positions – Group F

	P	W	D	L	F	A	Pts
ENGLAND	3	1	2	0	2	1	4
IRELAND	3	0	3	0	2	2	3
HOLLAND	3	0	3	0	2	2	3
Egypt	3	0	2	1	1	2	2

ROMANIA v IRELAND
Monday, 25 June 1990   *Luigi Ferraris Stadium, Genoa – 31,818*

Romania. There was a name to conjure with. Home to Dracula and all kinds of spooks. A football nation scoring high marks on raw material but low on results. Ever-presents in World Cups before the war, but appearing now for only the second time since. They had been in England's group in Mexico '70, losing 0-1, but had left several of Alf Ramsey's players black and blue. Romania were habitually dismissed, like all East European teams, as technically adept, dour in outlook, defensive in tactics, brutal in strategy.

In 1986, Steaua Bucharest had become the first communist representatives to win the European Cup. They reached the Final again three years later, losing to AC Milan. Three of the current national team – goalkeeper Silviu Lung, Iosif Ratariu, and multi-talented Georghe Hagi – had featured in that disappointing evening in Barcelona. Short in stature, dark of hair, sure of foot, Hagi was spoken of by Charlton as 'far and away the best player I have seen in the competition to date.' Another Steaua player, influential midfielder Marius Lacatus, had picked up two yellow cards and would sit out the match.

With President Ceausescu dead and the iron curtain about to be ripped away, Romania's stars would soon be scattered among the rich clubs of Spain and Italy. For the moment, most were tied to clubs at home. Players from the two Bucharest giants, Dinamo and Steaua, dominated the team.

Romania's was a curious route to the World Cup's last sixteen. They had beaten the Soviets, lost to Cameroon, then – with Argentina – staged another of the World Cups' regrettable sit-ins. Both sides knew their 1-1 score would take them through, and both sides all but lay down for a snooze.

The Irish party decamped from Sicily for the far north of the mainland, dragging their adoring fans in their wake. Team-wise, as Charlton had no new injuries, he saw no reason to mess around. This did not please Cascarino or Whelan, who could barely conceal their anguish.

Genoa's Luigi Ferraris Stadium, home to Sampdoria, had recently hosted Scotland's matches with Costa Rica and Sweden. It had brought mixed blessings to the Scots, who were finally eliminated by Brazil in Turin.

Romania had probably uttered a whoop of delight when they learned they would face Ireland and not Holland. Hagi, in particular, seemed unimpressed by these green-shirted hordes let loose upon them. Despite the intense heat, Romania had plenty of football in them, and early in the match Hagi provided his share of impromptu lessons. Twice he swung his left foot from twenty-five yards and twice Bonner had to move sharply.

But midway through the half, with Aldridge off with an Achilles injury, the tide began to turn. The Romanian sting had been drawn, and Sheedy brought the half to a close with a shot that Lung clawed to safety.

Second-half chances were few and evenly distributed, but a combination of heat and looming extra time meant that, long before the end, the game had slowed to walking pace. Nor did those extra thirty minutes look like breaking the deadlock. Players were tired, not wanting to make fatal mistakes, and prepared to let fate take its course. When Brazilian referee Ramiz Wright blew for time he released the players from their exhaustion and sent them into the unknown. Neither side had ever before faced a penalty shoot-out.

Exponents of ways to be rid of this dramatic but farcical system presented alternatives that were, we were told, being seriously entertained for future World Cups. The number of corner-kicks, for example. That would have favoured Romania to the tune of 9-4. The number of bookings, perhaps. That ended 2-2. But for the moment, nothing mattered except penalties.

Other than that Kevin Sheedy would open up for Ireland, Charlton left it to the players to decide who would take them and in what order. Aldridge and Whelan would have been naturals, but they were both on the bench.

McCarthy lost the toss (once again) for first go, and Hagi shot Romania into a 1-0 lead. Sheedy replied by smacking the ball over Lung's head, as he had promised Charlton he would. The tally reached 4-4, with Cascarino's third nearly saved. Daniel Timofte of Dinamo Bucharest had come on as an injury-time substitute, presumably because he was good at penalties. By standing almost parallel with the goal-line he telegraphed his intention to Bonner. It was not a difficult save, as penalties go, but a priceless one. Bonner was beside himself. Now it was down to Ireland's fifth taker.

All eyes swung to the centre circle to see who it was, and were astonished to find the tall figure of David O'Leary striding forward. O'Leary? A centre-half taking the most vital kick in Irish history? He had only taken one for Arsenal in his life. And he'd missed that! Like Timofte, O'Leary had only recently come on, seeing his first action of the tournament. He now sent Lung to the left, the ball to the right, and the Irish players, bench, supporters and the whole nation into delirium.

ROMANIA   (0) 0   **IRELAND** *   (0) 0
* Ireland won 5-4 on penalties   *After extra time*

ROMANIA: Lung (STEAUA), Rednic (DINAMO), Klein (DINAMO), Andonie (DINAMO), G Popescu (CRAIOVA), Rotariu (STEAUA), Sabau (DINAMO) (*sub* Timofte, DINAMO), Hagi (STEAUA), Lupescu (DINAMO), Raducioiu (DINAMO) (*sub* Lupu, DINAMO), Balint (STEAUA).
IRELAND: Bonner, Morris, Staunton (O'Leary), McCarthy, Moran, McGrath, Houghton, Townsend, Aldridge (Cascarino), Sheedy, Quinn.

ITALY v IRELAND
Saturday, 30 June 1990   *Olympic Stadium, Rome – 73,303*

Ireland already knew that, after Romania, Italy or Uruguay lay in wait. For every imaginable reason Ireland preferred Italy. Back in the 1920s, Italy had given Irish independence a fillip by being the first nation to play the Free State. Matches with Uruguay were likely to degenerate into blood-baths, as

Scotland would testify from 1986. Italy were giants of world football, the hosts to boot, focusing the eyes of the world on Ireland's 'little invincibles'.

Italy duly overcame Uruguay, 2-0, to direct Ireland to the Olympic Stadium. Arrangements behind the scenes fixed up an audience with the Pope, which warmed the hearts of the Catholics in the Irish party, left Charlton almost tongue-tied, for once, and gave rise to one of the many jokes to attend Italia '90. Inspecting a photograph of the Ireland manager next to the Pontiff, a wag asked: 'Who's that with our Jack?'

The quarter-final draw might be magical for Ireland. It filled Italy with trepidation, facing a side they knew nothing about, whom in the past they had beaten at every time of asking, yet to whom they dare not lose now.

Italy were seeking their fourth World Cup triumph, having in 1982 added a third to those they had won in pre-war times. Italy remains one of the few high-profile European nations not to export her great names. Each of Italy's battery of stars played for Italian clubs – Zenga, Ferri, Berti, and captain Bergomi with Internazionale; Baresi, Maldini, and Charlton's favourite, Roberto Donadoni, across the city with AC Milan. The most expensive of them all, Roberto Baggio, had cost a king's ransom when transferring from Fiorentina to Juventus. Baggio had so far scored just once in the finals, but what a goal to savour, burrowing deep into the Czech defence from the touchline, to bamboozle defenders this way and that. The bulk of Italy's scoring had been done by wild-eyed 'Toto' Schillaci, a Sicilian who came on as substitute in Italy's first match and never looked back.

Playing the hosts, with all the added pressures on referees, linesmen, and opponents, was akin to scaling Everest without oxygen. Needing his trusty mountaineers, Charlton once again fielded an unchanged side. Cascarino, Whelan, even hero O'Leary, were stuck on the bench. The manager told his players in no uncertain terms, go at them! 'You're two games away from the World Cup Final.'

Italy did not know how to approach these Johnny-come-latelies, and for half an hour Ireland's relentless pressure game had them at sixes and sevens. Ireland looked better, far better than they had during those desperate encounters with England and Egypt. To Ireland, in fact, fell the first two chances. McGrath's header from Sheedy's corner was comfortably gathered by Walter Zenga, who had yet to concede a goal in the tournament. But when Quinn's header from McGrath's cross brought a second save, it would prove to be the last effort Ireland directed on target.

More's the pity, for Ireland were shortly trailing. Baggio's earlier effort had been annulled by Portuguese referee, Silva Valente. But now, with Ireland's players pushing up, Sheedy's pass to Aldridge was cut out by de Napoli. Baggio and Giannini, at pace, conveyed the ball two thirds the length of the pitch, setting up Donadoni for a shot that Bonner could only parry.

Packie steered the ball wide of goal, but stumbled wide of it himself. He might have got away with it had the ball gone anywhere but to Schillaci, who side-footed it inside the far post with Bonner stranded at his near.

Though the game had nearly an hour to run, that strike effectively settled it. Ireland pressed gallantly, but theirs was the pressure of guts rather than guile, and they seldom looked like pulling it back.

Indeed, all the near misses were at the other end. Schillaci's thunderous free-kick would have gone in had it struck the crossbar one centimetre lower. As it was, it flew down and out for Toto to have a second pot, which he hit over. Late in the game Serena wasted a free header. Cascarino was, by this time, on for Quinn. The late introduction of Sheridan for Aldridge, and, with it, a switch to 4-5-1, was a brave gamble by a manager who had no more tricks up his sleeve. Bonner's legs prevented a Serena goal. Baresi and Donadoni might also have broken through, and in the closing seconds Schillaci bundled the ball into the net. This time, he was offside.

On near misses and chances created, Italy might have won handsomely. But that would have been cruel on Ireland, who were permitted to retire with dignity from a competition that had exceeded all expectations.

ITALY (1) 1   IRELAND (0) 0
Schillaci 37

ITALY: Zenga (INTER), Baresi (MILAN), Bergomi (INTER), de Agostini (JUVENTUS), Ferri (INTER), Maldini (MILAN), de Napoli (NAPOLI), Giannini (ROMA) (*sub* Ancelotti, MILAN), Baggio (JUVENTUS) (*sub* Serena, INTER), Donadoni (MILAN), Schillaci (JUVENTUS).
IRELAND: Bonner, Morris, Staunton, McCarthy, Moran, McGrath, Houghton, Townsend, Aldridge (Sheridan), Sheedy, Quinn (Cascarino).

This would not be a vintage World Cup. Goals were down, fouls were up. Excitement was minimal. Negativity paid off, for no one more than for defending champions Argentina, who somehow stumbled from match to match, past one opponent after another (twice after penalty shoot-outs, including Italy in the semi-final) until only Germany remained. The Germans had likewise required a shoot-out to get past troublesome England in the other semi. In the Final, Germany, indubitably the better team and worthy winners overall, nevertheless required a fantasy penalty to get past Argentina, who managed to get two men sent off.

'Don't cry for me Argentina,' went the song. Few did.

For Ireland, however, it was a case of national celebration. Half a million, according to some reports, turned out to welcome the team home. The reception would leave a lasting impression on manager and players.

FIFA ranks all World Cup competitors in a list from 1 to 24, based on points, goal-difference, goals scored etc. Matches that are settled by penalty shoot-outs are taken as draws. As losing quarter-finalists, Ireland would be placed somewhere between fifth and eighth. But as their record showed no wins, four draws and one defeat, Ireland were ranked lowest, in eighth place. Ireland, little Ireland, were officially the eighth best team in the world!

Cynics were less impressed. Indeed, how a team could march so far without winning a single match, scoring just two goals, both late equalisers brought about by pressurised defensive mistakes, was a quandary. Some might say a miracle.

'Ireland played one-two with the angels,' remarked Alfredo di Stefano.

Ireland appearances and goalscorers (substitute appearances in brackets)
World Cup qualifying rounds and final competition 1990

	Apps	Goals		Apps	Goals
Houghton R	13	2	Whelan R *†	6 (1)	1
Moran K *†	13	1	Hughton C *†	5	–
Bonner P *	12	–	O'Leary D *†‡	4 (2)	–
Sheedy K *	12	1	Quinn N	3 (3)	1
Aldridge J	11 (1)	2	Stapleton F *†‡	2	–
McGrath P *	11	1	Sheridan J	1 (1)	–
Staunton S	11	–	Galvin A *	1	–
Cascarino A *	10 (3)	2	Peyton G †	1	–
McCarthy M *	10	–	Brady L *†‡	– (2)	–
Morris C	9 (2)	–	McLoughlin A	– (2)	–
Townsend A	8 (2)	–	O'Brien L	– (1)	–
			(own-goals)		1

---

* Appeared in 1986 World Cup.

† Appeared in 1982 World Cup.

‡ Appeared in 1978 World Cup.

22 players used

163 apps   12 goals
118   English League
27   Scottish League
15   Spanish League
3   French League

14

THE 1994 WORLD CUP

Jack Charlton was now a towering figure in Irish life, fêted by one and all in ways unknown to sporting leaders across the water. He had earned little Ireland the attention and respect of the world. Few men had ever done that, except through fear, the bullet and the bomb. Irish prime ministers were proud to shake him by the hand, and to be seen doing so. The rank and file in 'Hill 16' were proud to buy his Guinness, and to keep his glass full. No one could be, or could want to be, more English than Jack Charlton, but here he was, incarnated as honorary Irishman.

Charlton couldn't go wrong. A combination of personal and professional qualities endeared him to Irish folk of every description. They loved his salt-and-pepper earthiness. Charlton called a spade a bloody spade. He was as far removed from the snootiness of imperial England as it was possible to be. He was a man of the people, who spoke their language, and who, in doing so, had turned a crop of demoralised footballers into World Cup heroes.

Put him behind a microphone and he became a star. He could amuse, he could enlighten, he could intimidate, and Ireland was hooked on his every word. In this media-dominated age, when presentational skills are as essential as professional ones, Charlton was blessed with the lot. They say the Irish have the gift of the gab. In Charlton, they found one of their own. He was a personality, and a huge one.

More importantly, he was as good at doing his job as he was talking about it. World Cup quarter-finalists might not earn medals – except invisible ones. But how many footballing nations had ever gone further?

Northern Ireland, Scotland, Denmark, Romania – none of these had ever done so. Nor had Spain since 1950, Hungary since 1966. In the post-war era, only East Germany, in 1974, could be said to have performed better on their World Cup debuts. Ireland's accomplishments should be seen in that light.

Few could seriously argue with what Charlton had achieved. Football is a matter of personnel and strategy. Jack already had the manpower; he supplied the strategy. In doing so he extracted the maximum that each player had to give and harnessed it to common cause.

It is tempting to say that no other man and no other tactics could have worked the wonders Charlton worked.

And yet ... Charlton and his players still attracted flak from some quarters. These criticisms took two forms. First, Ireland were lucky. Second, Charlton imposed a brand of disagreeable football upon the world.

The charge that Ireland enjoyed a measure of good fortune can hardly be contradicted. Gary Mackay had supplied the first dollop some years back. The lucky-dip that sent Ireland to play Romania instead of Germany was beyond the powers of man or god. And although penalty shoot-outs are settled by players, not dice, few would contest that it is a devilishly hard way to be knocked out.

When these considerations are added to the sum of Ireland's results – no wins and just two goals – the case is strengthened. No other team in the history of the World Cup has exploited a string of low-scoring draws to such advantage – and without the aid of lots and shoot-outs, nor would Ireland. In 1982, Algeria won two out of three, yet didn't survive her group. In 1990, Ireland won none out of five, yet got to within two matches of the Final.

But good fortune and just deserts are not incompatible. Luck is so bound up with sport that it is nonsensical to think of one without the other. No team ever won anything without a close shave here and there, a rebound off a post, a shortsighted linesman. Sometimes decisions can be manifestly wrong: witness Geoff Hurst's second 'goal' in 1966.

Cup competition is actually predicated upon luck. Whether opponents are mammoths or minnows is decided by blindfold, yet few of us are disposed to question the ultimate triumph. Luck is inbuilt, and is accepted as such.

Besides, Ireland had known misfortune under Charlton. Hadn't Holland's late winner in Gelsenkirchen been offside? On another day, another referee might have annulled it, sending Ireland into the semi-final.

Though, over time, 'luck' tends to even out, some would say that Ireland were about to gobble another chunk in the 1994 World Cup qualifiers. In any case, why apologise for being lucky? Far from insulting manager and players, it is that quality among others that endears Jack Charlton to the Irish people. They think he's lucky, and wouldn't have him any other way.

The charge of 'ugly' football is equally Janus-faced. It is made by those who lose, not those who win. To the extent that Ireland play the ball upfield in the air, not on the ground, this clearly lessens any role for dribbling, for the rat-a-tat-tat of rapid inter-passing. These are what excites crowds, but they do not excite Charlton, for he sees them as a recipe for dispossession and disaster. If Ireland were to play Ireland, one fears the game would not be a pretty sight. The point is, they do not.

Neutrals might not rush to watch Ireland, but who cares? Few managers are appreciated at home. They never expect kisses abroad.

Charlton would argue, persuasively, that no other system would have carried Ireland so far. He simply hadn't the players to compete with Holland or Italy in the fancy stuff.

But this begs the question. Even blessed with an army of ball-players, would he have modified his style to suit them? Or was he wedded to pressure tactics come what may?

As England had reached the semi-finals, criticism from that quarter could not be dismissed as sour grapes. That a few Jeremiahs sought to undermine Ireland's achievements wrapped a protective cloak around all concerned. No matter the questionable 'Irishness' of some, the players were above reproach. As for Charlton, he was 'Our Jack'. The tribute was immense, and it clearly warmed him.

Our Jack did not have long to sit on his laurels. Within four months of the World Cup Ireland were off and running in the Euros. It was an unwelcome hand that conjured up England for the third consecutive competition, not that England had unlocked the key to putting Charlton's boys in their place.

For much of the campaign Ireland looked on course for yet another summer carnival. But in the final analysis, they inflicted victories only on humble Turkey, drawing twice with England, twice with Poland. A late strike by Gary Lineker in Poznan propelled England into the Euro finals, where they disappeared without trace. Charlton was left to muse upon Ireland's endless capacity to draw, their lesser capacity to win.

Jack admits to knowing little about politics, or anything outside football or fishing. But one presumes he uttered a mild curse at the crumbling empire in eastern Europe that, at a stroke, multiplied the number of nations seeking a place in the World Cup. Cameroon's exploits in Italy had already increased Africa's representation in the '94 finals at Europe's expense. Now a hatful of mini-nations – some from the former Soviet Union, others with minuscule populations, like San Marino and the Faeroe Islands – would clutter Europe's qualifying zones to an unprecedented degree. Many argued that it was bad enough having Cyprus, Luxembourg and Malta to contend with, and that Europe's small fry should wage their own pre-qualification series to prune their numbers.

As always, eligible nations were seeded in ranks. Since the time of Noah, Ireland had been dumped among the lower seeds. But this time, hooray for Italia '90, Ireland occupied the second tier.

Above all, they wished to avoid England. This they did. Weighing his opponents, Charlton had more cause to smile than to snarl. Spain had come out of the hat again. That was bad news, but Ireland couldn't avoid all the top seeds. Northern Ireland were unwelcome, for obvious reasons. As for Denmark, better to face them now than in the 1980s. The Danes had the look of a shooting star burning itself out. But in a later, dramatic twist, Denmark enjoyed a sudden, unmerited summons to Euro '92, where they toppled the cream of the continent.

Three lesser footballing powers were also basketed in Group 3. Albania, Latvia, and Lithuania were all ex-communist states of one complexion or another. Ireland knew as little of them as *vice versa*.

Ireland, in other words, were dumped in the only group to comprise seven teams. That meant *twelve* qualifying games. No European team had ever known a schedule like that. For countries with a domiciled core of players, league commitments could be tailored accordingly. For Ireland, dependent on players in the UK, the inflated programme spelled bad news. The English season was the longest and most exhausting in Europe. Top clubs already demanded seventy-odd matches from their players. Those players who had declared for Ireland now had to squeeze in a dozen more.

It suited Ireland to play matches concurrently with England, profiting from the cancelled English league programme on the previous Saturday. But, being in a larger group, Ireland would not always be so fortunate.

Qualifying Group 3

IRELAND v ALBANIA
Tuesday, 26 May 1992   *Lansdowne Road – 29,727*

Ordinarily, World Cup qualifiers are spread over fifteen months or so, concluding by the Christmas prior to the finals. The tentacles of Group 3's monster, forty-two-match itinerary spread so far and so wide that those nations not competing in Euro '92 set sail as soon as possible. This delayed the start of Denmark, who had urgent if unexpected business in Sweden, while encouraging those who had fallen by the wayside – Spain and the two Irelands – to get cracking. Spain set the ball rolling, beating Albania 3-0.

That was one of the few yardsticks available to Jack Charlton, other than the knowledge that Bobby Robson's England had beaten Albania 2-0 away and 5-0 at home *en route* to Italia '90.

Albania could consider themselves a notch above the likes of Malta and Cyprus. Rarely did they capitulate by more than two goals, and in recent competitions had twice avoided the wooden spoon. With the dismantling of the Iron Curtain, the taint of Albania's everlasting leader – Enver Hoxha – had been swept away. Some Albanian players already performed in Greece and one – Demollari – in Romania. Soon, more would join the exodus.

With Albania lurching from one political crisis to another, her footballers arrived in Dublin minus kit, medical equipment, and a contingent of players holed up in Greece. Their squad had to be topped up by recruits from the Under-21s, which lost to Ireland's 1-3 the previous night. Demollari and full-back Zmijani were the sole remnants of the outfit crushed at Wembley in 1989. Demollari, to recall, had thumped a sweet volley past Peter Shilton, but the referee saw fit to disallow it.

Ireland had aggravated their European misery by losing to Wales at the Royal Dublin Society (RDS), though they had subsequently exacted revenge on Switzerland and the USA.

Most of the heroes of Italia '90 were still pulling on the green, buttressed here and there by stars of tomorrow. Denis Irwin – left-back at Old Trafford – had claimed the right-back shirt, while young Roy Keane's all-round drive would have commanded a place from anyone. Of the old brigade, Ronnie Whelan was nursing a torn hamstring. Mick McCarthy was now player-manager of Millwall. He was showing signs of wear and tear, and Charlton left him on the bench. David O'Leary's inclusion marked a personal milestone. It was his *fifth* World Cup campaign, equalling the record of Johnny Giles. Implausibly, and briefly, Paul McGrath was made captain.

The drain on Ireland's emotions, following their European demise, was reflected in the attendance – under 30,000. These turned up on a sunny evening expecting to see Albania, in their borrowed scarlet strip, sacrificed on the altar of capitalism.

What they saw was bags of huff and puff, Ireland running round in circles, and blazing away at goalkeeper Dani to his heart's content. He kept out raspers from Houghton and Keane, saw Quinn's header wobble his bar, and with an hour played was the most grudgingly admired player on view.

The limping Sheedy had been subbed by McCarthy shortly after half-time. Ireland kept pressing and were rewarded when Keane chipped the ball forward and Aldridge flung himself to meet it. This time Dani was in limbo.

McGrath claimed the second goal. Having been pushed into midfield to accommodate McCarthy, he climbed above a pack of defenders to meet one of the sub's ballistic throw-ins. For his rare goal, McGrath was voted man of the match. For his unstinting efforts, many would have given it to Houghton.

Goal-difference was always liable to determine Group 3. Ireland now stood one goal worse off than Spain. Not that the players had time to dwell. Reveille was at dawn next morning. The squad were off to America.

IRELAND (0) 2   **ALBANIA (0) 0**
Aldridge 60, McGrath 79

IRELAND: Bonner (CELTIC), Irwin (MAN U), McGrath (VILLA), O'Leary (ARSENAL), Staunton (VILLA), Houghton (LIVERPOOL), Townsend (CHELSEA), Keane (FOREST), Sheedy (NEWCASTLE) (*sub* McCarthy, MILLWALL), Quinn (MAN C), Aldridge (TRANMERE) (*sub* Coyne, CELTIC).
ALBANIA: Dani, Zmijani, Peqini, Vata, Abazi, Quendro (Pali), Vasi, Kushta, Demollari, Zela (Sokoli), Raklli.

IRELAND v LATVIA

Wednesday, 9 September 1992   *Lansdowne Road – 32,000*

The posh-sounding 'US Cup' necessitated a tour nobody really wanted. It was intended to be a dress rehearsal for the World Cup. Shaking off their jet lag, Ireland lost to the USA, then to Italy, where Bonner was red-carded. Ireland were spared their blushes by overcoming Portugal.

Latvia were one of three Baltic states enjoying the flush of independence. Another, Lithuania, was also in Ireland's group; the third Estonia, was in Scotland's. Latvia had entered the 1938 World Cup, but were denied by Austria. In 1940 Latvia and her neighbours were annexed by Moscow.

Maurice Setters flew to watch Latvia at home to Denmark. It was the Danes' first competitive match since their coronation, and despite twenty-three shots and fourteen corners they failed to score.

Latvian coach Janis Gilis had no funds with which to inspect opponents in person. He had to rely on press reports and, if lucky, video tapes. His players were drawn from Latvia's small domestic league, and one or two from Polish lower divisions.

England weren't in action this week, and Ray Houghton took a bad knock for Villa at the weekend. Andy Townsend – who had signed for Chelsea after Italia '90 – took the captaincy, and kept it. Alan Kernaghan made his debut.

The Latvians did their best to disorientate their hosts by turning out in propeller-patterned shirts of maroon and purple. Nevertheless, it took Ireland only twenty-one seconds to win the first of fifteen corners, and by closing time they had mustered twenty-six attempts on goal. Irwin crossed for the first goal. Sheedy pounced as one defender lunged from the left, another from the right. Irwin also made the last goal, from Aldridge two minutes from time. That, a towering header into the far corner, completed Aldridge's hat-trick. How times had changed. Aldridge had threatened a hat-trick against Albania, but now actually achieved it, his second for Ireland.

He was grateful even to be on the pitch. These days the veteran striker was rarely asked to play ninety minutes, and was customarily pulled off. He had opened his account with a header that beat Igoshnin to his left, and bagged his second from the spot after Bulders had clobbered Tommy Coyne.

The press duly voted Aldridge man of the match, for which they were put straight by Big Jack. The best player on the field, he scolded the assembled press, was Ronnie Whelan.

IRELAND (1) 4   **LATVIA (0) 0**
  Sheedy 31,
  Aldridge 59, 81 pen, 88

IRELAND: Bonner (CELTIC), Irwin (MAN U), Kernaghan (MIDDLESBROUGH), McGrath (VILLA), Staunton (VILLA), Keane (FOREST), Townsend (CHELSEA), Whelan (LIVERPOOL), Sheedy (NEWCASTLE) (*sub* Phelan, MAN C), Quinn (MAN C) (*sub* Coyne, CELTIC), Aldridge (TRANMERE).
LATVIA: Igoshnin, Bulders, Alexeenko, Gnedoi, Abzhinov, Glasov, Astafjev (Sidorov), Sprogis, Popkov (Semyonov), Linards, Jeliseev.

DENMARK v IRELAND
Wednesday, 14 October 1992   *Parken Stadium, Copenhagen – 40,100*

So far so good. Now came back-to-back trips to Denmark and Spain. Two wins would put Ireland in pole position; two defeats might bury them. In the interim Denmark and Spain had dipped their toes into the waters of Baltic football and found it nippy. Both had to settle for goalless draws. The Danes had missed a penalty, and had merely two points to show for their Baltic excursions. Judging from these results, Denmark's European title hung round their necks like a lead necklace. This was their first home match since their coronation, and in a spanking new stadium the crowd would surely lift them.

This was the fourth time Denmark had crossed Ireland's path in the World Cup. Ireland had beaten them home and away in the 1958 series, since when Denmark had dominated.

Denmark were a paradox. The side that slayed England in 1983, dissected Ireland twice under Eoin Hand, and toppled Scotland in the '86 finals was described by Scotland's manager Alex Ferguson as arguably the best in Europe. But, like cherry blossom, Denmark bloomed spectacularly, only to wilt overnight. They failed to make the finals of Italia '90 or Euro '92, and gave every indication of being nine-day wonders. Then they exploded into life in Sweden.

Denmark's English ties had strengthened. Once upon a time, Jan Mölby flew the flag alone. Johnny Sivebaek had come and gone from Old Trafford, goalkeeper Peter Schmeichel was still there. John Jensen had just signed for Arsenal and Torben Piechnik for Liverpool.

Coach Richard Moeller-Nielsen fielded nine of his European champions. That meant he was still without Michael Laudrup, elder brother of Brian and jewel of Denmark's team in Mexico. Laudrup disapproved of the more negative game-plan Moeller-Nielsen had foisted on the players, a difference of opinion that had kept him out of the side for two years.

Charlton described Denmark's tactics in Sweden as 'bouncing the ball off the opposition's back four.' But they had tried something new in Latvia and Lithuania and come unstuck. Charlton thought they would revert to type.

McGrath was out, so was Whelan, so was McCarthy, Staunton and Sheedy, plus a number of fringe players, and Charlton's patched-up side were soon in the thick of it. Quinn was booked early on for charging into

Schmeichel, but that was the extent of the Danish keeper's discomfort. Ireland didn't manage one shot on target. Mind you, that was not for want of trying. Ireland shaded the first half, whistling shots over the top or round the post. Houghton, for one, blasted a cracker inches too high.

Denmark began to assert themselves after the break, pinging balls over the back four, with novice Kernaghan and stalwart Moran standing tall. Bonner, prone to parrying shots instead of clutching them or deflecting them away, made fine stops from Povlsen, Brian Laudrup and others.

Ireland's last chance to take both points came when substitute David Kelly headed wide. The final whistle was greeted with roars of Irish approval.

On the same evening, Spain, handicapped by having a man sent off, drew 0-0 in Belfast. For Billy Bingham it was a second home point dropped (after Lithuania), and Northern Ireland were beginning to sag.

DENMARK   (0) 0   **IRELAND   (0) 0**

DENMARK: Schmeichel, Sivebaek, Rieper, Olsen, Piechnik, Heintze, Vilfort, Larsen, Jensen, B Laudrup, Povlsen (Christiansen).
IRELAND: Bonner (CELTIC), Irwin (MAN U), Kernaghan (MIDDLESBROUGH), Moran (BLACKBURN), Phelan (MAN C), Houghton (VILLA), Keane (FOREST), Townsend (CHELSEA), McGoldrick (PALACE), Quinn (MAN C), Aldridge (TRANMERE) (*sub* Kelly, NEWCASTLE).

SPAIN v IRELAND
Wednesday, 18 November 1992   Sánchez Pizjuán Stadium, Seville – 52,000

Ireland's record in Spain did not bear close examination. They had lost on their last seven visits, and it was something of an achievement even to score.

Two bookings in two games ruled out Kernaghan. Cascarino, McCarthy, Whelan and Sheridan were likewise sidelined, in their case through injury. In a recent book, Manchester United manager Alex Ferguson had written things about Paul McGrath to which the player took exception. He was on a downer, and was said to be flirting with quitting. Thankfully, he only flirted.

Spain's top seeding was reward for reaching the latter stages of the finals three times running. Xavier Clemente had taken control in the summer. Clemente relied heavily on players from Barcelona and the Basque region, less so on those from Real Madrid. He promptly recalled Butragueno and Salinas – the latter dropped by Barcelona. Clemente needed these older, wiser heads, and the compliment to Ireland did not go unheeded. Nor did the fact that Spain opted to play in their most impregnable fortress, the Sánchez Pizjuán Stadium, whose tiers reared up to the sky like a stairway to heaven.

Diego Maradona had just signed for the local club, Seville. He was affability itself, diplomatically declining to predict the outcome.

As in Copenhagen, Ireland started in a rush, hoping to score before the opposition could settle. The Belgian referee, Constantin, was quick to note the names of McGrath – upending the keeper as he collected a cross – and Moran, plus that of Goicoechea.

A flick from Aldridge put Quinn clear. The side-footed shot was slightly telegraphed, and Zubizarreta stuck out a toe to turn it behind. The best of the other openings fell to Spain. Martin Vazquez seemed sure to score, but Moran cleared with Butragueno buzzing over his shoulder.

In the second half the frizzy-haired Lopez, a constant irritant, dragged Aldridge back with an arm round the throat and a foot round the knee. Aldridge had eluded him and was bearing down on goal. The red card was flourished and Lopez slunk away.

Ireland would have preferred to be ahead on goals rather than manpower. All too often the depleted side summon the energy to fill the gaps and present their opponents with unwanted tactical problems.

The game's major talking point was not the sending off, but a linesman's flag that denied Ireland a priceless goal. The indefatigable Keane threaded the ball inside to Quinn, who tapped it ahead to Aldridge. In a flash Aldridge had rounded Zubizarreta to score. A linesman flagged, however, and no amount of post-match replays could undo the damage. Quinn had been onside. Even the Spanish press next day concurred.

Only once did Ireland catch their breath. Three minutes from time Martin Vazquez flipped the ball over Moran to the lurking Bakero. It had to be hit on the drop, difficult enough for anyone. Bakero sent the ball into space, and it would have been cruel on Ireland otherwise.

Back in Belfast, Northern Ireland had lost to Denmark, in a match punctuated by floodlight failure. Having consumed four home ties, Northern Ireland's threat was all but extinguished.

SPAIN (0) 0   IRELAND (0) 0

SPAIN: Zubizarreta, Ferrer, Lopez, Solozabal, Goicoechea, Michel, Hierro, Amor, Martin Vazquez, Butragueno (Beguiristain), Salinas (Bakero).
IRELAND: Bonner (CELTIC), Irwin (MAN U), McGrath (VILLA), Moran (BLACKBURN), Phelan (MAN C), Houghton (VILLA), Keane (FOREST), Townsend (CHELSEA) Staunton (VILLA), Aldridge (TRANMERE), Quinn (MAN C).

IRELAND v NORTHERN IRELAND
Wednesday, 31 March 1993   *Lansdowne Road – 33,000*

Spain rounded off 1992 by trouncing Latvia 5-0. In February they repeated the score against Lithuania, and Northern Ireland triumphed 2-1 in Albania.

While Northern Ireland were winning in Tirana – with Charlton looking on – Ireland squeezed in a friendly with Wales at Tolka Park. The match resulted in a fractured cheekbone for David O'Leary and a twenty-third and last cap for John Byrne. Strangely, not one had been in the World Cup.

A rugby match, scheduled for Lansdowne Road on the Saturday, pleased Jack and the FAI not one jot. They brought pressure to bear, and the match was switched, though not without stirring up further ill-feeling.

Kick-off was fixed for 1.45 pm, ensuring thousands of 'non-runners' north and south of the border. Only a tiny quota of Ulster fans had tickets.

This would be Billy Bingham's fortieth World Cup encounter, of which he had lost just thirteen. He hoped to field his strongest side, half of which languished in the reserve teams of their English clubs. Danny Wilson, so bright for Sheffield Wednesday, so dull for Northern Ireland, was omitted.

In view of the political situation, just the Republic's anthem *Amhrán na bhFiann* was played, just the Irish tricolour flew. Protocol would be reversed in Belfast. But common cause was made when all twenty-two players stood in the centre circle in respect for the victims of violence, and in particular those of the recent Warrington bombs. The drizzle was the only sound.

The absent Aldridge – recovering from an operation to repair torn stomach muscles – required Charlton's only team-change. Tommy Coyne deputised.

Local derbies, whether between clubs or nations, are traditionally tight, hard, low-scoring. The teams' strengths and weaknesses tend to cancel each other out. This particular match bucked the trend.

Andy Townsend signalled the mood with a wonderful weaving sortie. Minutes later he dabbed the ball to Niall Quinn, raced for the backheeled return, and with defenders converging sidefooted past Tommy Wright. Nineteen minutes had elapsed. Two minutes later, Houghton's banana cross was volleyed in by Quinn himself.

The Ulstermen, in their natty blue shirts with white pin-stripes, stood around dazed. But worse was to come. Ian Dowie intended to head Steve Staunton's inswinging corner behind for another, but he somehow missed it, and the full-back at the near post had no time to react as it swerved past him into the net. 3-0 to Ireland. Game, set and match.

In the second half Northern Ireland came out fighting. Ireland had done the necessaries and seemed content to sit back. Jimmy Quinn and Kingsley Black came on for the North, but made little difference. In truth, it got a bit tedious by the end, with the result wrapped up.

The one sour moment was when air-heads chanted: 'There's only one team in Ireland.' Jack's players could do without that needless provocation. They knew it would be revisited upon them, with interest, in Belfast.

Ray Houghton was narrowly voted man of the match. But it was that sort of day when half a dozen players could have claimed it.

Tommy Wright is on his knees in despair. Niall Quinn is on his knees with joy.

Billy Bingham told the waiting press: 'I think the finals are now becoming unreachable.' Meanwhile, Denmark saw off Spain, 1-0 in Copenhagen.

IRELAND (3) 3   **NORTHERN IRELAND   (0) 0**
Townsend 19, Quinn 21,
Staunton 28

IRELAND: Bonner (CELTIC), Irwin (MAN U), McGrath (VILLA), Moran (BLACKBURN), Phelan (MAN C), Houghton (VILLA), Keane (FOREST), Townsend (CHELSEA), Staunton (VILLA), N Quinn (MAN C) (*sub* McGoldrick, PALACE), Coyne (TRANMERE) (*sub* Cascarino, CHELSEA).
N IRELAND: Wright (FOREST), Donaghy (CHELSEA), Taggart (BARNSLEY), McDonald (QPR), Worthington (SHEFF W), O'Neill (HIBS) (*sub* Black, FOREST), Magilton (OXFORD) (*sub* J Quinn, READING), Morrow (ARSENAL), Hughes (STRASBOURG), Dowie (SO'TON), Gray (SUNDERLAND).

IRELAND v DENMARK
Wednesday, 28 April 1993   *Lansdowne Road – 33,000*

What a change from Denmark's last visit to Lansdowne, eight years earlier. Then they wore the mantle of choir boys about to raid a den of thieves. Ireland were the footballing vagabonds, whipped 1-4, denied tickets for the festival yet again. It was that defeat which opened the door to Jack Charlton. One thing was sure: Denmark would not wear a youthful swagger this time. Buoyed by wins over Spain and Latvia, which thrust them back into the frame, the Danes arrived in a happier state of mind. Like Ireland, they hadn't lost a goal so far. Denmark had nine points from six, Ireland eight from five. With two mean defences and goal-shy attacks, what price a goalless draw?

With FIFA insisting on Lansdowne Road being all-seater for World Cup-ties, which greatly reduced its capacity, thousands of loyal fans were denied entrance. The situation was worsened by Denmark taking up their full ticket allocation – Albania and Latvia hadn't, and Northern Ireland couldn't.

Full-back Terry Phelan, transferring from Wimbledon to Manchester City for a cool £2.5 million, had established himself as the costliest player ever to represent Ireland. But he had tweaked a hamstring and was out. In view of Brian Laudrup's pace – later exhibited at Rangers – Charlton couldn't fiddle with his midfield. He left well alone, bringing in Eddie McGoldrick at No. 3.

Matchday was Kevin Moran's thirty-seventh birthday. He stood to be one of three survivors from Denmark's 1985 visit, but succumbed to a late injury. Now only McGrath and Cascarino (on the bench) had that distinction. Moran was replaced by Kernaghan.

Charlton also recalled John Aldridge quicker than expected. The Tranmere striker had played his first league game for two months on the Saturday. One consolation to JC was that ace striker Flemming Povlson was out for the season, crocking his knee playing for Borussia Dortmund.

Ireland's home record under Charlton was now thirty-odd games with just two defeats, both against Wales. One was in his first match, when he allowed others to pick the side, the second was not at Lansdowne. In Jack's eyes, Ireland were unbeaten at Lansdowne Road, where, in World Cups, Ireland had won seven out of seven. Weighing these facts and the general state of Group 3, Moeller-Nielsen sent out a team even more defensive than usual.

For the second successive match, Lansdowne Road stood in silent respect before the kick-off. This time it was to honour the dead of Zambia's World Cup team, which had perished in an aircrash in the Atlantic.

Whereas Ireland were quickly away from the blocks against the North, this time it was Denmark who imposed an early grip. The pitch was hard, the ball bouncing like a beach-ball, but that did not stop Laudrup tormenting McGoldrick. It took Ireland fifteen minutes to stabilise, whereupon three quick corners and a near-miss by Houghton indicated better times ahead.

Denmark's goal was surprising only in that it came when it did. The French referee, Harrel, had dished out one yellow card apiece when the Irish defence was pierced. Olsen crossed and Bonner tentatively came to punch clear. McGrath either didn't hear him or didn't trust him, and headed out – to Kim Vilfort. Bonner was in limbo as the Dane killed the ball with one foot and flipped it with the other over the keeper's head. Bonner landed on his backside in the net, from which posture he aired his frustration at McGrath.

The goal was the first Ireland had lost at home in the World Cup since 1985, which was also attributable to Denmark. The Danes were well-capable of protecting their lead, and, with their swift breakouts, to extend it.

Ireland screamed 'penalty' when Rieper elbowed Quinn in the face as he challenged Schmeichel. Five minutes into the second half it was the Danes' turn. Kernaghan's desperate tackle from behind on Lars Elstrup sent hearts into stomachs. Once again the referee wasn't interested.

Ireland enjoyed only fleeting glimpses of goal, being outgunned by a five-man Danish midfield, and unable to string together any coherent moves. Cascarino took over from Aldridge, who had looked far from match-fit.

Even the most diehard Irish supporter could see Denmark winning. Jakob Kjeldbjerg, shortly to sign for Chelsea, was a colossus in defence, Vilfort and Arsenal's Jensen were bossing Townsend and Keane in midfield, and Laudrup continued to cause mayhem down the flank.

Ireland's equaliser was an unexpected as it was welcome. McGrath's persistence won a corner. It was taken short by Houghton to Staunton, whose curling cross was flicked into the far corner by the salmon-leaping Quinn. It was the merest deflection, but it beat Schmeichel.

Buoyed up, Ireland went in search of a second point, but they carried no greater punch than before, and Denmark experienced few scares.

'Maybe not the most beautiful football match I have seen,' expounded Moeller-Nielsen afterwards.

'In the end I'm absolutely delighted with the result. It was looking dodgy for a while,' said Jack. Far away, Spain were hammering the final nail in Northern Ireland's coffin, coming from behind to win 3-1.

IRELAND (0) 1   **DENMARK (0) 1**
Quinn 74   Vilfort 26

IRELAND: Bonner (CELTIC), Irwin (MAN U), McGrath (VILLA), Kernaghan (MIDDLESBROUGH), McGoldrick (PALACE), Houghton (VILLA), Townsend (CHELSEA), Keane (FOREST), Staunton (VILLA), Aldridge (TRANMERE) (*sub* Cascarino, CHELSEA), Quinn (MAN C).
DENMARK: Schmeichel, Friis-Hansen, Rieper, Olsen, Kjeldbjerg, Steen Nielsen, Vilfort, Jensen, Elstrup, B Laudrup, Pingel (Kristensen).

ALBANIA v IRELAND
Wednesday, 26 May 1993   *Qemal Stafa Stadium, Tirana – 10,000*

That dropped point changed the complexion of Ireland's three end-of-season excursions to eastern Europe. Three 'results' (in soccer-speak, 'draws') would ordinarily have been good enough. Not any more. To keep Denmark at arm's length it was necessary to go for three wins.

End of season matches were both a blessing and a curse. On the one hand, English clubs could no longer yell 'hands off'; Charlton could choose from a full complement of players. On the other, they were knackered after an exhausting season. Irish and British teams rarely sparkle in May and June. For that reason, Charlton was determined to keep those dates for the small fry, and tackle the big boys in the autumn when his players were fresh.

The domestic season ended with Manchester United claiming the first Premier League title, and extraordinary goings-on in the National League. A new format meant that – as Shelbourne, Bohemians and Cork City had tied on points – they engaged in a three-way play-off. That too ended deadlocked, and it took a second round-robin before the men of Cork claimed their prize.

Ireland were to play Albania, Latvia and Lithuania within the space of three weeks. For months it had been debated whether the Albania match could go ahead, and if so where. Northern Ireland's players and officials had endured a torrid time getting to Tirana.

Delicate negotiations with the FAI sorted out most of the pitfalls, but could do nothing to ameliorate the heat or the spartan conditions. Knowing it was not a trip to relish, unless players were likely to play, Charlton restricted the travelling party to just seventeen players. These excluded Sheridan, worn out following an endless series of Wembley cup finals against Arsenal, and McGrath, 'missing' again. Ray Houghton was set to win his fiftieth cap.

The Mustafa Qemal Stadium, with its bare concrete step-terracing, was frowned over by trees and mountains, and still bore the imprint of its Stalinist past, red flags, bas-reliefs of heroic workers. Albania's most famous result was the 0-0 draw that expelled West Germany from the 1968 European Championship. Albanians hankered after that match as if it signalled a golden past, less inclined to reflect upon the 0-6 drubbing in the away tie.

Satellite TV pictures were far from perfect, but it was just possible to pick out the one Albanian player most people had heard of, the sweeper, Rudi Vata, of Glasgow Celtic. It was a year to the day since the teams last met, during which time more Albanian players had found employment abroad.

If the first shock to the thousands of Irish congregating in specially hired theatres was the poor picture quality, the second was that Albania were no fools. They hadn't looked mugs in Dublin, either, but now they scored a super goal. Kushta was freed by Demollari, sprinted clear of Kernaghan's lumbering pursuit, and crashed the ball past Bonner at his near post.

Ireland needed to level quickly before Albania started getting ideas. Townsend was pulled down by Kushta. The free-kick was on the edge of the box and was exploited by Staunton. The wall was inexpertly positioned and Staunton – playing despite a tummy bug – found the gap.

The relief was palpable, but Ireland had come to Tirana to win, not to draw. Staunton entered the Italian referee's notebook a second time, this time for the novel offence of taking a free-kick before the referee was ready. Two Albanians were also booked, and the longer the match wore on the more frenetic it became. McGrath was badly missed, and Ireland created little.

Aldridge, as usual, had run his legs off. His replacement, Cascarino, had barely warmed up than he took up position at the far post for Staunton's corner and made clean headed contact. Musta was stranded, and the ball was over the line when Vata, attempting to clear, skied it high into the net. The keeper railed at the referee so fiercely he was lucky not to be ordered off.

Had Quinn's header not gone adrift of an untenanted goal, Ireland might have lived out those closing minutes more cosily. Afterwards, Charlton paid Albania their due: 'They played some good football'.

ALBANIA (1) 1
Kushta 7

IRELAND (1) 2
Staunton 12, Cascarino 77

ALBANIA: Musta, Zmijani (Fortuzi), Lekbello, Vata, Shala, Shulku, Peqini, Kushta, Demollari, Milori, Raklli (Bano).
IRELAND: Bonner (CELTIC), Irwin (MAN U), Moran (BLACKBURN), Kernaghan (MIDDLESBROUGH), Phelan (MAN C), Houghton (VILLA), Keane (FOREST), Townsend (CHELSEA), Staunton (VILLA), Aldridge (TRANMERE) (*sub* Cascarino CHELSEA), Quinn (MAN C).

LATVIA v IRELAND
Wednesday, 9 June 1993   *Dauvadas Stadium, Riga – 7,000*

Charlton's team arrived in the picturesque city of Riga seven days after Billy Bingham's. Northern Ireland had won 2-1, but for them it was too late.

Once again Charlton flew out with fewer than his permitted twenty-two, confident he had enough cover. Paul McGrath had turned up, and Moran had to make way for him. Niall Quinn was out of sorts with a stomach bug, or something, but would play. Latvia's doughty goalkeeper, Igoshnin, wouldn't.

Latvia had sprinted through their programme. This was their penultimate match, having drawn and lost five apiece. They were the only team in Group 3 still searching for a win. More to the point, both Spain and Denmark had been held to scoreless draws in the Dauvadas Stadium.

The pitch was surrounded by a running track, which in turn was surrounded by a moat. This kept spectators far from the action and dissipated any atmosphere. Those with binoculars were instantly popular.

Aldridge's goal after fourteen minutes looked good from any distance. The overlapping Irwin had crossed, allowing Aldridge to shed his marker by darting to the near post and heading inside the far.

Latvia were giving as much as they got, and Ainars Linards – sporadically prominent in Dublin – had a taste for running at McGrath, which the defender did not appreciate. Popkov fired over at one end, then blocked an Irish effort on his own goal-line.

As half-time beckoned, Ireland scored another. Houghton received a short free-kick from Staunton and eyed the field. Aldridge sprinted away, dragging defenders, leaving McGrath to duck into the gap and meet the cross with a firm header. McGrath had earlier apologised to everyone for his unexplained absence for the Albania match, and now the slate was wiped clean.

Townsend opened the second half with a pot-shot that Karavajev turned onto the bar and over. Charlton had evidently instructed his men to go for the jugular. Although the points looked safe, goal-difference could not be ignored. But Staunton kept over-hitting his crosses and chances went begging. Cascarino and Keane held their heads in frustration. Would Keane ever score for Ireland, some wondered?

Afterwards Charlton toasted his midfielders, Keane and Townsend: 'I often wonder where they get the energy from.'

LATVIA   (0) 0   **IRELAND   (2) 2**
                                       Aldridge 14, McGrath 42

LATVIA: Karavajev, Sarando (Gorjacilov), Gnedoi, Sevlakovs, Bulders, Erglis, Astafjev, Ivanov, Popkov, Linards, Babicev (Jeilejev).
IRELAND: Bonner (CELTIC), Irwin (MAN U), McGrath (VILLA), Kernaghan (MIDDLESBROUGH), Phelan (MAN C), Houghton (VILLA), Keane (FOREST), Townsend (CHELSEA), Staunton (VILLA), Quinn (MAN C) (*sub* Cascarino, CHELSEA), Aldridge (TRANMERE) (*sub* Sheridan, SHEFF W).

LITHUANIA v IRELAND
Wednesday, 16 June 1993   *Zalgirls Stadium, Vilnius – 5,000*

Lithuania were the one newcomers still to be faced. They were also competing in their first World Cup since the 1930s, having been beaten by Sweden in the 1934 eliminators and neighbours Latvia four years later. They now showed themselves the strongest of the three eastern minnows. They had beaten the other two. Defensively, Lithuania seemed sound enough; only Spain had put more than two past them. But as both Spain and Northern Ireland had won here in the past month, there would be few excuses.

Vilnius had less to offer by way of medieval majesty and Western enterprise than Riga. Ireland's players did, however, enjoy a few laughs at the match programme, which listed their names as 'Makgratas' (of Villa), 'Oldridzas' (of Tranmere), 'Kvinas' (of Manchester City), 'Boneras' (of Celtic). Ireland were apparently managed by one 'Dzekis Carltonas'.

Lithuania matched the Latvians' maroon and mauve with an alluring outfit of orange and green, with German-style zigzags across their chests. Their cymbal-crashing supporters were disheartened by the news that three players with Austria Vienna had not been released, as the Lithuanian FA couldn't raise the money to insure them. This pleased neither Spain nor Denmark, alarmed at Ireland's all-conquering path. Some wise-heads reckoned Spain had offered to pay the money themselves.

While a few intrepid Irish fans stayed on, meandering leisurely from one Baltic republic to the next, JC brought his players home to relax and prepare. When he announced his team, it was unchanged.

Two home corners inside two minutes confirmed that Lithuania were no pushovers. But Ireland were soon pounding forward. McGrath headed down at the far post for Keane, whose low drive was whacked clear by Baltusnikas, while Kernaghan's shot was repulsed by the keeper, Martinkenas. McGrath's late challenge cost him a booking and a place in the next match.

Irwin narrowly avoided an own-goal at one end, but Baltusnikas was not so fortunate at the other. Staunton's free-kick was either ingenious or scuffed, an ankle-trimmer that the sweeper powered high into his own net. A distaste for own-goals has led some to credit the strike to Staunton, but that seems excessively indulgent.

In fact, there was almost a contagion of own-goals. Full-back Ziukas tried to get in on the act, from Staunton's corner, but Martinkenas rescued.

Ireland looked stronger after half-time, McGrath and Phelan outstanding at the back, Houghton the pick of midfield. A one-goal lead left everyone on tenterhooks, and Baranauskas fired a free-kick round the wall and against the bottom of a post. The ball flew back against Bonner's head and out to safety.

Ronnie Whelan subbed for Aldridge, solidifying the midfield with a 4-5-1 formation, and slowly strangling the life out of the home side. The match finished with a replica booking to that in Riga. This time it was Houghton who took a free-kick without waiting for authorisation. At the final whistle Charlton strode onto the pitch and gave the Luxembourg referee a piece of his mind. One is unsure whether the official understood Geordie.

'The Spanish will be ******** themselves and I'm delighted,' said Jack.

LITHUANIA (0) 0   **IRELAND (1) 1**

Baltusnikas 40 (o.g.)

LITHUANIA: Martinkenas, Ziukas, Baltusnikas, Baranauskas, Mazeikis, Buzmakovas, Skarbalius (Zdancius), Urbonas (Ranelis), Kirilovas, Stumbrys, Slekys.
IRELAND: Bonner (CELTIC), Irwin (MAN U), McGrath (VILLA), Kernaghan (MIDDLESBROUGH), Phelan (MAN C), Houghton (VILLA), Keane (FOREST), Townsend (CHELSEA), Staunton (VILLA), Quinn (MAN C), Aldridge (TRANMERE) (*sub* Whelan, LIVERPOOL).

IRELAND v LITHUANIA

Wednesday, 8 September 1993   *Lansdowne Road – 33,000*

The season was closed, Ireland were out in front, having won three in a row away from home for the first time since the war. As it turned out, it was that triple whammy that eventually took Ireland to America.

Now, the new season less than one month old, it was time to see off Lithuania. A number of players had changed clubs. Most ventured north, Townsend from Chelsea to Villa, O'Leary from Arsenal to Leeds, Keane from Forest to Manchester United. Only one headed south. Alan Kernaghan didn't fancy life in the Endsleigh League and signed for Manchester City.

The FA Carling Premiership and the newly named National League of Ireland slipped anchors early (the European Under-16s were scheduled for Ireland in the spring). Not that the LOI's revamped image could tempt Charlton into fielding an Ireland-based player. Those days were gone. The emergence of Ireland's national side served to widen the gulf between British pros and Irish semi-pros. By comparison, the latter were short of fitness and experience, and, by being left out, the vicious circle could only widen.

Lithuania had gone down 0-4 in Copenhagen. Why they should arrive in Dublin with an all-green kit was a mystery. The FAI came to the rescue by supplying white shirts and black shorts. Coach Algmintas Liubinskas had further problems over the release of expat players, and his side showed four changes, among them a new goalkeeper.

McGrath – suspended – was missing from Charlton's first-team core, as was O'Leary (Achilles tendon) and Tommy Coyne. Coyne had suffered personal tragedy, the death of his wife in childbirth.

For the 33,000 who packed Lansdowne Road with its FIFA-restricted capacity, the finishing line was almost within reach. Two more points and it would be even nearer. It took just four minutes for Staunton's grass-trimming centre to be swept in by Aldridge, the 100th goal of Charlton's regime.

Threatened with capsize, poor Lithuania didn't know which way to turn. Quinn might have scored, but stumbled at the moment of shooting. Staunton's humdinger whizzed over the bar. Aldridge, Keane, Kernaghan and Moran were the next to chance their luck as Ireland queued up to score.

It was surely just a matter of time, and when Irwin chipped into the middle Kernaghan leapt up and over a defender to head number two.

Oddly, in the face of what had gone before, that goal killed not only the match but also Ireland's lust. In view of Denmark's goal-difference, the spectator in the stand or the viewer on his sofa could not fathom the complacency. The opposition were already dead; now mutilate the corpse.

It seldom works out like that, of course. Though Moran's header came back off a post, Ireland were in some disarray by half-time.

The second half, played in torrential rain, saw Ireland slip from bad to worse. Lithuania had their dander up. Baltusnikas, fall-guy of the first match, sprinted forty yards unopposed into Ireland's penalty box; Kivrolas's shot was saved, Slekys' slewed wide.

In an attempt to stop the rot, Charlton brought on Whelan and Cascarino. The rot continued. Stumbrys might have scored twice. Ireland were suddenly looking awful, standing off instead of pressurising, grateful that Lithuania hadn't the players to capitalise.

No one really deserved it, but Alan Kernaghan was nominated man of the match, more for his goal than his defensive contribution.

Jack had clearly felt the tension too. 'The worst performance for some time,' he admitted. Even he had got it wrong at half-time, emphasising negatives instead of positives. With a stack of yellow cards hanging over key players he had urged them *not* to get stuck in, *not* to commit themselves.

To cap it all, Denmark won 1-0 in Albania.

IRELAND (2) 2 **LITHUANIA (0) 0**
Aldridge 4, Kernaghan 25

IRELAND: Bonner (CELTIC), Irwin (MAN U), Moran (BLACKBURN), Kernaghan (MAN C), Phelan (MAN C), Houghton (VILLA), Keane (MAN U), Townsend (VILLA) (*sub* Whelan, LIVERPOOL), Staunton (VILLA), Quinn (MAN C) (*sub* Cascarino, CELTIC), Aldridge (TRANMERE).
LITHUANIA: Stauce, Ziukas, Baltusnikas, Kalvaitis, Tereskinas, Apanavicius, Baranauskas, Skarbalius (Staliynas), Stumbrys, Kirilovas (Maciulevicius), Slekys.

IRELAND v SPAIN
Wednesday, 13 October 1993 *Lansdowne Road – 33,000*

Five weeks later Spain came a-calling, having just won 5-1 win in Albania amid allegations of money changing hands and Albania fielding a makeshift side. Each of the big three had played ten games. Ireland had 17 points, Denmark 16, Spain 15. Denmark hosted Northern Ireland the same night.

The calculators were busy. If Ireland won, they were through (Spain could no longer overtake them). If Ireland drew, they would need another draw in Belfast to make sure. If Ireland lost? Oh hell. As for Spain, their target was a draw in Dublin, followed by victory over Denmark. A defeat by Ireland – should Denmark overcome Northern Ireland – would put Spain out.

For reasons both practical and sentimental, Charlton wanted to win this one. Get it over with here and now, and celebrate in Dublin. Last time, it was Malta. Celebrations in Belfast would carry unsavoury undercurrents.

The Spanish team showed key changes from that which drew in Seville. The old guard – Butragueno, Martin Vazquez and Michel – were absent. Key strikers Salinas and Bakero were present, as was goalkeeper Zubizarreta, winning his eighty-second cap. Barcelona provided five of the team. Real Madrid players were out of favour.

Ireland would be without their captain, Townsend having pulled a hamstring. He had, some said, gone off the boil of late, and his loss was felt to be more symbolic than strategic. Captains are captains. Moran had done the job before, and now – aged thirty-eight – he did it again. Townsend's replacement, Ronnie Whelan, was not in the best of spirits himself, having been shop-windowed at Anfield by Graeme Souness.

Pat Bonner had gone down with a kidney infection, but would play. Less fortunate was John Aldridge, sidelined at Tranmere for several weeks with a thigh strain. Aldridge was sad he didn't make it: he regarded Zubizarreta as a personal rabbit, scoring eight times against the Barcelona goalkeeper in five matches with Real Sociedad. To put the wind up the Spanish, who had yet to name their side, Aldridge was sent marching up and down outside their changing room wearing his customary No. 10 shirt.

On the domestic front, Cork City's euphoric league title was swiftly put into perspective by Galatasaray of Turkey. The Greeks of Panathinaikos were no kinder to Shelbourne in the Cup-Winners' Cup.

President of FIFA Joao Havelange attended the big match. This pleased the FAI, for it meant Ireland had come of age, and Spain, because the Italian referee, Fabio Baldas, would need to check any bias towards the home team.

For reasons not entirely clear, Charlton chose not to replace Aldridge with Cascarino, or otherwise keep faith with his usual formation. Instead, he played Niall Quinn alone up front and switched at the eleventh hour to 4-5-1. This introduced misgivings among many supporters. This was no time to fanny about with new formations. Look what had happened to Graham Taylor's England when he had done the same in Oslo. Whenever Charlton had imposed 4-5-1, Ireland had sprung leaks – 3-3 against Poland in Poznan; 1-3 against USA in Washington.

Moran won the toss and elected to face the wind. Ten minutes later, no alarms, and Ireland looking comfortable. Then Ferrer took a throw on the right, Julio Salinas nodded it on, and Caminero – Atletico Madrid's sole representative – launched into a left-footed volley. 0-1.

Three minutes later it was 0-2. Salinas outpaced Kernaghan, just as Kushta had done in Tirana. The pair sprinted down the left with Kernaghan unable to engage. As he reached the goal-line, Salinas pulled the ball inside, shooting past the partly culpable Bonner from a tight angle. Kernaghan covered his face, while the stadium – Spanish supporters aside – went deathly quiet.

Nor was the anguish over. Desperate to redeem himself, Kernaghan saw his header deflected on top of the bar. The resulting corner reached McGrath, but his shot whacked Zubizarreta's legs. Moran limped off, wearing an

John Sheridan's "consolation" goal against Spain would ultimately take Ireland to USA '94.

expression of utter woe, and was replaced by Sheridan. McGrath slipped on the captain's armband and slipped back into central defence. Whereupon Salinas seized upon Sheridan's interception and – cool as you like – took the ball round Bonner.

Nothing could prepare the Ireland team or supporters for such a score. Some fickle fans were already heading for the exits, with almost three-quarters of the match still to play.

Never mind the loss of two points, Ireland's crumbling goal-difference was handing Denmark another point on a plate. A nightmare was unfolding. Never count your chickens, but that very morning the nation had awoken to a plague of press supplements on how to travel to America. The merchandising industry was already in overdrive, just waiting for the green light.

Cascarino came out for the second half instead of the struggling Staunton, as Ireland reverted to their familiar 4-4-2. The real fans, proud to support their team in good times and bad, were shamed by the hushed stadium that permitted a few hundred delirious Spanish to outshout thirty thousand Irish.

Whelan had began brightly, but then vanished. Sheridan alone looked capable of presenting Spain with the unexpected, and to him fell the pride of salvaging a goal eighteen minutes from time. The 'roar' that greeted the goal was barely a whimper.

Ireland threatened just once more, Zubizarreta saving from Houghton. When the final whistle blew, the stadium was half-empty.

Spanish centre-back Nadal achieved the near-impossible, being one of the first opposition players at Dublin to be named man of the match.

'It wasn't our day,' said Charlton afterwards. A reporter reminded him that Ireland had played badly in their last match, against Lithuania, and before that, too. Maybe the team were no great shakes any more.

This was to be a bad night for Irish football. With twenty minutes to play in Copenhagen, Northern Ireland were drawing 0-0. Then Jimmy Quinn scored with his head, but the referee said no, mystifying everyone. Brian Laudrup snatched the winner with nine minutes left.

In Rotterdam, England were sunk by the Dutch. As things stood, USA '94 might be graced by no Irish or British team for the only time since the war.

IRELAND (0) 1   **SPAIN (3) 3**
Sheridan 72   Caminero 11, Salinas 14, 26

IRELAND: Bonner (CELTIC), Irwin (MAN U), Phelan (MAN C), Moran (BLACKBURN) (*sub* Sheridan, SHEFF W), Kernaghan (MAN C), Keane (MAN U), McGrath (VILLA), Houghton (VILLA), Quinn (MAN C), Whelan (LIVERPOOL), Staunton (VILLA) (*sub* Cascarino, CHELSEA).
SPAIN: Zubizarreta, Ferrer, Voro, Nadal, Giner, Hierro, Goicoechea, Camarasa, Salinas (Guardiola), Caminero (Bakero), Luis Enrique.

NORTHERN IRELAND v IRELAND
Wednesday, 17 November 1993   *Windsor Park – 10,500*

Ireland had to live through the fires of doubt for five weeks. They would be extinguished, for better or worse, in the worst possible setting, Belfast. Denmark would simultaneously take the field in Spain. The top three were now separated by just one point, but, crucially, Ireland had slipped to third.

	P	W	D	L	F	A	GD	Pts
Denmark	11	7	4	0	15	1	(+14)	18
Spain	11	7	3	1	26	4	(+22)	17
Ireland	11	7	3	1	18	5	(+13)	17

An Irish victory would secure second place, while an Irish defeat would spell oblivion. A draw would only be good enough provided the other match did not likewise finish all-square. If both matches ended level, it was bye-bye America. Unable to leave their fate to others, Ireland had to press for a win.

Ireland supporters could not flock to Belfast to back their team. This was down to the reciprocal agreement that, for security reasons, had prevented

Ulster fans descending on Dublin. Windsor Park was sited inside loyalist territory. FIFA regulations also closed the standing 'Kop' end, limiting the crowd to just 11,000. The cheering or weeping would be done in front of TV screens, apart from intrepid supporters who somehow got in anyway.

There were those in Spain and Denmark who reasoned that, blood being thicker than water, Northern Ireland would not do the dirty on the South. In theory, they had a point. England's spineless 0-0 Wembley draw with Northern Ireland, which took Bingham's team to Mexico '86, convinced the aggrieved Romanians, not to mention many spectators, that the result was preordained. The FIFA representative thought otherwise.

Anyone acquainted with the Ulster mentality knew it was unthinkable that the Republic might be granted easy passage. Some in the South argued that – were the positions reversed – they would treat a Northern victory more generously than the North would now treat a Southern one. Better one Irish team reached America than neither. Most English fans say the same about Scotland, applauding Scottish victories over everyone but themselves. Scots, however, like nothing better than England falling flat on their faces. In both cases it is the smaller that resents the larger. But these are deep waters.

Suffice to say, Ireland journeyed through the checkpoints and armed guards expecting no favours at their destination. Besides, there was that 0-3 hiding to avenge, not to mention the Lansdowne taunts.

'The O.K. Corral,' Billy Bingham described the match in prospect. It marked Bingham's send-off after seventeen years, off and on, at the helm. His association with Northern Ireland stretched back forty-two years. He had won fifty-six caps and managed the side 117 times.

As if the cards were not already stacked against Ireland, key players now began falling like rabbits. Staunton, injured against Spain, was despatched for surgery. More's the pity, since he was Ireland's International Player of the Year. Moran and Sheridan were next to call off, followed by Whelan and Sheedy. Aldridge just made it, having played his first full league match for seven weeks. Now he had to shrug off the flu, which struck down one or two of the Ireland party, including Charlton himself.

Baby-faced Leeds defender Gary Kelly and Coventry stopper Phil Babb were called into the squad as cover, though this was neither the time nor the place to blood them. Enough of Charlton's regular marauders were on their feet for him to field a patched-up side. Eddie McGoldrick assumed Staunton's left-flank duties. McGrath lined up in defence, alongside Alan Kernaghan.

Kernaghan's eligibility was both curious and, on his part, courageous. He and his parents had been born in England. His grandparents could be traced to Northern Ireland, for whom he had wished to play. But Northern Ireland adhered tightly to the birth principle. Just two of Bingham's squad were born outside Ulster. This meant Kernaghan's only chance of international honours was with England, or – exploiting the granny rule – for the Republic. This second option was somewhat easier to accomplish than the first. He got his wish, but at the cost of being cast in the North's eyes not just as a mercenary, but a traitor. This lent added venom to the taunts of Ulster supporters. They matched the South's 'There's only one team in Ireland' with their own 'You were never born in Ireland.'

Bingham had sharpened the cutting edge of the match by describing Charlton's team as a 'bunch of mercenaries'. Before the match was over rumours circulated that someone in the Northern camp had cast aspersions on blacks playing for the Republic.

Tension was bad enough already. In the weeks prior to the match, scores were murdered in Belfast in waves of sectarian violence. It got so bad there was talk of switching the match elsewhere. But that would have been in the South's interests, disadvantaging Spain and Denmark, who protested loudly.

There were some who said so, and more who thought it, but if things went wrong this might even be the end for Big Jack. History wasn't with him. The Republic had yet to score in Belfast, posting 0-1 and 0-0 scores on previous visits. It was fortunate that Pat Bonner was fit and able. The Celtic stalwart knew enough about sectarian hatreds not to be fazed by the intimidating atmosphere.

Bingham had no injury scares, naming a side that included thirty-four year old Jimmy Quinn, top scorer in English football, albeit with Reading from the Endsleigh League second division.

On this most dramatic of nights, the first shock came from elsewhere. Even before the match kicked-off, the grapevine told that San Marino had scored against England after just eight seconds.

Reciprocating the arrangement in Dublin, only one anthem was played: *God Save the Queen*. Where Northern Ireland had played in a second strip of blue and white, Ireland's was their usual reverse, white shirts, green shorts.

A gusty wind hampered the enterprise of both teams. The start was quiet, cautious, probing. For fifteen minutes little transpired that was memorable. Those Southern ears tuned in to Seville were alerted to the fact that Spanish keeper Zubizarreta had been expelled, magnifying Spain's task.

Half-time at Windsor Park. There had been barely a shot on goal, barely an incident of note. Phil Gray had come closest for the North, hooking wide. It was still goalless in Seville. Something had to give in the second half, otherwise Ireland were out.

Matches in other groups kicked off earlier. Those hoping for a broad sweep of Irish and British clubs in America were to be disappointed. Holland had won in Poland, putting England out of their misery. Wales were despatched, too, missing a penalty against Romania.

Ireland were the last 'home' nation still alive, but time was running out. With twenty minutes left, and both matches still 0-0, Ireland looked doomed.

But at least Ireland were pressing now. No doubt about it, the North were in retreat. Houghton had a chance, but Tommy Wright saved with his feet.

News from Seville. Ten-man Spain had scored through Hierro. That Peter Schmeichel had been blatantly obstructed was of little concern to an Irish nation jumping out of their seats. What a pity it wasn't Denmark who had scored. Spain were a man short and would be less able to hang on.

Cascarino assumed the job of town-crier, running up and down the line passing on the score. Houghton came off, replaced by Alan McLoughlin. It was only Charlton's crop of injuries that permitted McLoughlin a place on the bench. He hadn't featured in any of the previous qualifiers, and his main, perhaps his only, moment of glory had been when coming on as sub against England in Cagliari. McLoughlin somehow stirred things up.

McLoughlin was still attuning to the pace of the game when the world caved in. Jimmy Quinn uncorked a fabulous airborne volley that whistled over Bonner's head from twenty yards.

'There's only one team in Ireland,' mocked the Windsor Park faithful. Bingham celebrated so gustily from one dug-out that exception was taken in the other. Angry words were exchanged.

News of the goal must have come as a godsend to the beleaguered Danes. Their ecstasy, and Ireland's agonies, lasted three and a half minutes. That was the time it took for Irwin's free-kick to be headed out to McLoughlin. The substitute took the ball on his chest, and with defenders lunging struck it in an arc that veered away from Wright inside his right-hand post.

Pandemonium. McLoughlin was engulfed and the roar from Dublin, Cork and Galway doubtless carried to the moon. JC's substitutions once again appeared to bear the divine stamp.

All was not safe. McLoughlin's goal served only to restore parity. Parity was useless if Denmark, too, should equalise. Cascarino came on for the South, Kingsley Black for the North. With play going on, the public address announced 'joint' men of the match, Alan McDonald and Paul McGrath.

The Turkish referee's final whistle was greeted with a kind a spluttering hysteria, questioning faces turning to each other for news from Seville. Charlton delivered an earful to Billy Bingham that he instantly regretted and which later led him to interrupt Bingham's press conference to apologise.

Tommy Eglington remarked: 'I played twenty-four times for Ireland and six times for Northern Ireland, but that was the toughest match I have ever played.' After four minutes' purgatory, Denmark's defeat was confirmed.

Ireland had qualified on goals scored, the narrowest of margins, becoming the first European nation ever to qualify by such means. John Sheridan's late strike against Spain had not been a consolation, but a life-saver.

It was a feature of Group 3 that the big guns boasted remarkable defensive records. For Denmark, eighteen points from twelve matches, conceding just two goals, was among the worst hard-luck stories in the history of World Cup qualification. They had missed out in 1990 by a whisker, too.

What had kept Ireland afloat was their record against Albania, Latvia and Lithuania, and in particular the summer programme that saw them haul a maximum six points.

Put another way, Ireland had a poorish record against the stronger teams. Had Group 3 comprised just Spain, Denmark, and the two Irelands, the Republic, with just one win, would have finished a distant third.

NORTHERN IRELAND (0) 1   IRELAND (0) 1
Quinn 73   McLoughlin 76

N IRELAND: Wright (FOREST), Fleming (BARNSLEY), McDonald (QPR), Taggart (BARNSLEY), Worthington (SHEFF W), Wilson (NOTTS CO) (*sub* Black, FOREST), Donaghy (CHELSEA), Magilton (OXFORD), Hughes (STRASBOURG), Quinn (READING), Gray (SUNDERLAND) (*sub* Dowie, SO'TON).
IRELAND: Bonner (CELTIC), Irwin (MAN U), McGrath (VILLA), Kernaghan (MAN C), Phelan (MAN C), Houghton (VILLA) (*sub* McLoughlin, PORTSM'TH), Townsend (VILLA), Keane (MAN U), McGoldrick (ARSENAL), Quinn (MAN C), Aldridge (TRANMERE).

Qualifying Group 3

	P	W	D	L	F	A	W	D	L	F	A	Pts
				Home					Away			
SPAIN	12	5	1	0	17	1	3	2	1	10	3	19
IRELAND	12	4	1	1	13	4	3	3	0	6	2	18
Denmark	12	5	1	0	12	0	2	3	1	3	2	18
Northern Ireland	12	2	3	1	8	4	3	0	3	6	9	13
Lithuania	12	1	2	3	4	6	1	1	4	4	15	7
Latvia	12	0	3	3	2	6	0	2	4	2	15	5
Albania	12	1	1	4	5	11	0	1	5	1	15	4

Other group results

Spain v Albania	3-0	Denmark v Spain	1-0
N Ireland v Lithuania	2-2	Denmark v Latvia	2-0
Albania v Lithuania	1-0	Lithuania v Albania	3-1
Latvia v Lithuania	1-2	Spain v N Ireland	3-1
Latvia v Denmark	0-0	Latvia v Albania	0-0
N Ireland v Albania	3-0	Lithuania v N Ireland	0-1
Lithuania v Denmark	0-0	Denmark v Albania	4-0
Latvia v Spain	0-0	Lithuania v Spain	0-2
N Ireland v Spain	0-0	Latvia v N Ireland	1-2
Lithuania v Latvia	1-1	Denmark v Lithuania	4-0

Albania v Latvia	1-1
N Ireland v Denmark	0-1
Spain v Latvia	5-0
Albania v N Ireland	1-2
Spain v Lithuania	5-0

Albania v Denmark	0-1
N Ireland v Latvia	2-0
Albania v Spain	1-5
Denmark v N Ireland	1-0
Spain v Denmark	1-0

The World Cup finals – UNITED STATES   June-July 1994

Alan McLoughlin had revived the fortunes and possibly the career of Jack Charlton. The World Cup finals were never going to be as uproarious second time round. The footballing world wouldn't again be caught cold by a sucker punch from Charlton's little invincibles. Ireland's strengths were there for all to see, and to prepare for. No longer would opponents think they had landed a soft touch. FIFA's rankings consistently confirmed Ireland to be among the top ten soccer powers. The gung-ho, underdog spirit wouldn't fool anybody this time. Ireland were nobody's mugs, nobody's underdogs.

The late demise of England and Wales – while maybe welcomed by some Irish supporters – was always going to cost Ireland dear. On a personal level, Charlton was an Englishman, he'd won a World Cup medal with England, and their absence from the finals clearly pained him. On a practical level, Italia '90 had seen Bobby Robson and Andy Roxburgh absorb the flak of the British media, leaving the Irish party largely for the Irish.

How different it would be in the USA. With no teams of their own to scavenge upon, British hacks would prey upon Jack and company, exposing every trifle.

History showed what might lie in store. The last time England failed to qualify, in 1978, the media circus had swooped on Scotland, Britain's only representatives. Ally MacLeod made a pig's ear of the job, and his fall was as savage as his resignation was inevitable. Yet Scotland generally treated their managers sympathetically, and MacLeod might have survived but for the press onslaught from south of the border.

When English TV condescends to report on other 'British' teams, it seeks out familiar faces, players and managers who made it big in England. Were Ireland, say, still to be managed by Eoin Hand, he would have been cold-shouldered compared with Charlton. Jack's very celebrity commanded headlines in England as well as Ireland, and he did not always take kindly to that kind of hassle. In 1990, he carried the flag of Ireland. Like it or not, in 1994 he would also carry the flag of Britain.

In December 1993 eyes and ears turned to Washington for the final draw. Sending the finals to America in the first place owed more to politics than to football. Looking on the bright side, though Americans were indifferent to soccer, they sure knew how to put on a good show.

USA '94 was the first World Cup since 1950 not to allocate groups on a regional basis. Only nine stadia would be utilised, with continental distances between them. Wherever Ireland ended up, they could be sure of crossing a time zone or several lines of latitude *en route* from one match to another.

Long before the draw was made the rumour-factory was in overdrive. Officially, only the top seeds have their venues settled in advance. The rest must rely on rabbits pulled from hats. This does not stop star-gazers or sceptics insisting on knowing other nations' base-camps. In 1986, everyone said England – though not seeded – would land up in Monterrey. They did. In 1994, everyone said Ireland would end up in Boston. They did not.

Rather, Ireland found themselves based in the Big Apple in an ominously powerful group. It was headed by Italy, continuing the repetitive sequences that had bedevilled Ireland since Euro '88. Italy would be tough. So would Norway, who had topped England's group. Although Mexico might surrender meekly in Europe, they were unlikely to do so near to home.

Charlton arranged friendlies in Holland and Germany, of all places. Managers usually invite warm-ups against teams that failed to qualify, or which are unlikely to spring unwelcome surprises, like Bolivia, whom Ireland beat 1-0. No one wants to head off to the finals bruised by heavy defeats.

It says much for Charlton's confidence in his players that he never entertained that possibility. But did he anticipate the converse? Holland had squeezed England out of a place in USA '94, but they were bettered by Ireland (1-0) in Tilburg. The result resounded around the world. But not nearly as loudly as Ireland's next feat of arms – a 2-0 win in Hanover.

Either of these wins would have placed Ireland on a pedestal. Their conjunction stamped Charlton's team among the favourites for the trophy.

But was this in Ireland's best interests? Far from being the upstarts of 1990, they were now potential world-beaters. Charlton could hide no more aces up his sleeve. His clothes were being picked over by the Italians, the Mexicans, the Norwegians, by everyone in football.

The harder they come, the bigger they fall. The fairy-tale heroes of Euro '88 and Italia '90, fêted to the stars for winning just one match in eight, were now expected to roll everyone aside in America. Ireland had never known that kind of pressure. Should they lose three out of three, they might escape the tomatoes that would await Italy in such an eventuality, but there would be no partying, no heroic return in recognition of getting to the finals in the first place. Ireland were now in the big league. The cute, if patronising tag 'little invincibles' had been buried. Teams of Ireland's stature don't receive sympathy when things go wrong, only brickbats.

As such, one wonders how much the Dublin defeat by the Czech Republic – in Ireland's final warm-up – really hurt. No one likes to lose, especially

Jack Charlton and his fired-up players. But at least they were shown to be mortal after all, and to that extent the defeat probably did them a favour.

No	Name	Position	Club	Age	Caps	Goals
1	Pat Bonner	Goalkeeper	Celtic	34	73	–
2	Denis Irwin	Full-back	Manchester U	28	26	1
3	Terry Phelan	Full-back	Manchester C	27	22	–
4	Kevin Moran	Central defence	Blackburn	38	71	6
5	Paul McGrath	Defence/Midfield	Aston Villa	34	65	7
6	Roy Keane	Midfield	Manchester U	22	22	–
7	Andy Townsend (c)	Midfield	Aston Villa	30	45	4
8	Ray Houghton	Midfield	Aston Villa	32	58	3
9	John Aldridge	Forward	Tranmere	35	58	13
10	John Sheridan	Midfield	Sheffield Wed	29	20	3
11	Steve Staunton	Full-back/Midfield	Aston Villa	25	47	5
12	Gary Kelly	Full-back	Leeds	19	4	1
13	Alan Kernaghan	Central defence	Manchester C	27	11	1
14	Phil Babb	Central defence	Coventry	23	4	–
15	Tommy Coyne	Forward	Motherwell	31	14	4
16	Tony Cascarino	Forward	Chelsea	31	50	12
17	Eddie McGoldrick	Utility	Arsenal	29	11	–
18	Ronnie Whelan	Midfield	Liverpool	32	50	3
19	Alan McLoughlin	Midfield	Portsmouth	27	17	1
20	David Kelly	Forward	Wolves	27	16	7
21	Jason McAteer	Midfield	Bolton	23	5	–
22	Alan Kelly	Goalkeeper	Sheffield Utd	25	3	–
			Averages	*28.5*	*31.5*	

The average age of Ireland's squad was no younger than in 1990. Though McCarthy and O'Leary had slipped away, Bonner, McGrath, Moran and Aldridge were all integral to Charlton's plans. Each was approaching his footballing dotage. But for Moran's torn hamstring, he might have filled the stopper berths with McGrath. Their combined age was a mere seventy-two.

With an average of 31½ caps per man, Charlton's squad was even more experienced than that in Italy, and more experienced than any that England or Scotland had sent to the finals of a World Cup.

John Aldridge had at last found his goal-touch, and, provided he was used sparingly, he would be an important weapon in Charlton's arsenal. Aldridge had been used from the start in the qualifiers, and pulled off when his legs went. But America's soaring summer temperatures meant he would more likely come on rather than come off. This, despite the fact that injury to Niall Quinn had thrown Charlton's plans into disarray.

The 6ft 5in Quinn had been a bit-player in Italy, an unwanted Arsenal forward more renowned for missing chances than taking them. A move to Manchester City had enlivened him. He was sure of his place at Maine Road, his confidence had blossomed, and he was ever-present in the '94 qualifiers.

But torn cruciate ligaments had struck him down without time to recover. Denied Quinn's lofty head to aim at, Charlton found himself short of options. The choice of alternative target-men rested between Tony Cascarino and Tommy Coyne, two more thirty-something players, strong on elbow-grease, bereft of pace, short on goals. Neither would be short-listed for a place in a 'British' XI, and against the cream of the world's defenders they were liable to make little impact. Cascarino, besides, was bedevilled by a calf strain.

To counter, Charlton adopted a radical tactical change. Playing with just one forward would enable him to minimise the loss of Quinn and reinforce his midfield, without – he hoped – sacrificing Irish potency up front. Nor could he risk jeopardising Ireland's phenomenal defensive record – forty-six goals conceded in seventy-eight matches under his care.

The 4-5-1 strategy provoked mixed reactions from fans and pundits. Charlton's best results had come with 4-4-2. Ireland had been clobbered by Spain when Charlton changed the system, and grass-roots opinion was that he should stick with his tried and trusted format. The long ball might offend aesthetes, but it had got Ireland where they were. Paradoxically, the extra man in midfield could foster the shorter pass and brighten Ireland's play.

More to the point, Charlton no longer had two strikers up to the task of playing 4-4-2. To compensate, the rest of his squad was probably stronger than in 1990. Jack was blessed with midfield talent in abundance. Roy Keane had burst on the scene, burst the British record fee when transferring from Nottingham Forest to Manchester United, and would inject youth into a team not overflowing with that commodity. He would also hope to inject goals, but in twenty-two internationals he was still searching for his first.

Steve 'Stan' Staunton was another of Charlton's younger players, whose cultured left foot enabled him to slot in at full-back or, in oldie-worldie terms, left-half, to good effect.

Ray 'Razor' Houghton never seemed to pause for breath, and his short, piston-like strides carried him to all corners of the pitch. Like Charlton, he was one of those old-fashioned types who held that the player should do all the work, not the ball. On a good day, Houghton appeared always in the thick of things. On a bad day, the ball always seemed to be passing him by, and his frenetic chasing lent him the air of a headless chicken. A growing body of opinion at Villa Park thought him ruined by Charlton's hard-running game.

Andy Townsend, Charlton's captain, was one of Jack's granny rulers. He was refreshingly open about never harbouring ambitions to play for Ireland. Charlton asked him before England did. It was as simple as that.

'If Townsend's an Irishman, I'm Glenn Miller,' sneered one celebrity sports writer.

One could see sense in Townsend's captaincy. Townsend had been ever-present in Italia '90 and quietly established himself as another midfield workhorse. Townsend was a pro's pro. 'He's a hard man,' said Charlton, who knew one when he found one. He was a player whose weaknesses were fewer than his strengths. Outstanding at nothing, capable at everything. Much the same used to be said of Billy Wright, who played 105 times for England.

With his cheerful demeanour and chirpy London accent, Townsend would prove a find for the TV men, who would prop him in front of the camera in New York or Orlando and exploit the good vibes that emanated from him.

Charlton had no worries about either full-back, Denis Irwin of Manchester United and Terry Phelan of Manchester City. But when Moran's injury failed to respond, Jack drafted in young Phil Babb to partner the redoubtable McGrath. This meant three of Ireland's back four had African fathers.

If McGrath was supposed to be feeling his years, no one had bothered to tell the player. He looked as good as ever, and had picked up the PFA Player of the Year award for 1993. Now that Charlton was playing five in midfield, McGrath – who would play through the pain of a damaged shoulder – could drop back to central defence, where his legs would have less running to do, and where his experience would mask Babb's lack of it.

The big worry for Charlton was his last line of defence. Bonner was no longer the goalkeeper of old. He had lost confidence, was prone to blunders, and been shown the door at Parkhead. In such circumstances, international managers are apt to keep faith, arguing that so-and-so has never let his country down. Bingham said the same of Jennings in 1986, Andy Roxburgh of Jim Leighton in 1990. In the light of events, neither keeper remembered those finals favourably, and might have stood down for a younger man.

But No. 1 is the last position to be filled by a rookie in the World Cup finals. The only alternative to Bonner was young Alan Kelly Jnr of Sheffield United, son of the father who kept goal for Ireland, on and off, for seventeen years. But Kelly had only picked up three caps, and Italy would surely relish facing a greenhorn in their opener. Charlton did what almost every other manager would in that situation. He stuck with Bonner.

Bonner would relish facing penalties by Diana Ross. Compared with Italia '90, the opening ceremony was kitsch and tawdry. The singer was upstaged by O J Simpson, a man few in Ireland had heard of until his white van was pursued down a US freeway by a posse of police cars, helicopters, and TV cameras.

Meanwhile, soccer coaches were busy debating FIFA's rule changes. Tackling from behind was now a red-card offence, a ruling that seemed to inflame British more than global opinion. Players feigning injury would be booked. No injuries could be treated on the pitch. Instead the injured player would be conveyed to the touchline by means of an 'electric cart'. Three points for a win was antithetical to Ireland's interests, since they had shown themselves in Italy adept at harvesting points only in ones.

Before the gloves came off, the *Irish Independent* consulted an astrologer, Austin Byrne, to forecast Ireland's results. Byrne predicted a definite win over Italy, a probable defeat by Mexico, and a probable draw with Norway.

ITALY v IRELAND
Saturday, 18 June 1994   *Giants Stadium, New Jersey – 75,338*

Back-to-back matches with the same opponents in consecutive World Cups was an oddity. It was certainly the toughest of tasks for Ireland, who had lost all seven previous internationals against Italy. Italy were third favourites – behind Brazil and Germany – for the trophy.

Optimists could point to Ireland's recent victories over Holland and Germany, and to Italy's traditionally sluggish start to World Cup finals. They were rarely out of the gate quickly. When they last won the trophy, in 1982, they had failed to win any of their group games.

The fact that most third-place teams would survive meant that defeat in the opening match was not the disaster it once was. Even so, Charlton would be delighted to draw this one, and pick up the other necessary points against opponents to come. Four points looked to be the safety threshold.

Four years on, four Italians and six Irishmen lined up for Round 2. The Italians were Baresi, Maldini, Donadoni and Roberto Baggio (European and World Footballer of the Year); the Irish, Bonner, McGrath, Staunton, Houghton, Townsend, and Sheridan (substitute in Rome).

Italy's international team was not in the best of health. They were managed by Arrigo Sacchi, short, grey-haired, animated to the point of lunacy. He would be an icon of this World Cup, manic on the touchline, dressed more often than not in blue top and emerald green leggings.

Sacchi had been architect of Milan's domination of Italian and European football, weaning his players away from man-to-man marking, preferring to defend zonally, with a back four and no sweeper. Appointed to the hot seat in 1991, he was committed to employing the same tactics with Italy, pledging to introduce brighter football to the national team.

Despite Italy's fathomless ocean of talent, Sacchi appeared to be no nearer welding them into an efficient unit. They had qualified from Scotland's group, and although a transitional Scottish team did not extend them,

Paul McGrath once again gets the better of Italy's Giuseppe Signori.

Switzerland and Portugal did. In fact, it took an 82nd minute goal from Dino Baggio (no relation of Roberto) against Portugal to ensure a place in USA. Since then, defeats in warm-ups by France, Germany, and by an Italian fourth-division side, had heaped the pressure on him.

Sacchi identified Ireland as posing a physical threat, not a creative one, and picked his side accordingly. Italy's back four, plus two midfielders, were all plucked from his old club, who thrillingly won the European Cup in May.

Ireland's first and third matches were scheduled for the Giants Stadium in New Jersey, home to the New York Giants American Football team. The stadium could accommodate 77,000. At 4 pm, kick-off time, the temperature was touching ninety. Irish fans appeared to outnumber Italian ones.

It took Ireland ten seconds to close within range, but Staunton's volley was awry. The first ten minutes were as tense as might be expected, but Italy looked to be settling nicely when Ireland knocked them cold. It was a dramatic goal, part inspirational, part cock-up. Costacurta nodded Sheridan's long, forward ball up in the air, and Baresi, attempting a headed pass out, directed it straight at the onrushing Houghton. Razor was considered in some quarters fortunate to be playing. An unrewarding domestic season had seen his Ireland shirt coveted by Jason McAteer. For the time being, Charlton kept faith with the old guard. He would be glad he did.

What followed next was variously called genius (in Irish quarters) or fluke (in Italian ones). As Houghton was sideways to the ball, he could not make meaty contact, and the outcome was half lob, half shot. But Sampdoria goalkeeper Gianluca Pagliuca had positioned himself on his six-yard line. He was well placed to deal with a firmly struck shot, but not a half-hit dipping one. The ball came down over Pagliuca's head without his making the faintest attempt to save. It was almost as if he expected it to float over the bar.

Whatever its technicalities, the goal provided Houghton another moment to cherish. It was his first international goal for almost five years, and had elicited a plague of errors in the Italian defence. Italy promptly fell to pieces. Staunton found Townsend bang in front of the posts, but Townsend's first touch let him down and he couldn't take advantage.

Whenever Italy tried to attack, which was often, they ran into the brick wall of Paul McGrath and Phil Babb. Phelan was cautioned for a nasty tackle on Donadoni. Half-time arrived with Bonner having suffered few scares, and recommenced afterwards with Italy bringing on yet another Milan player, the ace goalscorer Daniele Massaro, and switching to 4-3-3.

Coaches knew in advance that referees were under orders to wave red and yellow cards at the slightest provocation, and that time-wasting was regarded as a cautionable offence. Even so, the booking of Tommy Coyne seemed unreasonable. He took a blow on the head, took a while to get to his feet, and when the pall-bearers who had come to fetch him departed empty handed, Dutch referee Van der Ende saw fit to wave a yellow card.

Roberto Baggio, the pony-tailed Buddhist, was continually short-changed by the fearsome 'black pearl' McGrath. Baggio's namesake, Dino, appeared on the evidence of this match to be the better player, and it was he who twice might have forced an equaliser. On both occasions he was tackled in the box. The second of these, by Denis Irwin, was perfectly timed and executed. The first, by Phil Babb, was borderline. He won the ball cleanly enough, but went through Baggio's legs from behind, a penalty offence according to new FIFA statutes. The Italians were not slow to remind Mr Van der Ende of this.

This was a difficult period for Ireland. Bonner beat out a shot straight at him from Signori, but otherwise he was well protected by McGrath and company in front of him. Indeed, once Italy had shot their bolt the better chances fell to Ireland. Houghton, waiting to be substituted, tested Pagliuca at the foot of the near post, before coming off to allow McAteer the perfect twenty-third birthday present.

Pagliuca was helpless when Keane, inspirational throughout, got to the by-line and pulled the ball back. Coyne dummied, leaving Sheridan – twelve yards out – to drive the ball against the top of the crossbar. It wasn't bad luck; it was a bad miss.

But not a costly one. Ireland survived four minutes' injury time to record their first victory over Italy and their first in the finals of the World Cup.

Equally important, the win was unambiguous. Italy had enjoyed 54% of possession, but managed just one shot on target. Ireland had created more chances, and defended like lions. A few flat-earthers still quibbled about Jack Charlton's place in the pantheon of great managers, but this was without reservation a tactical masterpiece. Charlton had been in the job eight years, longer than any other manager in the tournament, and he had just enjoyed his, and Ireland's, finest hour. As someone shrewdly observed, 'Charlton was the monkey in the cage laughing at the people laughing at him.'

In the space of a few weeks, Ireland had beaten Holland, Germany and now Italy. The odds against Ireland lifting the World Cup were duly slashed from 25/1 to 16/1.

Italy had never before lost their first match in a World Cup. 'A legendary fiasco,' wailed *La Stampa*.

'Give Ireland the first laugh and we'll have the last one,' an Italian fan winked.

ITALY (0) 0	IRELAND (1) 1
	Houghton 11

ITALY: Pagliuca (SAMPDORIA), Tassotti (MILAN), Baresi (MILAN), Costacurta (MILAN), Maldini (MILAN), Donadoni (MILAN), D Baggio (JUVENTUS), Albertini (MILAN), Evani (SAMPDORIA) (*sub* Massaro, MILAN), R Baggio (JUVENTUS), Signori (LAZIO) (*sub* Berti, INTERNAZIONALE).
IRELAND: Bonner, Irwin, Babb, McGrath, Phelan, Houghton (McAteer), Keane, Sheridan, Townsend, Staunton, Coyne (Aldridge).

MEXICO v IRELAND
Friday, 24 June 1994   *Citrus Bowl, Orlando – 61,219*

The next day Mexico largely outplayed Norway, yet lost to a very late goal. From Ireland's point of view it was pity the game hadn't stayed goalless, thus distributing two points instead of three. Nevertheless, Ireland and Norway sat proudly on top of Group E, and the pressure was piling on Italy and Mexico.

Ireland were not yet home and dry. Ten-man Italy had resurrected their own hopes by beating staid Norway 1-0. Two defeats could undo all Ireland's good work. They needed two more points to put them into the second round, and even one might do.

Ten years earlier, Ireland had entertained Mexico in Dublin in the only previous meeting between the sides. That result, 0-0, if repeated in Orlando's three-sided Citrus Bowl Stadium, would hurt Mexico more than Ireland. By having to play their second match down in Florida, Irish supporters would

have to fork out an arm and a leg to travel from New York to watch them –
provided they could procure tickets.

Mexico had been banned from Italia '90 on account of fielding over-aged
players in a youth tournament, but had been the first nation to qualify for
USA '94. Coach Miguel Mejia Baron had subsequently seen his team
hammered by Switzerland and Russia.

Mexico's frequent appearances in World Cup finals owed everything to
the feeble opposition encountered in the North and Central American
(CONCACEF) qualifying zone. In the finals, it was a different story. Only
when hosting the tournament, in 1970 and 1986, did Mexico not depart in a
hurry. Her record in those World Cups she hadn't hosted was apologetic: W1
D3 L16.

Against Norway, Mexico had just lost for the seventeenth time. Her dodgy
reputation did not imply she was short on talent. Hugo Sanchez had
illuminated the Real Madrid forward line for many years. But few Mexicans
widened their horizons by playing abroad. Mexicans also tended to slighter
physiques than Europeans or South Americans. This put them at a
disadvantage when the going got physical – as it had against Norway.

On the plus side, playing in the United States, in her own back yard,
guaranteed Mexico the vociferous support of local Hispanics and Mexican
supporters flooding over the Rio Grande. Mexico were expected to do better
in USA '94 than in any other 'foreign' tournament.

How they would have welcomed Hugo Sanchez in his prime. He was still
exciting crowds in Spain and had been in the side against Norway. He was
unlikely to relish Irish muscle, however, and was one of four changes, being
replaced by the younger, taller Carlos Hermosillo. With Italy still to come,
Mexico simply had to win.

The one other expatriate was Luis Garcia, fresh from transferring from
Atletico Madrid to John Aldridge's old stomping ground, Real Sociedad.
Luis Garcia was a lively, goalscoring midfielder who would need to be
carefully policed. Garcia Aspe also returned to midfield, having been banned
from Mexico's opening match.

Jorge Campos was a sight for sore eyes. The flamboyant goalkeeper, who
played centre-forward with his club a few seasons earlier, had a penchant for
dazzling opposing forwards with a day-glo strip adorned with black zigzags.

Coyne's dehydration and Townsend's allergy-related puffiness of the
knees soon cleared, enabling Charlton to field an unchanged team. The match
would kick off at 12.30 local time, when the sun was almost overhead. This
suited European television schedules, but more importantly avoided the
heavy downpours that are an afternoon feature of Florida's summers.

Both teams ordinarily played in green, and as Ireland were nominally the
away side it was they who were invited to change. They did not, however,

John Aldridge's life-saving header leaves goalkeeper Jorge Campos prostrate.

dispense with the green and white. Instead they introduced a new concept to connoisseurs of football gear, green stripes that petered out halfway down the chest.

The 'petering out' metaphor was apt, for Ireland were unrecognisable from the slayers of Italy. They began strongly, however, and Coyne should have scored from Phelan's wonderful overlap and cross. In front of the posts, Coyne and the ball missed each other like trains on different tracks.

Five minutes before half-time Staunton's long throw was inadvertently back-headed by a Mexican defender, presenting Townsend with a gaping goal. Townsend lunged awkwardly with his head, when he might have used his foot, but the ball was headed for the bottom corner when it was brilliantly turned behind by Campos.

The first sign that Ireland were up against it had come some time earlier, when Swiss referee Kurt Roethlisberger – who refereed the all-Ireland qualifier at Lansdowne Road, and had 'sent off' Manchester United's Eric Cantona *after* a European Cup-tie in Galatasaray – booked Denis Irwin for ostensibly delaying a throw-in. Having been cautioned against Italy, Irwin would now miss out against Norway.

Although they had as yet created nothing, the Mexicans were starting to run at the Irish defence. Ominously, cracks started to appear and errors made in that part of the field where Charlton forbids them. A Mexican wave was about to be unleashed.

Two minutes from the break, Mexico scored a super goal. Bernal cut inside Phelan on the touchline and speared goalwards. With Irish defenders backing off, Bernal threaded the ball to Hermosillo, whose deft lay off was swept by Luis Garcia low to Bonner's right.

The oppressive heat – over 100 degrees – was evidently contributing to Ireland's wilting display, but sympathy does not win matches. Ireland tried their best to regroup after half-time, but the game appeared to have slipped away from them. Even McGrath looked worryingly mortal, and Charlton was contemplating switching him with Kernaghan when Mexico scored a second. Denis Irwin was befuddled by a high bouncing ball, which was spirited away from him by Garcia Aspe, leaving Irwin looking leaden-footed. Aspe passed inside to Luis Garcia, who to his astonishment was given time to kill the ball with his left foot and strike it with the right. The shot flew past Bonner.

There was nothing for it but for Charlton to send on Aldridge for Coyne, and McAteer for poor Staunton, who, with his fair complexion, had suffered more than most. A communication problem with an Egyptian FIFA official delayed Aldridge's introduction by some minutes, leaving Ireland a man short, while treating millions of armchair viewers to a close-up of Aldridge's famed temper.

This was not the first altercation between officialdom and the Irish bench. Attempts to get water to the players provoked much shaking of heads and wagging of fingers, to the extent that the 'water issue' would be blown up in the press as a major incident. Curiously, it was only Ireland who felt hard done by. Belgium and Holland, for example, played several times in the Citrus Bowl, in similar temperatures, but found no need to litter the pitch with discarded cellophane bags.

None of this endeared FIFA to Ireland's cause. For allegedly abusing officials, Charlton would be fined £10,000 and banned from the touchline for the match with Norway. FIFA had evidently had enough of his 'ranting and raving'. Aldridge was fined a lesser amount for 'ill-mannered behaviour'.

For the moment, Ireland had even worse problems to confront. Had they lost 0-2 they would have gone bottom of the group on goal-difference. They would then have had no alternative but to beat Norway in their last match. The faces on the bench as the minutes slipped away told a miserable tale, reminiscent of that when Ireland trailed Holland in Palermo. It was all going horribly wrong, just when it seemed Ireland were on the crest of a wave. Ireland were being overrun in midfield, where Keane looked to be holding back the tide single-handedly.

Mexico had the chances to turn Irish defeat into humiliation. A dazzling run by Luis Garcia, culminated with an audacious chip over McGrath's head and a strong shot that Bonner clutched to deny Garcia his hat-trick. Two other close-range shots, one saved, one wide, were better than anything Ireland were managing at the other end. All Ireland had to show was a stubbed chip-shot by Sheridan that Campos plucked out of the air.

It was Aldridge's turn to steam to the rescue. Maybe the FIFA official unwittingly did him a good turn by getting him fired up. Six minutes remained when the two subs combined to throw Ireland a lifeline. McAteer's cross from the right was dropping towards the penalty spot when Aldridge's powerful downward header buried the ball in the net. It might have been 0-4. Instead, it was 1-2. Aldridge had scored Ireland's 100th World Cup goal.

Ireland dug deep, and the match might have ended famously. Townsend's last minute snap-shot brought a showy save from Campos.

MEXICO (1) 2   **IRELAND (0) 1**
Luis Garcia 43, 66   Aldridge 84

MEXICO: Campos (UNAM), Rodrigues (TOLUCA) (*sub* Gutierrez, ATLANTE), Suarez (UNAM), Perales (MONTEREY), Del Olmo (VERA CRUZ), Luis Garcia (REAL SOCIEDAD), Bernal (TOLUCA), Aspe (NECAXA), Ambriz (NECAXA), Alves (AMÉRICA), Hermosillo (GUAD'JARA) (*sub* Salvador, ATLANTE). IRELAND: Bonner, Irwin, Babb, McGrath, Phelan, Houghton, Sheridan, Keane, Townsend, Staunton (McAteer), Coyne (Aldridge).

NORWAY v IRELAND
Tuesday, 28 June 1994   *Giants Stadium, New Jersey – 76,322*

Orlando left a bad taste in Irish mouths. It was good to fly back to New Jersey where the temperature was a degree or two cooler and where Irish nerves could be soothed by the remembrance of victory.

Group E was so tight it was Sardinia revisited. The press always liked to dub the toughest, meanest, lowest-scoring section the 'Group of Death'. That tag always seemed to stick to England's, Scotland's, or Ireland's group. But never mind.

All four teams showed one win, one loss. Goal-differences were identical, but in such circumstances teams having scored most goals are given priority. That gave Ireland and Mexico the edge. Crucially, where goals scored are also equal, the victors take precedence. By such reasoning, Mexico were now top, Ireland second, Italy third.

Ever since Argentina, needing four, knocked six goals past Peru in the 1978 finals, FIFA had determined that concluding group matches should start simultaneously. Aldridge's goal had transformed Ireland's prospects. Without it, they would have needed to beat Norway. With it, they could draw. That would ensure that Norway finished beneath them.

A draw would serve Norway only in the event of the Italy v Mexico match producing a loser. Norway could hardly bank on that, and were expected to chase the game.

Ireland owed Norway one. After fourteen clashes, spread over half a century, Norway had just two wins to show. Both had been in World Cup qualifiers.

Norway had also vanquished England just twice. These, too, had been in the World Cup. In 1981 the damage had been humiliating but transitory. England got through anyway. In 1993 it was to prove catastrophic, sowing the seeds of England's later capitulation.

These were Norway's first finals since 1938. For all their triumph over England, they were a heavy-footed, ponderous side, bereft of glamour or adventure. They were coached by Egil Olsen, a lapsed Marxist who was now employed as a 'professor of football'. Olsen was an academic type who devoured facts and figures. For him, statistics confirmed that direct football was the way to win. Under Olsen's direction, Norway had lost just nine times in over forty matches, but they were conspicuous in USA '94 for putting the emphasis on defence, and few would mourn their departure.

In recent years Norway's players had become heavily Anglicised. Of the eleven to face Ireland, Erik Thorstvedt kept goal for Tottenham. Gunnar Halle, Henning Berg and Stig Bjornebye were defenders with, respectively, Oldham, Blackburn and Liverpool. Jostein Flo – at 6ft 5in the tallest outfield player in the World Cup – spearheaded Sheffield United's attack. Waiting in the wings were Erland Johnsen (Chelsea), Jan Fjortoft (Swindon), Roger Nilson (Sheffield United), Lars Bohinen (Nottingham Forest). Enough of these teams had been relegated from the FA Carling Premiership, or come close to it, to suggest that Norwegian players were made for sinking ships. All told, nine of Norway's squad were Anglos, most of them defenders, for that was where Norwegian strength was perceived to lie. On the pitch, a number of personal acquaintances were set to be renewed.

For that reason, both camps were half-hoping that English referee Philip Don would take charge. Instead, Colombian referee José Torres was chosen to run the game.

Charlton had to put his thinking cap on. He was clearly hurt by his banishment from the touchline, but had to conceal his anger from the players. The sense of injustice, that FIFA were somehow gunning for them, threatened to cocoon Ireland within an 'us against the world' siege mentality. This would be puerile and counter-productive, and Charlton wisely steered clear of any such gestures. More importantly, he had a team to pick. Both his full-backs had received two yellow cards.

'I'll have to find somebody else,' he had quipped, when questioned after the Mexico game.

The somebody else was Gary Kelly, at nineteen, Ireland's youngest ever competitor in the World Cup finals. Kelly had seized his chance at Leeds when David Kerslake was injured. Kelly stepped into the breach and impressed so much that Kerslake eventually had to move on.

Staunton filled the left-back slot vacated by Phelan, and Jason McAteer started the match in midfield. Aldridge also played, allowing Coyne a rest.

Except for those emotionally involved, to describe the match as grim is to understate. It was awful, pedestrian and predictable, Egypt revisited. It was the occasion, of course, that enabled Irish folk of every description to kick every ball with the players. So much hinged on the result that prettiness did not come into it.

The first half was so unremittingly bad that journalists' notebooks stayed empty. No shots, no saves, no nothing, just the curiosity of Houghton being booked for running about with a water bag in one hand.

It was little consolation that Norway bore the greater onus for the tedium. They had set out as if 0-0 was the summit of their ambitions, and with Charlton understandably wary of being caught on the break, Ireland had pushed few men forward.

Had Italy and Mexico not also been level at half-time, Norway would have thought themselves vindicated, though one shudders to think of what misery the second half would have inflicted.

As it was, Jack Charlton sat up in his sin-bin in the sky, up in the gods in a VIP box above the digital scoreboard. He sipped tea or something from plastic cups, no doubt enjoying the view, but not the long countdown from ninety minutes to zero. About the only time he needed to communicate by phone with Maurice Setters was to tell him to get McAteer to pipe down and stop arguing with the referee.

The best that can be said of the second half is that it was an improvement on the first. Keane's poor clearance enabled Mykland a low shot that Bonner was equal to. Norway's next sortie also required Irish assistance, but this time Ireland were beyond the assistance of man of god. Staunton, on the floor, deflected Sorloth's close-range shot into the air and down onto the crossbar.

These isolated efforts did not suggest Ireland were suddenly in retreat. They made chances, but managed not one shot on target. Aldridge headed Townsend's cross twenty yards wide, and McAteer's cross from the right might have brought a goal for substitute David Kelly. A fine move down the left saw Keane drift infield and slide the ball the Sheridan. Confronted by a wall of defenders, Sheridan tried to chip the stranded Thorstvedt and suffered the agony of seeing the ball land on top of the net. Sheridan had now come close in all three matches. But not close enough. An inch here and there, and he would have been acclaimed Ireland's player of the tournament.

Even in the knowledge that Italy and Mexico were drawing 1-1, Norway were unable to pack the closing minutes with anything other than plodding endeavour, and the match whimpered to a close. It was only the second goalless game of the tournament, and arguably the worst of all.

Four points would ordinarily be sufficient to survive, unless all four teams in a group ended with that total, in which case one of them must finish fourth and perish. That was the case in Group E, compounded by the fact that goal-differences were also identical. When all was settled, Mexico were placed top, on goals scored, and Ireland second, for having beaten Italy.

Italy had to rely on the third-place rule to survive, though with four points and a neutral goal-difference there was little doubt that they would. Only statistically was it possible to feel sympathy for Norway, the only team to be eliminated with four points.

So Ireland prospered on the goals-scored rule, introduced to encourage adventurous soccer. Norwegians thought there was some irony in this. They did not think Ireland at all adventurous. Charlton's luck had held again.

NORWAY (0) 0   IRELAND (0) 0

NORWAY: Thorstvedt (SPURS), Halle (OLDHAM) (*sub* Jakobsen, LIERSE), Berg (BLACKBURN), Bratseth (W BREMEN), Bjornebye (LIVERPOOL), Johnsen (CHELSEA), Leonhardsen (ROSENBORG) (*sub* Bohinen, FOREST), Mykland (START), Sorloth (BURSAPOR), Rekdal (LIERSE), Flo (SHEFF U).
IRELAND: Bonner, G Kelly, Babb, McGrath, Staunton, McAteer, Houghton, Keane, Sheridan, Townsend (Whelan), Aldridge (D Kelly).

Final positions – Group E

	P	W	D	L	F	A	Pts
MEXICO	3	1	1	1	3	3	4
IRELAND	3	1	1	1	2	2	4
ITALY	3	1	1	1	2	2	4
Norway	3	1	1	1	1	1	4

HOLLAND v IRELAND
Monday, 4 July 1994   *Citrus Bowl, Orlando – 61,355*

The World Cup had already exceeded all expectations. Goals were up, so were crowds, play was generally bright, and the Americans had wrapped up the whole in an effective, pleasing package. The USA team had actually beaten somebody, Colombia, and were into the second round. But at a heavy cost. Colombian defender Andres Escobar had put through his own goal. He flew home to be greeted by a dozen bullets in a Medallin carpark.

Oleg Salenko had scored five times in one match, against Cameroon, and Diego Maradona had been nicked taking drugs. Without him Argentina promptly sagged like a burst balloon.

Meanwhile, the good people of Ireland were in the throes of quasi-religious exultation. They had known nothing like it since the visit of the Pope in 1979. The tricolours, the team-photographs tacked to living-room windows, spoke of a nation besotted with the superhuman feats of their heroes. The national hysteria permeated through to young and old. Grandmothers with walking sticks talked of nothing else. They knew little of football, but the World Cup had brought joy, goodwill, and exuberance to everyone around them, and was cherished for that reason alone. Long might it continue.

There was something about Jack Charlton that wrapped his players in a cloak of indestructibility. Whether they played well or badly, they somehow squeezed through to fight another day.

The team finishing second in Group E was booked for another date with steamy Orlando, this time in the company of the Group F winners. Belgium looked to have that position sewn up, so much so that Jack Charlton flew to Washington to watch them tie up their group against Saudi Arabia.

He would wish he hadn't. Belgium lost to the most dazzling goal of the tournament. To cap it all, Charlton got waylaid overnight by a tropical storm. He should have gone to watch Holland beat Morocco. Brian Roy, bound for Nottingham Forest, scored the winner, tossing Ireland against Holland for the third time in recent championships.

This was depressing for all concerned. It was not that Belgium were necessarily weaker than Holland, just different. No one wanted to play the same opponents over and over again, and to cap it all Ireland had played the Dutch in April, winning 1-0 in Tilburg. Valuable though that win had seemed at the time, it now took on the aspect of an albatross. It was pointless beating teams for fun if you couldn't beat them for real. No one could use it as a pointer to this one, and talk of psychological advantages was so much hot air.

Outwardly, Ireland were content to face another north European team in Orlando, whose tropical conditions would not favour one side over the other. The Dutch, however, had been based in Orlando, had played two matches in the Citrus Bowl (beating Morocco there!), and were, to boot, in the habit of employing two wingers. Unlike Ireland, Holland kicked up no fuss about the heat. They just got on with it. Advocaat observed: 'Talking too much about the heat problem affects the players more than the heat does.' The Dutch also shrugged off the fact of having one day less than Ireland in which to recover.

Like Norway, Holland had qualified at the expense of England. It was their crunch victory in Rotterdam that closed the door on Graham Taylor's time at Lancaster Gate.

As always, the Dutch squad was at war with itself. In 1978, the team travelled to Argentina without Johann Cruyff, who put self before nation. Much the same happened now, with Ruud Gullit. Gullit was still only thirty-one, had come back from injury, but personal differences with Dutch coach Dick Advocaat had proved irreconcilable.

That Advocaat was still in charge took some by surprise. He had masterminded Holland through the qualifiers in the expectation that he would be deposed before the finals, by Cruyff, for example, someone more amenable to the likes of Gullit.

Without Gullit, Van Basten (a long-term absentee), and Jan Wouters (suspended), just three of the Dutch side from Palermo turned out in Orlando – Ronald Koeman, Frank Rijkaard, and Rob Witschge. In *lieu* of Van Basten, Holland had unearthed another goalscorer *extraordinaire*. Dennis Bergkamp had broken the bank when signing for Internazionale, and his volleyed chip over Chris Woods' head at Wembley demonstrated the kind of skill that could not be defended against. He had had a quiet World Cup to date, just one goal, but that did nothing to disguise his menace.

Ronald Koeman's menace these days lay more in his free-kicks than in his defending – both aspects being aired against England in Rotterdam. The Barcelona sweeper scored from an exquisite free-kick, at a time when he should have been off the field for clattering David Platt. In defence, however, Koeman had slowed to such an extent that he was forced to defend too deeply, dropping off his attacker for fear of being turned and outpaced.

Whilst Advocaat, in common with every other judge, had the utmost respect for Ireland's defence and midfield, he was not running scared at the thought of Ireland's powder-puff attack. Here was a match in which the first goal – provided there was one – would surely settle it.

Charlton brought back Coyne at the expense of Aldridge. Although Jack was happy to reinstate Phelan at left back, there was no way he could leave out young Kelly. This was no disrespect to Irwin, who could probably have laid claim to a place in half the teams in the tournament. Charlton appeared to be spoiled for choice.

Other good judges begged to differ. Italy had earmarked Ireland's full-backs as weak links, and although Arrigo Sacchi had paid for his presumption, Dick Advocaat was evidently of the same mind. Under a dark, brooding sky, the Dutch widemen, Marc Overmars and Peter van Vossen, ripped into Phelan and Kelly, leaving poor Phelan, in particular, to wish he had sat this one out.

Mercifully, it was cooler than before, though Ireland derived no obvious comfort. They looked shaky from the off, but had never yet given away goals of the kind about to be visited upon them. Eleven minutes had passed when Phelan, facing his own goal, plopped a dinky header into the path of

'Overdrive' Overmars. Babb was taken aback, otherwise he might have beaten the winger to it. But Overmars had wings on his heels. Infield, Bergkamp had reacted quicker than McGrath, and was sprinting for the penalty box. Overmars squared, and the inrushing Bergkamp swept the ball past Bonner.

Ireland were stunned, and for the rest of the half survival was their only option. Rijkaard just failed to connect at the foot of a post, and Overmars drove straight at Bonner.

The interval was four minutes away, and Charlton was already rehearsing his verbal demolition when Wim Jonk glided contemptuously past Sheridan, carried the ball on, was checked by McGrath, and tried his luck from twenty-five yards. Bonner – who had had a flawless World Cup – did not have to move. Had he been a tailor's dummy the ball would have bounced back off him. But he got his hands all wrong, and the ball slipped through into the net.

Bonner thumped the earth with his fists, kneeling with head bowed as his team-mates clutched theirs in their hands. The gestures were symptomatic of the general malaise. Other than the first half against Spain at Lansdowne Road, one was hard pressed to recall a more wretched half for Ireland. Bonner would be man enough to shoulder the blame, thankful no doubt that he was not Colombian, but he knew he'd scuppered Ireland's hopes.

One was not privy, but one suspects Charlton's half-time words were calmer than had it stayed at 0-1. After all, the party was over. Few teams in the world could chase two goals against Holland, and Ireland had too little firepower at the best of times. They had trouble scoring once, and in eleven matches in finals had never managed two.

Not that they went down without a fight. With a handsome lead under their belts, and with a tough quarter-final looming, Holland pressed the cruise button. Territory was surrendered to Ireland, and with it the odd glimpse of goal. Houghton headed over under pressure, and later, when given the chance to score with that now-famous left foot, his shot trundled into nothingness. Babb, too, wasted a chance of glory, smashing substitute Cascarino's knock-down wide of the post.

These chances were cancelled out by those around Bonner's goal, the best of which fell to substitute Brian Roy. Bonner had parried Bergkamp's angled drive, but Roy blazed the loose ball over the bar.

McGrath brought the match to a close by kicking Rijkaard in the head and netting. The 'goal' was ruled out for high-kicking.

Ireland could hold their heads up, though the self-inflicted nature of defeat momentarily detracted from their sense of achievement. It was, perish the thought, a reminder of the bad old days BC, before Charlton, when such howlers were par for the course for an Ireland team.

Just think, had Ireland won they would have faced Brazil in the last eight.

HOLLAND (2) 2   IRELAND   (0) 0
Bergkamp 11, Jonk 41

HOLLAND: De Goey (FEYENOORD), Koeman (BARCELONA), Valckx (SPORTING LISBON), F de Boer (AJAX), Rijkaard (AJAX), Winter (LAZIO), Jonk (INTER), Witschge (FEYENOORD) (*sub* Numan, PSV), Overmars (AJAX), Bergkamp (INTER), Van Vossen (AJAX) (*sub* Roy, FOGGIA).
IRELAND: Bonner, Kelly, McGrath, Babb, Phelan, Houghton, Keane, Townsend, Sheridan, Staunton (McAteer), Coyne (Cascarino).

This exhilarating World Cup continued to inspire all the way to the Final, whence it went a bit flat. *En route*, Holland fell to Brazil, who, abetted with a bit of steel in defence, were sweeping all before them. In the Final, Brazil met Italy, the same Italy whom Ireland vanquished in the opening match, yet who had derived nourishment from defeat.

The Final itself was anticlimactic, Italy reverting to type, falling back to protect their goal. It would have been a travesty had such tactics prevailed. For the good of football they did not. Brazil won the penalty shoot-out to lift the World Cup for the first time since 1970.

Most Irish fans who attended both Italia '90 and USA '94 concurred that the former had been the most fun. The innocence and the thrill of competing in the big time had somehow been replaced by the hard sell and the tyranny of raised expectations. Sure, Irish supporters partied and mingled as good-naturedly as before, but there was undeniably something missing second time round. Next time, the laughs would surely be yet fewer, the expectations higher.

Next time? It was achievement enough to reach two World Cup finals. By France '98 Jack Charlton would surely be just a wondrous memory. His successor would face a daunting task. Living in the shadow of Our Jack might prove to be Charlton's most damning legacy.

As for the talent on the field, it is unevenly distributed, as is always a risk for small countries. Ireland's deficiencies in attack were rudely confirmed by their meagre total of four goals in nine World Cup matches. History may turn upon itself. The time may come when grass-roots opinion demands that Ireland cease to search far and wide for granny rule candidates, and comforts itself – as does Northern Ireland – with players who are proud to be Irishmen.

All things run in cycles, and maybe two successive finals constitutes the ceiling for Ireland's achievements. For Northern Ireland '82, '86, read the Irish Republic '90, '94. The combined records are almost identical, both Irelands winning one, losing three, drawing most. The North found the strain of making it three in a row, with a transitional team, beyond their means. The same could conceivably happen to the South.

All the same, it was disappointing to hear Jack fall into the oft-repeated trap.

'We are a nation of only three million people,' he said. 'We shouldn't even be competing here at all.'

In this, Charlton is mistaken. Uruguay (population two million) twice won the World Cup. Denmark (population five million) won the European Championship. Even Holland, twenty years at the top, is a 'small' nation compared with England, France, Germany, Italy. Quality of player is what matters, and that is not always commensurate with size of population.

Roy Keane, Gary Kelly, Phil Babb, Steve Staunton, Jason McAteer. These are the players who may spearhead the assault on France '98. And there lies Ireland's greatest weapon.

Ireland appearances and goalscorers (substitute appearances in brackets)
World Cup qualifying rounds and final competition 1994

	Apps	Goals		Apps	Goals
Bonner P *†	16	–	Sheridan J *	4 (2)	1
Keane R	16	–	Babb P	4	–
Houghton R *	15	1	McGoldrick E	3 (1)	–
Townsend A *	15	1	Whelan R *†‡	2 (3)	–
Irwin D	14	–	Kelly G	2	–
Staunton S *	14	2	Sheedy K *†	2	1
McGrath P *†	13	2	McAteer J	1 (3)	–
Phelan T	13	–	O'Leary D *†‡§	1	–
Quinn N *	12	2	Cascarino A *†	– (7)	1
Aldridge J *	11 (2)	7	Kelly D	– (2)	–
Kernaghan A	9	1	McCarthy M *†	– (1)	–
Moran K *†‡	6	–	McLoughlin A *	– (1)	1
Coyne T	4 (2)	–	(own-goals)		1

---

* Appeared in 1990 World Cup.
† Appeared in 1986 World Cup.
‡ Appeared in 1982 World Cup.
§ Appeared in 1978 World Cup.
25 players used

201 apps   21 goals
179 English League
22 Scottish League

Appendix 1

Clubs supplying players in World Cups 1934-1994 (includes qualifying rounds and final stages). Note: all statistics *exclude* abandoned match with Denmark in 1968.

	Club	Caps	Players	Caps	Other clubs
1	**Manchester Utd**	88	Irwin D	14	
	15 players		McGrath P	9	+19 Villa
			Stapleton F	9	+9 Arsenal, +2 Le Havre
			Brennan S	8	
			Cantwell N	7	+5 West Ham
			Keane R	7	+9 Forest
			Moran K	6	+8 Sporting Gijon, +11 Blackburn
			Carey J	5	
			Dunne A	5	
			Givens D	5	+7 QPR, +3 Birmingham,+1 Neuchatel
			Giles J	4	+6 Leeds, +3 WBA,+1 Shamrock R
			Dunne P	3	
			Whelan L	3	
			Martin M	2	+1 Bohemians, +3 WBA, +4 Newcastle
			Grimes A	1	
2	**Liverpool**	79	Whelan R	19	
	8 players		Houghton R	14	+14 Villa
			Staunton S	14	+11 Villa
			Heighway S	10	+1 Minnesota Kicks
			Lawrenson M	9	+6 Brighton
			Beglin J	6	
			Aldridge J	5	+7 R Sociedad, +13 Tranmere
			Robinson M	2	+5 Brighton, +3 QPR
3	**Aston Villa**	67	McGrath P	19	+9 Man U
	8 players		Houghton R	14	+14 Liverpool
			Staunton S	11	+14 Liverpool
			Martin C	7	
			Townsend A	6	+10 Norwich, +9 Chelsea
			Cascarino A	5	+3 Gillingham, +8 Millwall, +7 Chelsea
			Saward P	3	
			Walsh D	2	
4	**Arsenal**	47	O'Leary D	23	
	7 players		Stapleton F	9	+9 Man U, +2 Le Havre
			Haverty J	6	+2 Blackburn,+1 Bris R,+2 Shelbourne
			Brady L	5	+7 Juventus, +8 Inter,+2 W Ham
			Quinn N	2	+16 Man C
			Devine J	1	+2 Norwich
			McGoldrick E	1	+3 Palace
5	**Celtic**	46	Bonner P	29	
	4 players		Morris C	11	
			McCarthy M	4	+4 Man C,+1 Olymp Lyon,+6 Millwall
			Coyne T	2	+1 Tranmere, +3 Motherwell
6	**Shamrock Rov**	43	O'Neill F	8	
	20 players		Mulligan P	5	+1 Chelsea,+3 Palace,+4 WBA
			Leech M	4	
			Nolan R	4	
			O'Connor T	3	
			Dunne J	2	

Club	Caps	Players	Caps	Other clubs
		Gaskins P	2	
		Godwin T	2	+3 Leicester, +1 Bournemouth
		Mackey G	2	
		Byrne P	1	
		Coad P	1	
		Daly P	1	
		Foy T	1	
		Fullam J	1	
		Giles J	1	+4 Man U, +6 Leeds, +3 WBA
		Herrick T	1	
		Kinsella O	1	
		Munroe L	1	
		O'Leary P	1	
		Williams J	1	
7 **Manchester City**	37	Quinn N	16	+2 Arsenal
5 players		Phelan T	13	
		McCarthy M	4	+4 Celtic,+1 Olymp Lyon,+6 Millwall
		Kernaghan A	3	+6 Middlesbrough
		Walsh W	1	
8 **Everton**	35	Sheedy K	16	+2 Newcastle
9 players		Farrell P	5	
		Eglington T	4	
		O'Neill J	4	
		Clinton T	2	
		Corr P	1	
		Donovan D	1	
		McDonagh S	1	+2 Bolton, +3 Notts Co,+1 Birmingham, +1 Gill'ham,+1 Sunderland,+1 Wichita
		Meagan M	1	+2 Huddersfield
9 **Blackburn Rov**	27	Moran K	11	+6 Man U, +8 Sporting Gijon
5 players		McEvoy A	5	
		Rogers E	5	+1 Charlton
		McGrath M	4	
		Haverty J	2	+6 Arsenal,+1 Bris R,+2 Shelbourne
9 **Tottenham**	27	Hughton C	15	
4 players		Kinnear J	5	
		Galvin A	4	+1 Sheff W
		Holmes J	3	+4 Coventry
11 **West Brom Alb**	24	Grealish A	6	+6 Luton, +1 Brighton
7 players		Mulligan P	4	+5 Sham R, +1 Chelsea,+3 Palace
		Ryan R	4	
		Giles J	3	+4 Man U, +6 Leeds, +1 Shamrock R
		Martin M	3	+1 Bohs, +2 Man U,+4 Newcastle
		Walsh D	3	+2 Villa
		Treacy R	1	+ 4 Charlton, +4 Swindon
12 **Luton**	21	Grealish A	6	+1 Brighton, +6 WBA
5 players		Cummins G	5	
		Dunne S	5	
		Aherne T	4	
		McNally B	1	

	Club	Caps	Players	Caps	Other clubs
13	**Chelsea**	20	Townsend A	9	+10 Norwich, +6 Villa
	4 players		Cascarino A	7	+3 Gillingham, +8 Millwall, +5 Villa
			Dempsey J	3	
			Mulligan P	1	+5 Shamrock R, +3 Palace,+4 WBA
13	**Millwall**	20	Cascarino A	8	+3 Gillingham,+5 Villa,+7 Chelsea
	5 players		McCarthy M	6	+4 Man C, 4 Celtic, +1 Olymp Lyon
			Dunphy E	4	+1 York
			Hurley C	1	+7 Sunderland, +1 Bolton
			Saward P	1	+3 Villa, +1 Huddersfield
15	**Middlesbrough**	18	Fitzsimons A	8	
	4 players		Kernaghan A	6	+3 Man C
			Desmond P	3	
			Hartnett J	1	
16	**Birmingham**	17	Langan, D	7	+2 Oxford
	5 players		Carroll T	3	+1 Ipswich
			Daly G	3	+5 Derby, +4 Coventry
			Givens D	3	+5 Man U,+7 QPR,+1 Neuchatel
			McDonagh S	1	+2 Bolton, +3 Notts Co,+1 Birmingham, +1 Gill'ham,+1 Sunderland,+1 Wichita
17	**Norwich**	16	Townsend A	10	+9 Chelsea, +6 Villa
	3 players		Gavin J	4	
			Devine J	2	+1 Arsenal
18	**Brighton**	15	Lawrenson M	6	+9 Liverpool
	4 players		Robinson M	5	+2 Liverpool, +3 QPR
			Ryan G	3	
			Grealish A	1	+6 Luton, +6 WBA
18	**Tranmere**	14	Aldridge J	13	+5 Liverpool, +7 Real Sociedad
	2 players		Coyne T	1	+2 Celtic, +3 Motherwell
20	**West Ham**	13	Cantwell N	5	+7 Man U
	6 players		Moroney T	3	+1 Evergreen
			Brady L	2	+5 Arsenal, +7 Juventus, +8 Inter
			Kearns F	1	
			McGowan D	1	
			O'Farrell F	1	
21	**Coventry**	12	Babb P	4	
	3 players		Daly G	4	+5 Derby, +3 Birmingham
			Holmes J	4	+3 Spurs
21	**Fulham**	12	Peyton G	6	+1 Bournemouth
	3 players		Conway J	4	
			Lawlor J	2	
21	**Nott'm Forest**	12	Keane R	9	+7 Man U
	3 players		Dennehy M	2	
			Kelly N	1	
21	**Preston**	12	Kelly A	9	+1 Drumcondra
	3 players		McGee P	2	
			O'Farrell, F	1	+1 West Ham

	Club	Caps	Players	Caps	Other clubs
21	**QPR**	12	Givens D	7	+5 Man U, +3 Birm'ham, +1 Neuchatel
	3 players		Robinson M	3	+2 Liverpool, +5 Brighton
			Waddock G	2	
21	**Sheffield Wed**	12	Sheridan J	7	+1 Leeds
	3 players		Gannon E	4	
			Galvin A	1	+4 Spurs
27	**Sunderland**	11	Hurley C	7	+1 Millwall, +1 Bolton
	3 players		Fogarty A	3	
			McDonagh S	1	+1 Everton,+2 Bolton,+3 Notts Co, +1 Birm'ham,+1 Gillingham,+1 Wichita
28	**Leeds**	10	Giles J	6	+4 Man U, +3 WBA, +1 Shamrock R
	4 players		Kelly G	2	
			Fitzgerald P	1	+2 Chester
			Sheridan J	1	+7 Sheff W
29	**Internazionale**	8	Brady L	8	+5 Brady,+7 Juventus,+2 W Ham
29	**Newcastle**	8	Martin M	4	+1 Bohemians, +2 Man U, +3 WBA
	4 players		Sheedy K	2	+16 Everton
			Kelly D	1	+1 Wolves
			O'Brien L	1	
29	**Portsmouth**	8	Hand E	5	
	3 players		O'Callaghan K	2	+2 Ipswich
			McLoughlin A	1	+2 Swindon
29	**Shelbourne**	8	Haverty J	2	+6 Haverty,+2 Blackburn,+1 Bris R
	7 players		Barber E	1	
			Carroll B	1	
			Curtis D	1	+3 Bris C, +1 Ipswich
			Hennessy J	1	
			Newman W	1	
			Squires J	1	
29	**Sporting Gijon**	8	Moran K	8	+6 Man U, +11 Blackburn
34	**Bolton**	7	McAteer J	4	
	3 players		McDonagh S	2	+1 Everton, +3 Notts Co,+1 Birm'ham, +1 Gill'gham,+1 Sunderland,+1 Wichita
			Hurley C	1	+1 Millwall, +7 Sunderland
34	**Crystal Palace**	7	McGoldrick E	3	+1 Arsenal
	3 players		Mulligan P	3	+5 Sham R, +1 Chelsea, +4 WBA
			Murphy J	1	
34	**Juventus**	7	Brady L	7	+5 Arsenal, +8 Inter,+2 W Ham
34	**Real Sociedad**	7	Aldridge J	7	+5 Liverpool, +13 Tranmere
38	**Bohemians**	6	Jordan W	2	
	5 players		Horlacher F	1	
			Martin M	1	+2 Man U,+3 WBA,+ 4 Newcastle
			O'Connor T	1	
			O'Flanagan K	1	

	Club	Caps	Players	Caps	Other clubs
38	**Derby**	6	Daly G	5	+4 Coventry, +3 Birmingham
	2 players		Fagan F	1	
38	**Stoke**	6	Conroy T	6	
38	**Swansea**	6	Dwyer N	4	
	3 players		Keane T	1	
			O'Driscoll T	1	
38	**Swindon**	6	Treacy R	4	+1 WBA, +4 Charlton
	2 players		McLoughlin A	2	+1 Portsmouth
38	**Waterford**	6	McConville T	4	
	3 players		Arrigan T	1	
			Hale A	1	
44	**Charlton**	5	Treacy R	4	+1 WBA, +4 Swindon
	2 players		Rogers E	1	+5 Blackburn
44	**Cork**	5	Foley J	2	
	4 players		Burke T	1	
			Chatton H	1	
			O'Keeffe T	1	
44	**Drumcondra**	5	Byrne P	1	
	5 players		Coffee T	1	
			Donnelly T	1	
			Kelly A	1	
			Meehan P	1	
44	**Limerick**	5	Finucane A	4	
	2 players		Fitzpatrick K	1	
44	**St James's Gate**	5	Kennedy W	2	
	3 players		O'Reilly J	2	+2 Aberdeen
			Geoghegan M	1	
44	**Southampton**	5	Byrne A	4	
	2 players		Traynor T	1	
44	**Southend Utd**	5	McKenzie G	2	
	3 players		Turner C	2	
			Scannell T	1	
51	**Aberdeen**	4	Moore P	2	
	2 players		O'Reilly J	2	+2 St James's Gate
51	**Gillingham**	4	Cascarino A	3	+8 Millwall, 5 Villa, +7 Chelsea
	2 players		McDonagh S	1	+1 Everton,+2 Bolton,+3 Notts Co,
					+1 Birm'ham,+1 Sunderland,+1 Wichita
51	**Ipswich**	4	O'Callaghan K	2	+2 Portsmouth
	3 players		Carroll T	1	+3 Birmingham
			Curtis D	1	+1 Shelbourne, +3 Bris C
51	**Porto**	4	Walsh M	4	+1 Blackpool
51	**Sheffield Utd**	4	Ringstead A	4	

Club	Caps	Players	Caps	Other clubs
51 **Wolves**	4	Kelly P	3	
2 players		Kelly D	1	
57 **Bristol City**	3	Curtis D	3	+1 Shelbourne, +1 Ipswich
57 **Dundalk**	3	Donnelly J	1	
3 players		Hoy M	1	
		O'Neill W	1	
57 **Fortuna Cologne**	3	Campbell N	3	
57 **Huddersfield**	3	Meagan M	2	+1 Everton
2 players		Saward P	1	+1 Millwall, +3 Villa
57 **Leicester**	3	Godwin T	3	+2 Shamrock R, +1 Bournemouth
57 **Motherwell**	3	Coyne T	3	+2 Celtic, +1 Tranmere
57 **Notts Co**	3	McDonagh S	3	+1 Everton, +2 Bolton,+1 Birmingham, +1 Gill'gham,+1 Sunderland,+1 Wichita
57 **Walsall**	3	Kearns M	3	
65 **Bournemouth**	2	Godwin T	1	+2 Sham R, +3 Leicester
2 players		Peyton G	1	+6 Fulham
65 **Chester**	2	Fitzgerald P	2	+1 Leeds
65 **Dolphin**	2	Kendrick J	2	
65 **Le Havre**	2	Stapleton F	2	+9 Arsenal, +9 Man U
65 **Northampton**	2	Foley T	2	
65 **Oxford**	2	Langan D	2	+7 Birmingham
65 **St Patrick's Ath**	2	Dunne T	1	
2 players		Gibbons S	1	
72 **Blackpool**	1	Walsh M	1	
72 **Bristol Rov**	1	Haverty J	1	+6 Arsenal, +2 Blackburn,+2 Shelb'ne
72 **Bury**	1	Gorman W	1	
72 **Coleraine**	1	Byrne D	1	
72 **Cork Bohemians**	1	Lynch M	1	
72 **Derry City**	1	Kelly J	1	
72 **Evergreen Utd**	1	Moroney T	1	+3 West Ham
72 **Hibernian**	1	Gallagher M	1	
72 **Minnesota Kicks**	1	Heighway S	1	+10 Liverpool
72 **Neuchatel Xamax**	1	Givens D	1	+5 Man U, +7 QPR, +3 Birmingham

	Club	Caps	Players	Caps	Other clubs
72	**Newport Co**	1	Duggan H	1	
72	**Olympique Lyon**	1	McCarthy M	1	+4 Man C, +4 Celtic, +6 Millwall
72	**Peterborough**	1	Conmy O	1	
72	**Philadelph Furies**	1	O'Brien F	1	
72	**Port Vale**	1	O'Keefe E	1	
72	**Wichita Wings**	1	McDonagh S	1	+1 Everton,+2 Bolton,+3 Notts Co, +1 Birm'ham,+1 Gill'ham,+1 Sunderl'd
72	**York City**	1	Dunphy E	1	+4 Millwall
	88 clubs	*985*			

Appendix 2
Ireland World Cup goalscorers 1934-94 (includes qualifying rounds and final stages)

Name	Goals	Apps	Name	Goals	Apps
Aldridge, John	9	25	Duggan, Harry	1	1
Moore, Paddy	5	2	Geoghegan, Matt	1	1
Stapleton, Frank	5	20	O'Flanagan, Kevin	1	1
Curtis, Dermot	3	5	Squires, Johnny	1	1
Martin, Con	3	7	O'Farrell, Frank	1	2
Robinson, Michael	3	10	Fogarty, Ambrose	1	3
Daly, Gerry	3	12	McLoughlin, Alan	1	3
Grealish, Tony	3	13	Eglington, Tommy	1	4
Givens, Don	3	16	Ringstead, Alf	1	4
Quinn, Niall	3	18	Farrell, Peter	1	5
Sheedy, Kevin	3	18	McEvoy, Andy	1	5
Cascarino, Tony	3	23	Walsh, Mickey	1	5
Houghton, Ray	3	28	Rogers, Eamonn	1	6
McGrath, Paul	3	28	Sheridan, John	1	8
Dunne, Jimmy	2	2	Kernaghan, Alan	1	9
McGee, Paul	2	2	Treacy, Ray	1	9
Gavin, Johnny	2	4	Martin, Mick	1	10
Ryan, Reg	2	4	Haverty, Joe	1	11
Cummins, George	2	5	Giles, John	1	14
Walsh, Davy	2	5	Hughton, Chris	1	15
Conroy, Terry	2	6	Whelan, Ronnie	1	19
Fitzsimons, Arthur	2	8	Brady, Liam	1	22
Lawrenson, Mark	2	15	Moran, Kevin	1	25
Staunton, Steve	2	25	Townsend, Andy	1	15
			(own-goals)	4	
			Total	*100*	

N.B. Noel Cantwell scored 14 goals for Ireland, but none in World Cups.

Appendix 3
Ireland World Cup goalkeepers 1934-94 (includes qualifying rounds and final stages)

Name	World Cups	Apps	Goals	Ave per match
Scannell, Tom	1954	1	0	0.00
Bonner, Pat	1986, '90,* '94	29	15	0.52
Peyton, Gerry	1978, '82, '90	7	6	0.86
Godwin, Tommy	1950, '58	6	8	1.33
Kearns, Mick	1978	3	4	1.33
McDonagh, Seamus	1982, '86	10	15	1.50
Dunne, Pat	1966	3	5	1.67
O'Neill, Jimmy	1954, '58	4	7	1.75
Kelly, Alan	1958, '70, '74	10	21	2.10
McKenzie, George	1938	2	6	3.00
Fitzpatrick, Kevin	1970	1	3	3.00
Dwyer, Noel	1962	4	17	4.25
Foley, Jim	1934	2	9	4.50
* Extra time matches	Totals	82	116	

Appendix 4
Ireland's full World Cup record 1934-1994 (all wins are treated as awarding 2 points)

	P	W	D	L	F	A	Pts
France	8	3	1	4	10	14	7
Denmark	8	2	3	3	7	12	7
Northern Ireland	4	2	2	0	7	1	6
Spain	7	2	1	4	4	10	5
Cyprus	2	2	0	0	9	2	4
Latvia	2	2	0	0	6	0	4
Luxembourg	2	2	0	0	5	0	4
Malta	2	2	0	0	4	0	4
Albania	2	2	0	0	4	1	4
Lithuania	2	2	0	0	3	0	4
Holland	5	1	2	2	7	11	4
Finland	2	1	1	0	4	1	3
Switzerland	2	1	1	0	3	0	3
Hungary	4	1	1	2	3	6	3
Norway	5	0	3	2	5	7	3
Italy	2	1	0	1	1	1	2
Belgium	3	0	2	1	5	6	2
England	3	0	2	1	3	7	2
Soviet Union	4	1	0	3	2	5	2
Egypt	1	0	1	0	0	0	1
Romania *	1	0	1	0	0	0	1
Bulgaria	2	0	1	1	1	2	1
Mexico	1	0	0	1	1	2	0
Sweden	2	0	0	2	2	6	0
Scotland	2	0	0	2	1	7	0
Czechoslovakia	4	0	0	4	3	15	0
26 nations	82	27	22	33	100	116	76

* 1990 match taken as 0-0

	P	W	D	L	F	A	Pts
World Cup finals	9	1	5	3	4	7	5
World Cup qualifiers	73	26	17	30	96	109	69
Home record in qualifiers	36	19	8	9	68	43	46
Away record in qualifiers	36	7	9	20	28	65	23
Qualifiers on neutral ground	1	0	0	1	0	1	0

Appendix 5
Ireland World Cup captains 1934-1994 (includes qualifying rounds and final stages)

Captain	World Cups	Captain	W	D	L
Andy Townsend	1994	14	7	5	2
Noel Cantwell	1958 (Eng H, Den A), '62, '66	9	2	1	6
Liam Brady	1982	8	4	2	2
Mick McCarthy	1990	7	2	4	1
Frank Stapleton	1986	7	1	2	4
Johnny Giles	1974 (France H, USSR A) '78	6	2	1	3
Kevin Moran	1990, '94 (Spain H)	6	2	2	2
Johnny Carey	1950	4	1	1	2
Shay Brennan	1970 (Czech A, Denmark H)	2	0	1	1
Tommy Eglington	1954 (Luxembourg H, France A)	2	1	0	1
Peter Farrell	1954 (France H) '58 (England A)	2	0	0	2
Paddy Gaskins	1934	2	0	1	1
Charlie Hurley	1970 (Czech H, Hungary H)	2	0	0	2
Charlie Turner	1938	2	0	1	1
John Dempsey	1970 (Denmark A)	1	0	0	1
Seamus Dunne	1958 (Denmark H)	1	1	0	0
Tony Dunne	1970 (Hungary A)	1	0	0	1
Tony Grealish	1986 (USSR H)	1	1	0	0
Alan Kelly	1974 (USSR H)	1	0	0	1
Paul McGrath	1994 (Albania H)	1	1	0	0
Con Martin	1954 (Luxembourg A)	1	1	0	0
Paddy Mulligan	1974 (France A)	1	0	1	0
Ronnie Whelan	1990 (Malta A)	1	1	0	0

Appendix 6
Irish World Cup appearances from 'Irish, English and other leagues 1934-1994 (includes qualifying rounds and final stages)

World Cup	Caps	League Ireland	English League	Scottish League	Irish League	German League	Italian League	US League	Port' League	Swiss League	Spain League	French League	% League of Ireland
1934	23	18		4	1								78%
1938	22	15	7										68%
1950	45	9	36										20%
1954	44	3	40	1									7%
1958	44	7	37										16%
1962	44	4	40										9%
1966	33	7	26										21%
1970	71	19	52										27%
1974	50	7	41		2								14%
1978	46	1	44		1								2%
1982	97	1	85			7	2	1	1				1%
1986	102	1	88	1		8	1	3					1%
1990	163		118	27							15	3	–
1994	201		179	22									–
Totals	985	92	793	55	1	3	15	3	4	1	15	3	9%

The percentage of players drawn from the League of Ireland fell steeply, from 78% for the 1934 World Cup down to 'zero' for the 1990 World Cup. This downward spiral included a brief upsurge for the 1970 World Cup. The last League of Ireland player to be capped in the World Cup was Pat Byrne of Shamrock Rovers, who came on as substitute against Denmark in November 1985.

Appendix 7

Ireland appearances and goalscorers in the World Cup 1934-1994
(includes qualifying rounds and final stages)

Apps	Player	1934 A	1934 G	1938 A	1938 G	1950 A	1950 G	1954 A	1954 G	1958 A	1958 G	1962 A	1962 G	1966 A	1966 G	1970 A	1970 G	1974 A	1974 G	1978 A	1978 G	1982 A	1982 G	1986 A	1986 G	1990 A	1990 G	1994 A	1994 G
29	Bonner, Pat																					1		12		16			
28	Houghton, Ray																							13	2	15	1		
28	McGrath, Paul																					4		11	1	13	2		
25	Aldridge, John																							12	2	13	7		
25	Moran, Kevin																			5		1		13	1	6			
25	Staunton, Steve																									11		14	2
25	Townsend, Andy																									10		15	1
23	Cascarino, Tony																							3		13	2	7	1
23	O'Leary, David																	4		4		8		6		1			
22	Brady, Liam																	4	1	8		8		2					
20	Stapleton, Frank																	3		8	3	7	2	2					
19	Whelan, Ronnie																			2		5		7	1	5			
18	Quinn, Niall																							6	1	12	2		
18	Sheedy, Kevin																					4	1	12	1	2	1		
16	Givens, Don													5	2	3		4	1	4									
16	Keane, Roy																											16	
15	Hughton, Chris																			6	1	4		5					
15	Lawrenson, Mark																	1		7	2	7							
15	McCarthy, Mick																							4		10		1	
14	Giles, John											4	1	3		1		2		4									
14	Irwin, Denis																											14	
13	Grealish, Tony																					7	2	6	1				
13	Mulligan, Paddy															6		3		4									
13	Phelan, Terry																											13	
12	Cantwell, Noel							1		4		4		3															
12	Daly, Gerry																			4		5	3	3					
11	Haverty, Joe							4		4	1	3																	
11	Heighway, Steve																	1		4		6							
11	Morris, Chris																									11			
10	Kelly, Alan (Snr)									1				5		4													
10	McDonagh, S																					3		7					
10	Martin, Mick																	3	1	3		4							
10	Robinson, M																					5	3	5					
9	Hurley, Charlie									2		4		1		2													
9	Kernaghan, Alan																											9	1
9	Langan, David																					7		2					
9	Treacy, Ray															4		4	1	1									
8	Brennan, Shay													2		6													
8	Fitzsimons, A					1		3	2	4																			
8	O'Neill, Frank											2		3		3													
8	Sheridan, John																									2		6	1

Apps	Name	1934 A	1934 G	1938 A	1938 G	1950 A	1950 G	1954 A	1954 G	1958 A	1958 G	1962 A	1962 G	1966 A	1966 G	1970 A	1970 G	1974 A	1974 G	1978 A	1978 G	1982 A	1982 G	1986 A	1986 G	1990 A	1990 G	1994 A	1994 G
7	Holmes, Jimmy																	3		4									
7	Martin, Con					4	3	3																					
7	Peyton, Gerry																			1		5				1			
6	Beglin, Jim																							6					
6	Conroy, Terry													3		3	2												
6	Coyne, Tommy																											6	
6	Godwin, Tommy					4				2																			
6	Rogers, Eamonn													5	1	1													
5	Carey, Johnny			1		4																							
5	Cummins, George							2	1	1	1	2																	
5	Curtis, Dermot									4	3	1																	
5	Dunne, Seamus							2		3																			
5	Dunne, Tony													3		2													
5	Dunphy, Eamon													1		4													
5	Farrell, Peter					2	1	2		1																			
5	Galvin, Tony																							4		1			
5	Hand, Eoin													1		4													
5	Kinnear, Joe													3		2													
5	McEvoy, Andy											2		3	1														
5	Saward, Pat							1		3		1																	
5	Walsh, Davy					3	1	2	1																				
5	Walsh, Mickey																			1		1		3	1				
4	Aherne, Tommy					3		1																					
4	Babb, Phil																											4	
4	Byrne, Tony													1		3													
4	Carroll, Tommy													1		3													
4	Conway, Jimmy													4															
4	Dwyer, Noel											4																	
4	Eglington, T					1		3	1																				
4	Finucane, Al													4															
4	Gannon, Eddie					2		2																					
4	Gavin, Johnny					2	1	1		1	1																		
4	Leech, Mick															3		1											
4	McAteer, Jason																											4	
4	McConville, Tom																	4											
4	McGoldrick, E																											4	
4	McGrath, Mick											2		2															
4	Moroney, T					3		1																					
4	Nolan, Ronnie									2		2																	
4	O'Callaghan, K																							4					
4	O'Neill, Jimmy									3		1																	
4	O'Reilly, Joe	2		2																									
4	Ringstead, Alf							1		3	1																		
4	Ryan, Reg					1		3	2																				
3	Campbell, Noel																	2		1									
3	Dempsey, John															3													

Apps	Name	1934		1938		1950		1954		1958		1962		1966		1970		1974		1978		1982		1986		1990		1994	
---	---	A	G	A	G	A	G	A	G	A	G	A	G	A	G	A	G	A	G	A	G	A	G	A	G	A	G	A	G
3	Desmond, Peter					3																							
3	Devine, John																					1		2					
3	Dunne, Pat													3															
3	Fitzgerald, Peter											3																	
3	Fogarty, Ambrose											3	1																
3	Kearns, Mick																				3								
3	Kelly, Phil											3																	
3	McLoughlin, A																									2		1	1
3	Meagan, Mick													1		2													
3	O'Connor, T					3																							
3	Ryan, Gerry																					3							
3	Whelan, Liam									3																			
2	Clinton, Tommy							2																					
2	Dennehy, Miah																	2											
2	Dunne, Jimmy			2	2																								
2	Foley, Jim	2																											
2	Foley, Theo													2															
2	Gaskins, Paddy	2																											
2	Jordan, Billy	1		1																									
2	Kelly, David																											2	
2	Kelly, Gary																											2	
2	Kendrick, Joe	2																											
2	Kennedy, Billy	2																											
2	Lawler, Joseph							2																					
2	Mackey, Gerry									2																			
2	McGee, Paul																					2	2						
2	McKenzie, G			2																									
2	Moore, Paddy	2	5																										
2	O'Farrell, Frank							1	1	1																			
2	Turner, Charlie			2																									
2	Waddock, Gary																							2					
1	Arrigan, Tom			1																									
1	Barber, Eric													1															
1	Burke, Tom	1																											
1	Byrne, David	1																											
1	Byrne, Paddy	1																											
1	Byrne, Pat																					1							
1	Carroll, Brendan					1																							
1	Chatton, Harry	1																											
1	Coad, Paddy					1																							
1	Coffey, Timmy					1																							
1	Conmy, Oliver															1													
1	Corr, Peter			1																									
1	Daly, Pat					1																							
1	Donnelly, Joey	1																											
1	Donnelly, Tom	1																											
1	Donovan, Don									1																			
1	Duggan, Harry			1	1																								

Apps	Name	1934		1938		1950		1954		1958		1962		1966		1970		1974		1978		1982		1986		1990		1994	
		A	G	A	G	A	G	A	G	A	G	A	G	A	G	A	G	A	G	A	G	A	G	A	G	A	G	A	G
1	Dunne, Tommy									1																				
1	Fagan, Fionan											1																		
1	Fitzpatrick, Kevin																	1												
1	Foy, Tom			1																										
1	Fullam, Johnny																	1												
1	Gallagher, Matt							1																						
1	Geoghegan, Matt	1	1																											
1	Gibbons, Shay							1																						
1	Gorman, Bill			1																										
1	Grimes, Ashley																							1						
1	Hale, Alfie																	1												
1	Hartnett, Jim							1																						
1	Hennessy, Jackie											1																		
1	Herrick, John																			1										
1	Horlacher, Fred	1																												
1	Hoy, Mick			1																										
1	Keane, Tom					1																								
1	Kearns, Fred							1																						
1	Kelly, Jimmy	1																												
1	Kelly, Noel							1																						
1	Kinsella, Owen					1																								
1	Lynch, Miah	1																												
1	McGowan, Dan							1																						
1	McNally, B													1																
1	Meehan, Paddy	1																												
1	Munroe, Liam									1																				
1	Murphy, Jerry																					1								
1	Newman, Billy													1																
1	O'Brien, Fran																					1								
1	O'Brien, Liam																											1		
1	O'Connor, Turlough																			1										
1	O'Driscoll, Jackie					1																								
1	O'Flanagan, K			1	1																									
1	O'Keefe, Eamonn																							1						
1	O'Keeffe, Tim	1																												
1	O'Leary, Pierce																					1								
1	O'Neill, William			1																										
1	Scannell, Tom							1																						
1	Squires, Johnny	1	1																											
1	Traynor, Tommy									1																				
1	Walsh, Willie							1																						
1	Williams, Joe			1																										
	own-goals																		1			1					1		1
82 games		2		2		4		4		4		4		3		6		4		4		8		8		13		16	
100 goals			6		5		6		8		6		3		2		3		4		2		17		5		12		21
177 different players		17		18		23		27		20		18		15		25		20		16		24		25		22		25	
985 caps			23		22		45		44		44		44		33		71		50		46		97		102		163		201

Appendix 8
Results of World Cup finals 1930-1994

URUGUAY – 1930

Pool I

			P	W	D	L	F	A	Pts
France v Mexico	4-1	ARGENTINA	3	3	0	0	10	4	6
Argentina v France	1-0	Chile	3	2	0	1	5	3	4
Chile v Mexico	3-0	France	3	1	0	2	4	3	2
Chile v France	1-0	Mexico	3	0	0	3	4	13	0
Argentina v Mexico	6-3								
Argentina v Chile	3-1								

Pool II

Yugoslavia v Brazil	2-1	YUGOSLAVIA	2	2	0	0	6	1	4
Yugoslavia v Bolivia	4-0	Brazil	2	1	0	1	5	2	2
Brazil v Bolivia	4-0	Bolivia	2	0	0	2	0	8	0

Pool III

Romania v Peru	3-1	URUGUAY	2	2	0	0	5	0	4
Uruguay v Peru	1-0	Romania	2	1	0	1	3	5	2
Uruguay v Romania	4-0	Peru	2	0	0	2	1	4	0

Pool IV

United States v Belgium	3-0	UNITED STATES	2	2	0	0	6	0	4
United States v Paraguay	3-0	Paraguay	2	1	0	1	1	3	2
Paraguay v Belgium	1-0	Belgium	2	0	0	2	0	4	0

Semi-finals

Argentina v United States	6-1	Uruguay v Yugoslavia	6-1

Final

Uruguay v Argentina	4-2

ITALY – 1934

1st Round		*2nd Round*	
Italy v United States	7-1	Germany v Sweden	2-1
Germany v Belgium	5-2	Italy v Spain	1-1 1-0 (replay)
Spain v Brazil	3-1	Austria v Hungary	2-1
Sweden v Argentina	3-2	Czechoslovakia v Switz'land	3-2
Czechoslovakia v Romania	2-1		
Austria v France	3-2 (aet)		
Switzerland v Holland	3-2		
Hungary v Egypt	4-2		

Semi-finals			
Czechoslovakia v Germany	3-1	Italy v Austria	1-0

Third/Fourth play-off		*Final*	
Germany v Austria	3-2	Italy v Czechoslovakia	2-1 (aet)

FRANCE – 1938

1st Round		*2nd Round*	
Switzerland v Germany	1-1 4-2 (replay)	Sweden v Cuba	8-0
Cuba v Romania	3-3 2-1 (replay)	Italy v France	3-1
Hungary v Dutch E Indies	6-0	Hungary v Switzerland	2-0
France v Belgium	3-1	Brazil v Czechoslovakia	1-1 2-1 (replay)
Czechoslovakia v Holland	3-0 (aet)		

Brazil v Poland	6-5 (aet)		
Italy v Norway	2-1 (aet)		

Semi-finals

Italy v Brazil	2-1	Hungary v Sweden	5-1

Third/Fourth play-off		*Final*	
Brazil v Sweden	4-2	Italy v Hungary	4-2

BRAZIL – 1950

Pool I

			P	W	D	L	F	A	Pts
Brazil v Mexico	4-0	BRAZIL	3	2	1	0	8	2	5
Yugoslavia v Switzerland	3-0	Yugoslavia	3	2	0	1	7	3	4
Yugoslavia v Mexico	4-1	Switzerland	3	1	1	1	4	6	3
Brazil v Switzerland	2-2	Mexico	3	0	0	3	2	10	0
Brazil v Yugoslavia	2-0								
Switzerland v Mexico	2-1								

Pool II

Spain v United States	3-1	SPAIN	3	3	0	0	6	1	6
England v Chile	2-0	England	3	1	0	2	2	2	2
United States v England	1-0	Chile	3	1	0	2	5	6	2
Spain v Chile	2-0	United States	3	1	0	2	4	8	2
Spain v England	1-0								
Chile v United States	5-2								

Pool III

Sweden v Italy	3-2	SWEDEN	2	1	1	0	5	4	3
Sweden v Paraguay	2-2	Italy	2	1	0	1	4	3	2
Italy v Paraguay	2-0	Paraguay	2	0	1	1	2	4	1

Pool IV

Uruguay v Bolivia	8-0	URUGUAY	1	1	0	0	8	0	2
		Bolivia	1	0	0	1	0	8	0

Final Pool

		Final Positions							
Uruguay v Spain	2-2	1 URUGUAY	3	2	1	0	7	5	5
Brazil v Sweden	7-1	2 Brazil	3	2	0	1	14	4	4
Uruguay v Sweden	3-2	3 Sweden	3	1	0	2	6	11	2
Brazil v Spain	6-1	4 Spain	3	0	1	2	4	11	1
Sweden v Spain	3-1								
Uruguay v Brazil	2-1								

SWITZERLAND – 1954

Pool I

			P	W	D	L	F	A	Pts
Yugoslavia v France	1-0	BRAZIL	2	1	1	0	6	1	3
Brazil v Mexico	5-0	YUGOSLAVIA	2	1	1	0	2	1	3
France v Mexico	3-2	France	2	1	0	1	3	3	2
Brazil v Yugoslavia	1-1 (aet)	Mexico	2	0	0	2	2	8	0

Pool II

Hungary v South Korea	9-0	HUNGARY	2	2	0	0	17	3	4
W Germany v Turkey	4-1	W GERMANY	2	1	0	1	7	9	2
Hungary v W Germany	8-3	Turkey	2	1	0	1	8	4	2
Turkey v South Korea	7-0	South Korea	2	0	0	2	0	16	0
W Germany v Turkey	7-2 (play-off)								

Pool III

Austria v Scotland	1-0	URUGUAY	2	2	0	0	9	0	4
Uruguay v Czechoslovakia	2-0	AUSTRIA	2	2	0	0	6	0	4
Austria v Czechoslovakia	5-0	Czechoslovakia	2	0	0	2	0	7	0
Uruguay v Scotland	7-0	Scotland	2	0	0	2	0	8	0

Pool IV

England v Belgium	4-4 (aet)	ENGLAND	2	1	1	0	6	4	3
Switzerland v Italy	2-1	SWITZERLAND	2	1	0	1	2	3	2
England v Switzerland	2-0	Italy	2	1	0	1	5	3	2
Italy v Belgium	4-1	Belgium	2	0	1	1	5	8	1
Switzerland v Italy	4-1 (play-off)								

Quarter-finals

| W Germany v Yugoslavia | 2-0 | Austria v Switzerland | 7-5 |
| Uruguay v England | 4-2 | Hungary v Brazil | 4-2 |

Semi-finals

| W Germany v Austria | 6-1 | Hungary v Uruguay | 4-2 (aet) |

| *Third/Fourth play-off* | | *Final* | |
| Austria v Uruguay | 3-1 | W Germany v Hungary | 3-2 |

SWEDEN – 1958

Pool I

			P	W	D	L	F	A	Pts
W Germany v Argentina	3-1	W GERMANY	3	1	2	0	7	5	4
N Ireland v Czechoslovakia	1-0	N IRELAND	3	1	1	1	4	5	3
W Germany v Czecho'vakia	2-2	Czechoslovakia	3	1	1	1	8	4	3
Argentina v N Ireland	3-1	Argentina	3	1	0	2	5	10	2
W Germany v N Ireland	2-2								
Czechoslovakia v Argentina	6-1								
N Ireland v Czechoslovakia	2-1 (play-off, aet)								

Pool II

France v Paraguay	7-3	FRANCE	3	2	0	1	11	7	4
Yugoslavia v Scotland	1-1	YUGOSLAVIA	3	1	2	0	7	6	4
Yugoslavia v France	3-2	Paraguay	3	1	1	1	9	12	3
Paraguay v Scotland	3-2	Scotland	3	0	1	2	4	6	1
France v Scotland	2-1								
Yugoslavia v Paraguay	3-3								

Pool III

Sweden v Mexico	3-0	SWEDEN	3	2	1	0	5	1	5
Hungary v Wales	1-1	WALES	3	0	3	0	2	2	3
Wales v Mexico	1-1	Hungary	3	1	1	1	6	3	3
Sweden v Hungary	2-1	Mexico	3	0	1	2	1	8	1
Sweden v Wales	0-0								
Hungary v Mexico	4-0								
Wales v Hungary	2-1 (play-off)								

Pool IV

England v Soviet Union	2-2	BRAZIL	3	2	1	0	5	0	5
Brazil v Austria	3-0	SOVIET UNION	3	1	1	1	4	4	3
England v Brazil	0-0	England	3	0	3	0	4	4	3
Soviet Union v Austria	2-0	Austria	3	0	1	2	2	7	1
Brazil v Soviet Union	2-0								
England v Austria	2-2								
Soviet Union v England	1-0 (play-off)								

Quarter-finals

France v N Ireland	4-0	W Germany v Yugoslavia	1-0
Sweden v Soviet Union	2-0	Brazil v Wales	1-0

Semi-finals

Brazil v France	5-2	Sweden v W Germany	3-1

Third/Fourth play-off   *Final*

France v W Germany	6-3	Brazil v Sweden	5-2

CHILE – 1962

Group 1

			P	W	D	L	F	A	Pts
Uruguay v Colombia	2-1	SOVIET UNION	3	2	1	0	8	5	5
Soviet Union v Yugoslavia	2-0	YUGOSLAVIA	3	2	0	1	8	3	4
Yugoslavia v Uruguay	3-1	Uruguay	3	1	0	2	4	6	2
Soviet Union v Colombia	4-4	Colombia	3	0	1	2	5	11	1
Soviet Union v Uruguay	2-1								
Yugoslavia v Colombia	5-0								

Group 2

			P	W	D	L	F	A	Pts
Chile v Switzerland	3-1	W GERMANY	3	2	1	0	4	1	5
W Germany v Italy	0-0	CHILE	3	2	0	1	5	3	4
Chile v Italy	2-0	Italy	3	1	1	1	3	2	3
W Germany v Switzerland	2-1	Switzerland	3	0	0	3	2	8	0
W Germany v Chile	2-0								
Italy v Switzerland	3-0								

Group 3

			P	W	D	L	F	A	Pts
Brazil v Mexico	2-0	BRAZIL	3	2	1	0	4	1	5
Czechoslovakia v Spain	1-0	CZECHOSLOVAKIA	3	1	1	1	2	3	3
Brazil v Czechoslovakia	0-0	Mexico	3	1	0	2	3	4	2
Spain v Mexico	1-0	Spain	3	1	0	2	2	3	2
Brazil v Spain	2-1								
Mexico v Czechoslovakia	3-1								

Group 4

			P	W	D	L	F	A	Pts
Argentina v Bulgaria	1-0	HUNGARY	3	2	1	0	8	2	5
Hungary v England	2-1	ENGLAND	3	1	1	1	4	3	3
England v Argentina	3-1	Argentina	3	1	1	1	2	3	3
Hungary v Bulgaria	6-1	Bulgaria	3	0	1	2	1	7	1
Argentina v Hungary	0-0								
England v Bulgaria	0-0								

Quarter-finals

Yugoslavia v W Germany	1-0	Chile v Soviet Union	2-1
Brazil v England	3-1	Czechoslovakia v Hungary	1-0

Semi-finals

Brazil v Chile	4-2	Czechoslovakia v Yugoslavia	3-1

Third/Fourth play-off   *Final*

Chile v Yugoslavia	1-0	Brazil v Czechoslovakia	3-1

ENGLAND – 1966

Group 1			P	W	D	L	F	A	Pts
England v Uruguay	0-0	ENGLAND	3	2	1	0	4	0	5
France v Mexico	1-1	URUGUAY	3	1	2	0	2	1	4
Uruguay v France	2-1	Mexico	3	0	2	1	1	3	2
England v Mexico	2-0	France	3	0	1	2	2	5	1
Uruguay v Mexico	0-0								
England v France	2-0								

Group 2									
W Germany v Switzerland	5-0	W GERMANY	3	2	1	0	7	1	5
Argentina v Spain	2-1	ARGENTINA	3	2	1	0	4	1	5
Spain v Switzerland	2-1	Spain	3	1	0	2	4	5	2
Argentina v W Germany	0-0	Switzerland	3	0	0	3	1	9	0
Argentina v Switzerland	2-0								
W Germany v Spain	2-1								

Group 3									
Brazil v Bulgaria	0-0	PORTUGAL	3	3	0	0	9	2	6
Portugal v Hungary	3-1	HUNGARY	3	2	0	1	7	5	4
Hungary v Brazil	3-1	Brazil	3	1	0	2	4	6	2
Portugal v Bulgaria	3-0	Bulgaria	3	0	0	3	1	8	0
Portugal v Brazil	3-1								
Hungary v Bulgaria	3-1								

Group 4									
Soviet Union v North Korea	3-0	SOVIET UNION	3	3	0	0	6	1	6
Italy v Chile	2-0	NORTH KOREA	3	1	1	1	2	4	3
Chile v North Korea	1-1	Italy	3	1	0	2	2	2	2
Soviet Union v Italy	1-0	Chile	3	0	1	2	2	5	1
North Korea v Italy	1-0								
Soviet Union v Chile	2-1								

Quarter-finals				
England v Argentina	1-0	Portugal v North Korea	5-3
W Germany v Uruguay	4-0	Soviet Union v Hungary	2-1

Semi-finals			
W Germany v Soviet Union	2-1	England v Portugal	2-1

Third/Fourth play-off		*Final*	
Portugal v Soviet Union	2-1	England v W Germany	4-2 (aet)

MEXICO – 1970

Group 1			P	W	D	L	F	A	Pts
Mexico v Soviet Union	0-0	SOVIET UNION	3	2	1	0	6	1	5
Belgium v El Salvador	3-0	MEXICO	3	2	1	0	5	0	5
Soviet Union v Belgium	4-1	Belgium	3	1	0	2	4	5	2
Mexico v El Salvador	4-0	El Salvador	3	0	0	3	0	9	0
Soviet Union v El Salvador	2-0								
Mexico v Belgium	1-0								

Group 2									
Uruguay v Israel	2-0	ITALY	3	1	2	0	1	0	4
Italy v Sweden	1-0	URUGUAY	3	1	1	1	2	1	3
Uruguay v Italy	0-0	Sweden	3	1	1	1	2	2	3
Israel v Sweden	1-1	Israel	3	0	2	1	1	3	2

Sweden v Uruguay	1-0
Israel v Italy	0-0

Group 3

England v Romania	1-0	BRAZIL	3	3	0	0	8	3		6
Brazil v Czechoslovakia	4-1	ENGLAND	3	2	0	1	2	1		4
Romania v Czechoslovakia	2-1	Romania	3	1	0	2	4	5		2
Brazil v England	1-0	Czechoslovakia	3	0	0	3	2	7		0
Brazil v Romania	3-2									
England v Czechoslovakia	1-0									

Group 4

Peru v Bulgaria	3-2	W GERMANY	3	3	0	0	10	4		6
W Germany v Morocco	2-1	PERU	3	2	0	1	7	5		4
Peru v Morocco	3-0	Bulgaria	3	0	1	2	5	9		1
W Germany v Bulgaria	5-2	Morocco	3	0	1	2	2	6		1
W Germany v Peru	3-1									
Bulgaria v Morocco	1-1									

Quarter-finals

Uruguay v Soviet Union	1-0 (aet)	Brazil v Peru	4-2
Italy v Mexico	4-1	W Germany v England	3-2 (aet)

Semi-finals

Italy v W Germany	4-3 (aet)	Brazil v Uruguay	3-1

Third/Fourth play-off		*Final*	
W Germany v Uruguay	1-0	Brazil v Italy	4-1

WEST GERMANY – 1974

Group 1

			P	W	D	L	F	A	Pts
W Germany v Chile	1-0	E GERMANY	3	2	1	0	4	1	5
E Germany v Australia	2-0	W GERMANY	3	2	0	1	4	1	4
W Germany v Australia	3-0	Chile	3	0	2	1	1	2	2
E Germany v Chile	1-1	Australia	3	0	1	2	0	5	1
E Germany v W Germany	1-0								
Chile v Australia	0-0								

Group 2

Brazil v Yugoslavia	0-0	YUGOSLAVIA	3	1	2	0	10	1	4
Scotland v Zaire	2-0	BRAZIL	3	1	2	0	3	0	4
Brazil v Scotland	0-0	Scotland	3	1	2	0	3	1	4
Yugoslavia v Zaire	9-0	Zaire	3	0	0	3	0	14	0
Scotland v Yugoslavia	1-1								
Brazil v Zaire	3-0								

Group 3

Holland v Uruguay	2-0	HOLLAND	3	2	1	0	6	1	5
Sweden v Bulgaria	0-0	SWEDEN	3	1	2	0	3	0	4
Holland v Sweden	0-0	Bulgaria	3	0	2	1	2	5	2
Bulgaria v Uruguay	1-1	Uruguay	3	0	1	2	1	6	1
Holland v Bulgaria	4-1								
Sweden v Uruguay	3-0								

Group 4

Italy v Haiti	3-1	POLAND	3	3	0	0	12	3	6
Poland v Argentina	3-2	ARGENTINA	3	1	1	1	7	5	3
Argentina v Italy	1-1	Italy	3	1	1	1	5	4	3
Poland v Haiti	7-0	Haiti	3	0	0	3	2	14	0

| Argentina v Haiti | 4-1 |
| Poland v Italy | 2-1 |

Pool A

Brazil v E Germany	1-0
Holland v Argentina	4-0
Holland v E Germany	2-0
Brazil v Argentina	2-1
Holland v Brazil	2-0
Argentina v E Germany	1-1

	P	W	D	L	F	A	Pts
HOLLAND	3	3	0	0	8	0	6
Brazil	3	2	0	1	3	3	4
East Germany	3	0	1	2	1	4	1
Argentina	3	0	1	2	2	7	1

Pool B

Poland v Sweden	1-0
W Germany v Yugoslavia	2-0
Poland v Yugoslavia	2-1
W Germany v Sweden	4-2
Sweden v Yugoslavia	2-1
W Germany v Poland	1-0

	P	W	D	L	F	A	Pts
W GERMANY	3	3	0	0	7	2	6
Poland	3	2	0	1	3	2	4
Sweden	3	1	0	2	4	6	2
Yugoslavia	3	0	0	3	2	6	0

Third/Fourth play off

| Poland v Brazil | 1-0 |

Final

| W Germany v Holland | 2-1 |

ARGENTINA – 1978

Group 1

Italy v France	2-1
Argentina v Hungary	2-1
Italy v Hungary	3-1
Argentina v France	2-1
France v Hungary	3-1
Italy v Argentina	1-0

	P	W	D	L	F	A	Pts
ITALY	3	3	0	0	6	2	6
ARGENTINA	3	2	0	1	4	3	4
France	3	1	0	2	5	5	2
Hungary	3	0	0	3	3	8	0

Group 2

W Germany v Poland	0-0
Tunisia v Mexico	3-1
Poland v Tunisia	1-0
W Germany v Mexico	6-0
Poland v Mexico	3-1
W Germany v Tunisia	0-0

	P	W	D	L	F	A	Pts
POLAND	3	2	1	0	4	1	5
W GERMANY	3	1	2	0	6	0	4
Tunisia	3	1	1	1	3	2	3
Mexico	3	0	0	3	2	12	0

Group 3

Austria v Spain	2-1
Brazil v Sweden	1-1
Austria v Sweden	1-0
Brazil v Spain	0-0
Spain v Sweden	1-0
Brazil v Austria	1-0

	P	W	D	L	F	A	Pts
AUSTRIA	3	2	0	1	3	2	4
BRAZIL	3	1	2	0	2	1	4
Spain	3	1	1	1	2	2	3
Sweden	3	0	1	2	1	3	1

Group 4

Peru v Scotland	3-1
Holland v Iran	3-0
Scotland v Iran	1-1
Holland v Peru	0-0
Peru v Iran	4-1
Scotland v Holland	3-2

	P	W	D	L	F	A	Pts
PERU	3	2	1	0	7	2	5
HOLLAND	3	1	1	1	5	3	3
Scotland	3	1	1	1	5	6	3
Iran	3	0	1	2	2	8	1

Group A

W Germany v Italy	0-0	HOLLAND	3	2 1 0		9	4	5
Holland v Austria	5-1	Italy	3	1 1 1		2	2	3
Italy v Austria	1-0	W Germany	3	0 2 1		4	5	2
Holland v W Germany	2-2	Austria	3	1 0 2		4	8	2
Holland v Italy	2-1							
Austria v W Germany	3-2							

Group B

Brazil v Peru	3-0	ARGENTINA	3	2 1 0		8	0	5
Argentina v Poland	2-0	Brazil	3	2 1 0		6	1	5
Poland v Peru	1-0	Poland	3	1 0 2		2	5	2
Argentina v Brazil	0-0	Peru	3	0 0 3		0	10	0
Brazil v Poland	3-1							
Argentina v Peru	6-0							

Third/Fourth play-off   *Final*

Brazil v Italy   2-1   Argentina v Holland   3-1 (aet)

SPAIN – 1982

Group 1

			P	W	D	L	F	A	Pts
Italy v Poland	0-0	POLAND	3	1	2	0	5	1	4
Peru v Cameroon	0-0	ITALY	3	0	3	0	2	2	3
Italy v Peru	1-1	Cameroon	3	0	3	0	1	1	3
Poland v Cameroon	0-0	Peru	3	0	2	1	2	6	2
Poland v Peru	5-1								
Italy v Cameroon	1-1								

Group 2

Algeria v W Germany	2-1	W GERMANY	3	2	0	1	6	3	4
Austria v Chile	1-0	AUSTRIA	3	2	0	1	3	1	4
W Germany v Chile	4-1	Algeria	3	2	0	1	5	5	4
Austria v Algeria	2-0	Chile	3	0	0	3	3	8	0
Algeria v Chile	3-2								
W Germany v Austria	1-0								

Group 3

Belgium v Argentina	1-0	BELGIUM	3	2	1	0	3	1	5
Hungary v El Salvador	10-1	ARGENTINA	3	2	0	1	6	2	4
Argentina v Hungary	4-1	Hungary	3	1	1	1	12	6	3
Belgium v El Salvador	1-0	El Salvador	3	0	0	3	1	13	0
Belgium v Hungary	1-1								
Argentina v El Salvador	2-0								

Group 4

England v France	3-1	ENGLAND	3	3	0	0	6	1	6
Czechoslovakia v Kuwait	1-1	FRANCE	3	1	1	1	6	5	3
England v Czechoslovakia	2-0	Czechoslovakia	3	0	2	1	2	4	2
France v Kuwait	4-1	Kuwait	3	0	1	2	2	6	1
France v Czechoslovakia	1-1								
England v Kuwait	1-0								

Group 5

Spain v Honduras	1-1	N IRELAND	3	1	2	0	2	1	4
Yugoslavia v N Ireland	0-0	SPAIN	3	1	1	1	3	3	3
Spain v Yugoslavia	2-1	Yugoslavia	3	1	1	1	2	2	3
Honduras v N Ireland	1-1	Honduras	3	0	2	1	2	3	2
Yugoslavia v Honduras	1-0								
N Ireland v Spain	1-0								

Group 6

Brazil v Soviet Union	2-1	**BRAZIL**	3	3	0	0	10	2	6
Scotland v New Zealand	5-2	SOVIET UNION	3	1	1	1	6	4	3
Brazil v Scotland	4-1	Scotland	3	1	1	1	8	8	3
Soviet Union v New Zealand	3-0	New Zealand	3	0	0	3	2	12	0
Soviet Union v Scotland	2-2								
Brazil v New Zealand	4-0								

Group A

Poland v Belgium	3-0	**POLAND**	2	1	1	0	3	0	3
Soviet Union v Belgium	1-0	Soviet Union	2	1	1	0	1	0	3
Soviet Union v Poland	0-0	Belgium	2	0	0	2	0	4	0

Group B

W Germany v England	0-0	**W GERMANY**	2	1	1	0	2	1	3
W Germany v Spain	2-1	England	2	0	2	0	0	0	2
England v Spain	0-0	Spain	2	0	1	1	1	2	1

Group C

Italy v Argentina	2-1	**ITALY**	2	2	0	0	5	3	4
Brazil v Argentina	3-1	Brazil	2	1	0	1	5	4	2
Italy v Brazil	3-2	Argentina	2	0	0	2	2	5	0

Group D

France v Austria	1-0	**FRANCE**	2	2	0	0	5	1	4
Austria v N Ireland	2-2	Austria	2	0	1	1	2	3	1
France v N Ireland	4-1	N Ireland	2	0	1	1	3	6	1

Semi-finals

Italy v Poland	2-0	W Germany v France	3-3 (aet)
		(W Germany won on penalties)	

Third/Fourth play-off | | *Final* | |
| Poland v France | 3-2 | Italy v W Germany | 3-1 |

MEXICO – 1986

Group A

			P	W	D	L	F	A	Pts
Bulgaria v Italy	1-1	**ARGENTINA**	3	2	1	0	6	2	5
Argentina v South Korea	3-1	**ITALY**	3	1	2	0	5	4	4
Italy v Argentina	1-1	**BULGARIA**	3	0	2	1	2	4	2
South Korea v Bulgaria	1-1	South Korea	3	0	1	2	4	7	1
Argentina v Bulgaria	2-0								
Italy v South Korea	3-2								

Group B

Mexico v Belgium	2-1	**MEXICO**	3	2	1	0	4	2	5
Paraguay v Iraq	1-0	**PARAGUAY**	3	1	2	0	4	3	4
Mexico v Paraguay	1-1	**BELGIUM**	3	1	1	1	5	5	3
Belgium v Iraq	2-1	Iraq	3	0	0	3	1	4	0
Paraguay v Belgium	2-2								
Mexico v Iraq	1-0								

Group C

France v Canada	1-0	**SOVIET UNION**	3	2	1	0	9	1	5
Soviet Union v Hungary	6-0	**FRANCE**	3	2	1	0	5	1	5
Soviet Union v France	1-1	Hungary	3	1	0	2	2	9	2
Hungary v Canada	2-0	Canada	3	0	0	3	0	5	0
France v Hungary	3-0								
Soviet Union v Canada	2-0								

Group D

Brazil v Spain	1-0	BRAZIL	3	3	0	0	5	0	6
Algeria v N Ireland	1-1	SPAIN	3	2	0	1	5	2	4
Spain v N Ireland	2-1	Northern Ireland	3	0	1	2	2	6	1
Brazil v Algeria	1-0	Algeria	3	0	1	2	1	5	1
Spain v Algeria	3-0								
Brazil v N Ireland	3-0								

Group E

Uruguay v W Germany	1-1	DENMARK	3	3	0	0	9	1	6
Denmark v Scotland	1-0	W GERMANY	3	1	1	1	3	4	3
Denmark v Uruguay	6-1	URUGUAY	3	0	2	1	2	7	2
W Germany v Scotland	2-1	Scotland	3	0	1	2	1	3	1
Uruguay v Scotland	0-0								
Denmark v W Germany	2-0								

Group F

Morocco v Poland	0-0	MOROCCO	3	1	2	0	3	1	4
Portugal v England	1-0	ENGLAND	3	1	1	1	3	1	3
England v Morocco	0-0	POLAND	3	1	1	1	1	3	3
Poland v Portugal	1-0	Portugal	3	1	0	2	2	4	2
England v Poland	3-0								
Morocco v Portugal	3-1								

Eighth-finals

Mexico v Bulgaria	2-0	Brazil v Poland	4-0
W Germany v Morocco	1-0	France v Italy	2-0
Belgium v Soviet Union	4-3 (aet)	Argentina v Uruguay	1-0
Spain v Denmark	5-1	England v Paraguay	3-0

Quarter-finals

W Germany v Mexico	0-0 (aet. W Germany won on penalties)
Belgium v Spain	1-1 (aet. Belgium won on penalties)
France v Brazil	1-1 (aet. France won on penalties)
Argentina v England	2-1

Semi-finals

W Germany v France	2-0	Argentina v Belgium	2-0

Third/Fourth play-off		*Final*	
France v Belgium	4-2	Argentina v W Germany	3-2

ITALY – 1990

Group A

			P	W	D	L	F	A	Pts
Italy v Austria	1-0	ITALY	3	3	0	0	4	0	6
Czechoslovakia v USA	5-0	CZECHOSLOVAKIA	3	2	0	1	6	3	4
Italy v United States	1-0	Austria	3	1	0	2	2	3	2
Czechoslovakia v Austria	1-0	United States	3	0	0	3	2	8	0
Italy v Czechoslovakia	2-0								
Austria v United States	2-1								

Group B

Cameroon v Argentina	1-0	CAMEROON	3	2	0	1	3	5	4
Romania v Soviet Union	2-0	ROMANIA	3	1	1	1	4	3	3
Argentina v Soviet Union	2-0	ARGENTINA	3	1	1	1	3	2	3
Cameroon v Romania	2-1	Soviet Union	3	1	0	2	4	4	2
Argentina v Romania	1-1								
Soviet Union v Cameroon	4-0								

Group C

Brazil v Sweden	2-1
Costa Rica v Scotland	1-0
Brazil v Costa Rica	1-0
Scotland v Sweden	2-1
Brazil v Scotland	1-0
Costa Rica v Sweden	2-1

BRAZIL	3	3	0	0	4	1	6
COSTA RICA	3	2	0	1	3	2	4
Scotland	3	1	0	2	2	3	2
Sweden	3	0	0	3	3	6	0

Group D

Colombia v UAE	2-0
W Germany v Yugoslavia	4-1
Yugoslavia v Colombia	1-0
W Germany v UAE	5-1
W Germany v Colombia	1-1
Yugoslavia v UAE	4-1

W GERMANY	3	2	1	0	10	3	5
YUGOSLAVIA	3	2	0	1	6	5	4
COLOMBIA	3	1	1	1	3	2	3
United Arab Emirates	3	0	0	3	2	11	0

Group E

Belgium v South Korea	2-0
Spain v Uruguay	0-0
Spain v South Korea	3-1
Belgium v Uruguay	3-1
Spain v Belgium	2-1
Uruguay v South Korea	1-0

SPAIN	3	2	1	0	5	2	5
BELGIUM	3	2	0	1	6	3	4
URUGUAY	3	1	1	1	2	3	3
South Korea	3	0	0	3	1	6	0

Group F

England v Rep Ireland	1-1
Egypt v Holland	1-1
England v Holland	0-0
Egypt v Rep Ireland	0-0
England v Egypt	1-0
Rep Ireland v Holland	1-1

ENGLAND	3	1	2	0	2	1	4
REP IRELAND	3	0	3	0	2	2	3
HOLLAND	3	0	3	0	2	2	3
Egypt	3	0	2	1	1	2	2

Eighth-finals

Cameroon v Colombia	2-1 (aet)
England v Belgium	1-0 (aet)
Czechoslovakia v Costa Rica	4-1
W Germany v Holland	2-1

Argentina v Brazil	1-0
Yugoslavia v Spain	2-1 (aet)
Italy v Uruguay	2-0
Rep Ireland v Romania	0-0 (aet)
(Rep Ireland won on penalties)	

Quarter-finals

| England v Cameroon | 3-2 (aet) |
| W Germany v Czecho'vakia | 1-0 |

Italy v Rep Ireland	1-0
Argentina v Yugoslavia	0-0 (aet)
(Argentina won on penalties)	

Semi-finals

| Argentina v Italy | 1-1 (aet. Argentina won on penalties) |
| W Germany v England | 1-1 (aet. W Germany won on penalties) |

Third/Fourth play-off

| Italy v England | 2-1 |

Final

| W Germany v Argentina | 1-0 |

UNITED STATES – 1994

Group A

United States v Switzerland	1-1
Romania v Colombia	3-1
Switzerland v Romania	4-1
United States v Colombia	2-1
Romania v United States	1-0
Colombia v Switzerland	2-0

					(3 pts for a win)		
	P	W	D	L	F	A	Pts
ROMANIA	3	2	0	1	5	5	6
SWITZERLAND	3	1	1	1	5	4	4
UNITED STATES	3	1	1	1	3	3	4
Colombia	3	1	0	2	4	5	3

Group B

Cameroon v Sweden	2-2								
Brazil v Russia	2-0	BRAZIL	3	2	1	0	6	1	7
Brazil v Cameroon	3-0	SWEDEN	3	1	2	0	6	4	5
Sweden v Russia	3-1	Russia	3	1	0	2	7	6	3
Brazil v Sweden	1-1	Cameroon	3	0	1	2	3	11	1
Russia v Cameroon	6-1								

Group C

Germany v Bolivia	1-0								
Spain v South Korea	2-2	GERMANY	3	2	1	0	5	3	7
Germany v Spain	1-1	SPAIN	3	1	2	0	6	4	5
South Korea v Bolivia	0-0	South Korea	3	0	2	1	4	5	2
Germany v South Korea	3-2	Bolivia	3	0	1	2	1	4	1
Spain v Bolivia	3-1								

Group D

Argentina v Greece	4-0								
Nigeria v Bulgaria	3-0	NIGERIA	3	2	0	1	6	2	6
Argentina v Nigeria	2-1	BULGARIA	3	2	0	1	6	3	6
Bulgaria v Greece	4-0	ARGENTINA	3	2	0	1	6	3	6
Bulgaria v Argentina	2-0	Greece	3	0	0	3	0	10	0
Nigeria v Greece	2-0								

Group E

Ireland v Italy	1-0								
Norway v Mexico	1-0	MEXICO	3	1	1	1	3	3	4
Italy v Norway	1-0	IRELAND	3	1	1	1	2	2	4
Mexico v Ireland	2-1	ITALY	3	1	1	1	2	2	4
Norway v Ireland	0-0	Norway	3	1	1	1	1	1	4
Mexico v Italy	1-1								

Group F

Belgium v Morocco	1-0								
Holland v Saudi Arabia	2-1	HOLLAND	3	2	0	1	4	3	6
Belgium v Holland	1-0	SAUDI ARABIA	3	2	0	1	4	3	6
Saudi Arabia v Morocco	2-1	BELGIUM	3	2	0	1	2	1	6
Saudi Arabia v Belgium	1-0	Morocco	3	0	0	3	2	5	0
Holland v Morocco	2-1								

Eighth-finals

Germany v Belgium	3-2	Holland v Ireland	2-0
Spain v Switzerland	3-0	Brazil v United States	1-0
Sweden v Saudi Arabia	3-1	Italy v Nigeria	2-1 (aet)
Romania v Argentina	3-2	Bulgaria v Mexico	1-1 (aet)
		(Bulgaria won on penalties)	

Quarter-finals

Italy v Spain	2-1	Bulgaria v Germany	2-1
Brazil v Holland	3-2	Sweden v Romania	2-2 (aet)
		(Sweden won on penalties)	

Semi-finals

Italy v Bulgaria	2-1	Brazil v Sweden	1-0

Third/Fourth play-off   *Final*

Sweden v Bulgaria	4-0	Brazil v Italy	0-0 (aet)
		(Brazil won on penalties)	